ELMER H. ANTONSEN

THE
ORIGINS
OF
WRITING

Edited by Wayne M. Senner

UNIVERSITY OF NEBRASKA PRESS   LINCOLN AND LONDON

Copyright © 1989 by the
University of Nebraska Press
All rights reserved
Manufactured in the United States of America
The paper in this book meets the minimum require-
ments of American National Standard for Information
Sciences—Permanence of Paper for Printed Library
Materials, ANSI Z39.48-1984.

Designed by Mary Mendell

Library of Congress Cataloging-in-Publication Data
The Origins of writing / edited by Wayne Senner.
p.   cm.
Includes bibliographies.
ISBN 0-8032-4202-6 (alk. paper)
1. Writing—History.   I. Senner, Wayne M.
P211.075   1990
411—dc19   89-30400 CIP

Contents

Preface

......

The Origins of Writing began as a lecture series held at Arizona State University in 1984. The lectures complemented and enhanced a traveling exhibit on the origins of writing—"Sign, Symbol, Script"—which received major funding from the National Endowment for the Humanities and essential support from a variety of private, public, and institutional sources. The intent of the project, directed by Keith N. Schoville, was to present to the public artifacts representative of major aspects and stages in the five-thousand-year history of writing. It is our hope that this book will perpetuate the results of this nationwide project and deepen the general public's knowledge of this cornerstone of the human heritage.

Wayne M. Senner brought the exhibit to Arizona State University and supplemented it by arranging for distinguished lecturers to appear in Phoenix. The lectures highlighted each of the exhibit's seven sections, which represent the major geographic and cultural areas important to the world history of writing.

The decision to transform the lectures into chapters in a collection took into account the desirability of expanding the original conception to include essays on as many major scripts as possible. Nevertheless, a focus on the educated interests of an English-speaking audience coupled with a limited time schedule and availability of qualified scholars made it necessary to impose restrictions on the scope of the expansion. Some scholars will miss intrinsically interesting chapters on writing in the Indian subcontinent, on African writing systems, the Korean Han'gul, or the mystery of the Easter Island tablets, to name just a few. The absence of essays on these scripts will not in any way obscure the essential story of how and why the world's major writing systems in the Middle East (Sumerian cuneiform, Egyptian hieroglyphics, Hebrew, and Arabic), the Far East (Chinese), Europe (Greek, Latin, ogham, and runes), and Middle America (Mayan) came into existence.

The essays in this volume are by scholars from a variety of scholarly disciplines, including history, philology, linguistics, anthropology, art, and literature, and the methodologies they apply will be familiar to most of the readers from those fields. The essays will also be of interest to students and teachers concerned with the increasing problem of literacy and the social functions of writing. In this regard, readers who have generally linked the study of languages and writing to that of belles-lettres will encounter hypotheses on the primary uses of writing in early societies that are both enlightening and provocative.

Even though the essays are directed to the educated lay reader, this focus does not diminish the book's usefulness to specialists, who in some chapters will discover new theses presented and defended. Specialists in the history of scripts may choose to go directly to the chapters on individual writing systems. Readers in search of additional information on any of the areas in the collection will find the Further Readings sections at the end of the chapters helpful.

Finally, we ask the reader to keep in mind that the essays endeavor to shed light on the earliest stages of writing systems; they do not attempt to offer thorough discussions of the historical development of scripts and their expansion. Topics like the imposing of borrowed scripts upon native languages, the development of cursive writing in ancient Egypt, or the issue of the evaluative relativity of writing systems were not included, as interesting and important as they, and others, are to the history of writing.

Keith N. Schoville
Department of Hebrew and Semitic Studies
University of Wisconsin–Madison

W.M. Senner
Department of Foreign Languages
Arizona State University

The Origins of Writing

Theories and Myths on the Origins of Writing: A Historical Overview

......

Wayne M. Senner

......

Twentieth-Century Scholars on the Origins of Writing

Empirical evidence or speculation?

For much of the twentieth century, European and American students of linguistics have generally ignored the origins of the world's major writing systems. Linguists have tended to regard language basically as speech, which is held to be more natural, universal, and older and therefore more closely related anatomically to the neural evolution of man than the written word, which is used only by a minority of speakers. In part, this attitude came about as a reaction against a long tradition of philology that approached language on a prescriptive, evaluative basis and focused on historical etymology and grammatology rather than on the actual popular usage of language. It was also a consequential reaction against millennia of speculative adventurism that occluded an empirical understanding of the original stages of writing. This chapter offers a historical sketch of pre-twentieth-century views on the origins of writing and relates them to the current stage of research as represented in the following eleven chapters.

One compelling reason for the study of the origins of writing is precisely the aforementioned argument against it: writing is relatively new to man. In contrast to spoken languages, which evolved over tens of thousands of years and left few traces of their beginnings, written languages offer access to nearly the entire history of some scripts. A case in point is cuneiform writing in Mesopotamia. As the earliest script known to man and long considered the ancestor of all writing, Sumerian cuneiform offers an abundance of documented evidence about its beginnings. Similar claims can also be made for several alphabetic scripts, such as ancient Greek and Latin or even the Korean Han'gul, all of which provide ample sources for mapping their evolution. Empirical evidence for other alphabetic as well as nonalphabetic scripts is, however, not as sufficiently extant. Elmer H. Antonsen (chapter 9 of this book) and David N. Keightley (chapter 11) both stress the value of further archaeological finds in order fully to understand the earliest origins of these writing systems, which in their primal documents already appear in a state of maturity. James A. Bellamy (chapter 6) notes that the existence of only five Arabic inscriptions from the date of the earliest find in 328 A.D. until the Koran in the seventh century precludes any exact account of the origins of the Arabic script. At the outset of the discussion of Egyptian hieroglyphics, Henry George Fischer emphasizes that in spite of the great progress that has been made in Egyptology since the decipherments by Champollion in the nineteenth century, very much still remains unknown.

Even for the historically young ogham alphabet, which Celtic scribes secretively guarded as a sacred trust, scholars have felt compelled to resort to fanciful speculation. And as Ronald S. Stroud reminds us in his discussion of the Linear A script discovered on Crete, we know practically nothing of the origins of this mysterious writing from Mycenaean civilization.

Thus, in spite of the immense extant documentation for the writing systems discussed in this volume, major lacunae in factual information necessitate linguistic reconstruction and at least some philological detective work if not cautious speculation.

The origin or origins of writing?

Fundamental to the discussion of the major writing systems included in this book is the question of a single or multiple origins of writing. Since the dawn of history scholars have struggled with this desideratum and until the nineteenth century almost universally accepted the monogenetic theory of writing, which asserts that all scripts derive from a single ancestor. To the detriment of scientific study, this theory became entangled in the peripheral question of cultural and religious primacy early in the history of writing. The authors of the chapters on early alphabets agree that alphabetic scripts most likely derive from a single ancestor, Old Canaanite. The authors of the chapters on cuneiform, Mycenaean, Chinese, and Mayan, however, reject the validity of linguistic monogeneticism, finding no evidence to support it in spite of the presence of many closely related common features,

such as phoneticism, the rebus principle, determinatives, early pictographic elements, elitist scribal castes, large sign inventories, and morphological multivalency.

Prewriting

Arguments for the independent origins of the Sumerian, Chinese, and Mayan scripts are bolstered by worldwide archaeological discoveries of prewriting artifacts. Some twentieth-century linguists and historians of writing see the earliest precursors of writing in the innumerable cave drawings and carvings of the Upper Paleolithic (35,000 to 15,000 B.C.).[1] Scattered throughout the world from the famous caves at Lascaux, France, to the rock shelters of central India and the far outreaches of southern Zimbabwe, these durable products of the imagination of prehistoric man seem to lend credence to the theory that the human need to communicate is too universal and diversified to admit of a single source (fig. 1).

But do these extraordinary fragments have any direct relationship to writing? David Diringer argues that the rock paintings are "isolated, arbitrary and unsystematic" and as a form of "embryo-writing" must be differentiated from "*conscious* writing."[2] Although petrograms (rock paintings) and petroglyphs (rock carvings) fail the generally recognized definition that true writing is "*a system of human intercommunication by means of conventional visible marks*," Naomi S. Baron cautions that the presence of lexicon and productivity cannot be completely ruled out.[3] On the basis of evidence collected from central India, Baron pos-

(a)

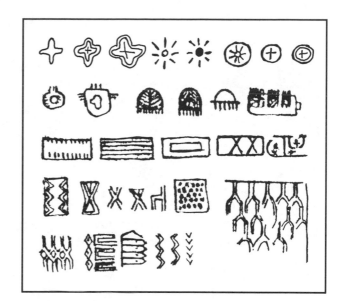

(c)

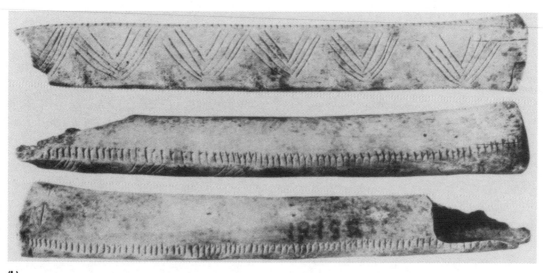

(b)

Figure 1 Three examples of prewriting. (a) Rock painting from southern Zimbabwe depicting rain ceremony. (b) The three faces of an engraved fragment of eagle bone from the site of Le Placard (Charente), Middle Magdalenian. (c) Stone Age painting from India, style six. Fig. 1(a) courtesy of Frobenius-Institut, Frankfurt am Main; fig. 1(b) reprinted from Alexander Marshack, *The Roots of Civilization: The Cognitive Beginnings of Man's First Art, Symbol and Notation* (New York: McGraw-Hill, 1972), 148, copyright © 1972 by Alexander Marshack; fig. 1(c) reprinted from Robert R. R. Brooks and Vishnu S. Wakankar, *Stone Age Painting in India* (New Haven: Yale University Press, 1976), 97.

tulates that rock paintings do not depict meaningless doodles or scratches but reveal stratified representational purposes.[4] In certain cases they even demonstrate a degree of productive combination, a major criterion of syntactic writing.

Far distant from India, Alexander Marshak found evidence of an earlier symbolic clustering in calendrical notations in Cro-Magnon Europe. Marshak concluded that the natural sequence of lunar appearances had been rendered in a symbolic sequence of vertical scratches or marks on eagle wing-bones (see fig. 1) that essentially could be "read" and were, therefore, precursors of writing.[5]

In terms of the motor action involved in the incising and drawing of paleolithic pictures and notations, rock painting more closely approaches the beginnings of true writing than contemporaneous and later systems of mnemonic communications such as the knot devices used by the Incas for counting and recording, the color symbolism of the wampum of the North American Iroquois, or the cowrie mussels employed by the African Yoruba to communicate simple phrases (e.g., two shells together = "meeting," two apart = "separation"). The first-century B.C. grammarian Dionysios Thrax recognized the etymological and semantic relationship between "scratching" and "writing" in one of the earliest systematic grammatical treatises in the Western world: "There are twenty-four letters from a to w. They are called letters (γράμματα) from being formed of lines and scratches. For to write (γράφαι), among the ancients meant to scratch (ξυθαι), as in Homer."[6]

Similar relationships are found in other languages. For example, English "to write" reflects the etymology of γράφαι in its correspondence to Old High German *rízan*, "to scratch," and Modern German *einritzen*, "to incise." Elmer Antonsen (chapter 9) also notes that the word "rune" is derived from an Indo-European root meaning "to scratch, dig, or make grooves." Modern German *schreiben*, "to write," from Latin *scribere* is the cognate of Modern Icelandic *skrifa*, which in Old Icelandic meant "to scratch" or "to paint." For other cultures, writing was more closely associated with "painting." For example, in Gothic the verb *meljan*, "to paint," was also used in the sense of "to write," and in Egyptian the same verb *zs3* meant both "to paint" and "to write." Henry George Fischer and David N. Keightley illustrate in the fourth and eleventh chapters of this book that the aesthetic use of brush and ink in the Chinese and Egyptian scripts brought about an almost complete amalgamation of art and writing and reflects the representational nature of earliest writing.

The impact of writing

Another important issue dealt with in the following chapters is the value of writing to the development of the human race. Diringer believes that the emergence of systematic codes of writing "represented an immense stride forward in the history of mankind, more profound in its own way than the discovery of fire or the wheel: for while the latter have facilitated man's control over his physical environment, writing has been the foundation for the development of his consciousness and his intellect, his comprehension of himself and the world about him, and in the very widest sense possible, of his critical spirit—indeed, of all that we today regard as his unique heritage and his *raison d'être*."[7] Walter Ong points out that the technology of writing, in particular that of the alphabetic writing of ancient Greece, freed the human mind from the arduous tasks of memorization necessary to store knowledge gained through natural speech.[8] At the same time it opened the door to more original analytical thought, which could be stored by artificial means in a permanent coded system of communication, thereby changing the very nature of human consciousness itself. And as Frank Moore Cross emphasizes in chapter 5, the alphabet not only brought about profound changes in individual and collective consciousness, it also effected the rapid and broad spread of literacy ("in centuries rather than millennia") and advanced the democratization of learning and cultural institutions. And finally, as the examination of the early Middle Eastern myths will show, historical speculation on the origins of languages was often influenced by the medium that fostered it. That is to say, the very act of speculating on the nature of a phenomenon from an oral culture and subjecting it to the scrutiny of an analytical mind-set from a literate culture presupposes fundamental changes in human perspective as mentally distant from Homer as Plato was.

Pictography and the rebus principle

The term "pictography" is an important cornerstone in the theoretical argumentation of most of the chapters on nonalphabetic writing in this volume. Diringer extends the terms "pictography" and "pictogram" to the early stages of true writing and links them directly to the development of phonetic scripts.[9] Pictograms are not unique to ancient writing systems and, in fact, can be found nearly everywhere in today's literate world, from the signs in national parks to the familiar silhouettes on the doors of restrooms. In ancient pictography, a circle, for example, could represent the sun and gradually assume additional abstract notions and become ideograms of ideas, such as "heat" or "light" (fig. 2).

The final stage was achieved when pictograms, logograms, and ideograms became phonograms, that is, when the phonetic value of the sign became independent of the original referent of the sign (and eventually of the external shape) and could be combined productively in a conventional system to intercommunicate (fig. 3). The chapter on cuneiform illustrates this graphic process as well as the rebus principle. In simplified terms, the final stage in the development of writing was something like a rebus process whereby pictograms and ideograms were arranged in sequential order to create a very rudimentary form of written communication. For example, a rebus of logograms (symbols representing entire words, i.e., $, %, +, etc.) containing pictures of an eye, a tin can, a knot, a piece of meat, and a ewe would yield in contemporary English, "I can't meet you." A rebus combining pictograms to create new words, such as a bee plus a leaf to form "belief," provides elementary insight into how signs became

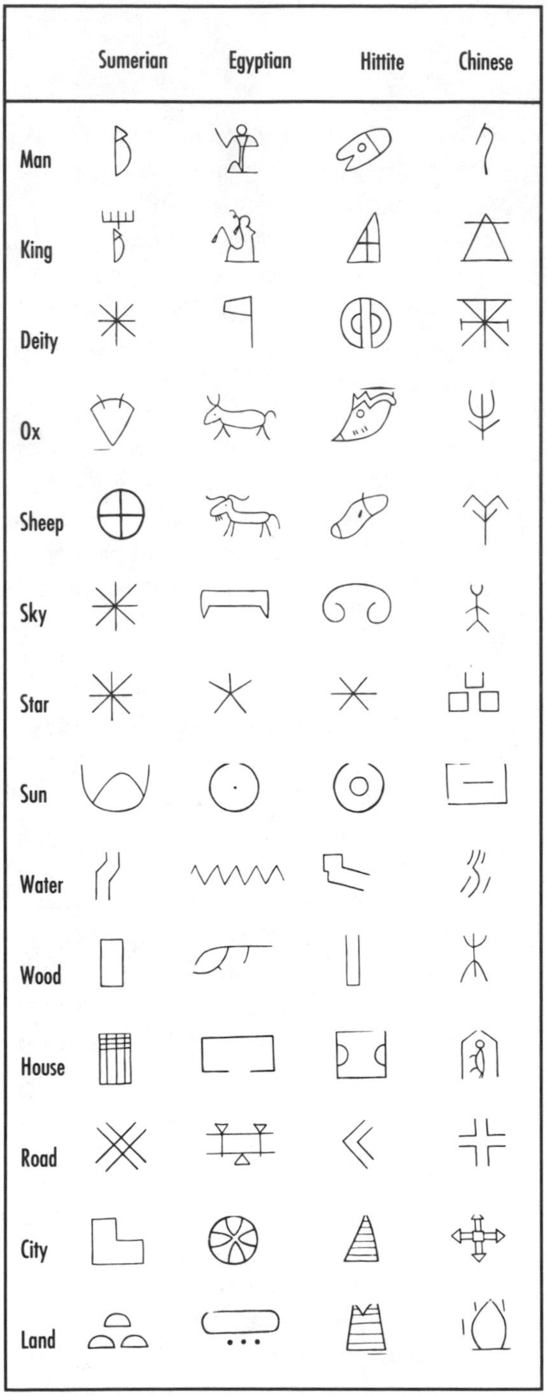

	Sumerian	Egyptian	Hittite	Chinese
Man				
King				
Deity				
Ox				
Sheep				
Sky				
Star				
Sun				
Water				
Wood				
House				
Road				
City				
Land				

Figure 2 Pictorial signs. From Keith Schoville, *Sign, Symbol, Script: An Exhibition on the Origins of Writing and the Alphabet* (Madison: University of Wisconsin, 1984), 3; copyright © 1984 by the Board of Regents of the University of Wisconsin.

associated with syllables, a process (presented here in a simplified form) that represented the crowning achievement of the Sumerians, the inventors of true writing. Since many signs in ancient rebus writing could refer to several different words, determinatives (or classifiers) were employed to indicate the semantic class of the sign. For example, in Egyptian the mace sign followed by a single vertical line (which meant something like "the thing itself") indicated simply "mace," but when followed by a sparrow (which indicated a negative idea) it meant "damage." In Chinese, the graph for *lai,* which meant "growing grain," was differentiated from the homophone *lai,* "to come," by means of a classifier which associated it with the idea of vegetation.

One should not think of the rebus concept as a uniformly applied principle in all nonalphabetic scripts. Each system evolved unique characteristics with distinct graphic and semantic features. For example, cuneiform writing developed a polyphonic system whereby a single sign could represent a range of semantically related words, such as "mouth," "speech," or "tooth," which were differentiated by means of supplementary determinatives. In Chinese this feature was unknown; one graph could also represent a range of different words, but they were not based on semantic relationships and were often the product of what Keightley calls the "componential principle." According to this principle, semantic and phonetic graphs were combined and fused to create new words in a way that allowed for an immense proliferation of graphic elements. In contrast to Chinese, Egyptian hieroglyphics avoided the fusing of parts and maintained a naturalistic quality that permitted the parts of composites to remain clearly recognizable. Thus, instead of using thousands of characters, Egyptian hieroglyphics existed with hundreds.

Given the fact of such great differences in the total reservoir of available characters, one might ask how the scribes of the complex Chinese and Egyptian civilizations managed to deal equally well with the vast intricacies of economic and social administration which their writing systems were designed to serve. The answer may lie in the fact that while Chinese had developed thousands of characters to deal with the complexities of urban society, Egyptian scribes maintained a stable and relatively unchanging system of hieroglyphic writing with the aid of a parallel, cursive writing system, the so-called hieratic script, to deal with administrative business.

The rebus principle also existed in Mayan hieroglyphics, which, like Egyptian hieroglyphics, were also strongly naturalistic and representational. As in cuneiform, Mayan signs were multivalent and a single sign could represent such radically different words as *be'n, ah,* and *ahaw*. F. G. Lounsbury (chapter 12) also points out, however, that multivalency (referred to as polyphony in the chapter on cuneiform) in Mayan hieroglyphics may have been founded on precise numerical relationships rather than on naturalistic representation.

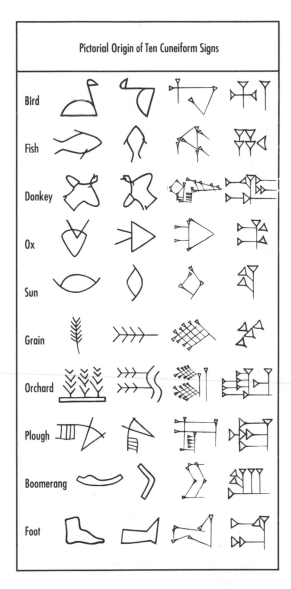

Figure 3 Development of Mesopotamian cuneiform script. From Keith Schoville, *Sign, Symbol, Script: An Exhibition on the Origins of Writing and the Alphabet* (Madison: University of Wisconsin, 1984), 16; copyright © 1984 by the Board of Regents of the University of Wisconsin.

Functions of nonalphabetic writing

The system of numerical calculation employed in Mayan hieroglyphics for calendrical and chronological recording is diagnostic not only of writing in Middle America but also of the evolution of writing throughout the world. Fischer informs us that in Egypt writing was essential for the dating of the regnal year, and for China, Keightley predicates the origins of writing upon the necessity of a script for exact mensuration and bureaucratic control of large-scale public works as well as such cultural functions as lineage-related activities, magic, and a form of divination known as plastromancy.

The functions of nonalphabetic writing discussed by the authors in this book parallel Keightley's analysis of ancient Chinese. A detailed discussion of the functions of writing at its earliest-known stage is offered in the following chapter on clay tokens. Here, Denise Schmandt-Besserat demonstrates the remarkable resemblance of "plain tokens," some of which date from 8,000 B.C., to the earliest pictographic signs employed in Sumerian writing of the fourth millennium B.C. She attributes the origins of the later "complex tokens" to the growing need for elaborate and efficient administrative recordkeeping which arose during the establishment of southern Mesopotamian cities like Uruk, Nippur, and Susa (in chapter 7 Ronald S. Stroud offers a similar explanation for the emergence of writing on Crete). M. W. Green (chapter 3) buttresses this theory with evidence that 90 percent of the Archaic period Uruk tablets were clerical records.

This brings us to the question of why writing systems did not evolve in other cultures with similar skills of representation and mensuration. On the basis of the hypotheses presented above, it appears that although the preconditions of writing, mensuration and pictographic representation, were present in Cro-Magnon Europe as well as many other places throughout the world, the necessary social and economic conditions had not yet evolved to the state that required the kind of intricate and complex administrative recording indicative of early nonalphabetic writing systems. There may have been isolated, individual surges toward the art of writing, but its practical and organizational potentiality had not yet become a necessity.

The authors of writing

In the chapter on cuneiform, Green points out that while the productivity of writing pervaded all forms of daily life in early Mesopotamia, literacy remained the exclusive domain of a special scribal system which had powerful control of the procedures and operations of communication throughout all social and economic strata of Mesopotamian civilization. Similar elitist scribal castes are documented for other nonalphabetic writing systems, including Egyptian hieroglyphics, ancient Chinese, and Mayan as well as some alphabetic systems, such as ogham and Han'gul (fig. 4). With these facts in mind, one should carefully consider the hypothesis that the invention and acquisition of the alphabet brought about the democratization of writing for the masses and ensured the founda-

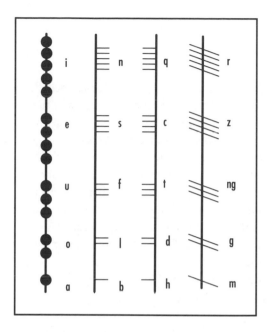

Figure 4 Symbols for vowels and consonants in the ogham script

tions for universal literacy. The examples provided by Chinese, a nonalphabetic script which spawned one of the most literate cultures of the world, and ogham, an alphabetic script which remained the exclusive property of a handful of scribes, raise some important questions about the preconditions and presumptions of literacy for the masses. James A. Bellamy adds historical complexity to the debate with the observation that for the period A.D. 328 to 643, only five inscriptions exist for Arabic, one of the most widely used alphabets in the world. The need for a closer and more precise analysis of the social and economic conditions for literacy becomes all the more apparent when one considers the fact that the world's most illiterate countries use alphabetic scripts while one of the most literate nations, Japan, does not. Nevertheless, as the authors of the chapters on alphabetic writing systems point out, the invention of

the alphabet ushered in a uniquely personalized and individualized means of written communication.

The functions of alphabetic writing

It would, of course, be an exaggeration to claim that the emergence of all major writing systems can be attributed to purely economic or religious functions. Time brings changes in cultural needs, and the conditions surrounding the emergence of scripts are far more complex than the earliest historical records indicate. Stroud (chapter 7) explains that nothing in extant materials suggests that the invention of the Greek alphabet was sparked by trade or commerce. The earliest Greek texts seem to imply that the Greeks first acquired the alphabet simply to establish ownership of objects and to show off writing skills. Rex Wallace (chapter 8) echoes Stroud's point of view and surmises that the wealthiest class in Latium and Etruria acquired writing not for keeping accounts but as a symbol of prestige. Yet both authors agree that very soon after the earliest appearances of writing in Greece and Italy, the Greek and Latin scripts were employed in the service of the state in a way that reflects the functions of writing in Mesopotamia, Egypt, and China. Nevertheless, the apparent functional differences between the earliest alphabetic and nonalphabetic writing systems seem to lend credence to hypotheses suggested by Cross and Stroud that the alphabet personalized writing at a level of self-expression that seems to make the origins of Western writing inseparable from the origins of poetry. Bellamy finds similar social conditions surrounding the earliest documents of Arabic writing, which were used to express such personal feelings as grief, sorrow, mourning, and love.

······

The History of Theories and Myths on the Origins of Writing up to the Twentieth Century

Early Mesopotamian and Egyptian myths

Twentieth-century accounts of the origins of writing differ substantially from the earliest myths, which generally credit the gift of writing to divinity. In a multivolume study of the diversity of languages in early cultures, Arno Borst found such accounts common to all cultures in the process of completing the transition from oral tradition to historical consciousness. As in the Tower of Babel myth, they are the product of a universal belief in religion as the justification for existence.[10] It was, therefore, natural to seek a relationship between language and religion, to believe that language was a gift of God to man and that God granted the gift of writing to bridge man's growing separation from his origins. One should not reject early myths out of hand as irrational effusions of unscientific minds. In many cases, early myths contain concepts which today have become essential to our views of the past; in others, they reveal historical perceptions that can aid our comprehension of the early stages of writing.

Unfortunately for posterity, Sumerian mythographers did not devise a systematic formulation of their cosmological beliefs, and information about the origins of their writing must be gleaned from their myths piece by piece. Political and social changes, historical and regional shifts in the pantheon of divine beings occlude even more the cosmology of the land that came to be known first as Sumer, later as Sumer and Akkad, and still later as Babylonia. This in part helps clarify why the creation of language and writing was attributed in varying degrees to Nabû, Tashmetum (Nabû's consort), Nidaba ("great scribe of heaven"), and Enlil. There is, however, consistent evidence that Sumerian theologians, like those in Egypt and Canaan, believed in the creative power of the divine word ("Your [Enlil's] word—it is plants, your word—it is grain, / Your word is the floodwater, the life of all the lands") and that most Sumerian scribes attributed that power to their patron Nabû (the biblical Nebo [Is. 46.01]).[11] Nabû, foremost son of the highest deity of the pantheon, after whom kings such as Nebuchadnezzar (562 B.C., 2 Kgs 24.01) were named, was revered as "the inventor of the writing of scribes," "the unrivaled scribe," "the scribe of the gods, wielder of the reed-pen" (fig. 5).[12]

As in Sumer, the birth of writing in Egypt was associated with several deities, including a goddess of writing (Seshat) and even a deity of perverse speech. Most Egyptian documents name Thoth as the creator of writing. Thoth, or Tehuti, has been linked through his Egyptian name "Dḥwt(y)" ("messenger" or "measurer") and one of his many mythical functions as son and representative of the sun god, Re, to the Greek messenger of the gods,

(a)

(b)

Figure 5 Emblems associated with the Mesopotamian god of writing, Nabû. (a) Akkadian
cylinder-seal. (b) Three emblems. Nabû's emblems were the table and the stylus which could
be rendered by a single wedge or two vertical
wedges, the lower pierced by the upper one.
On boundary stones the wedge or stylus could
be depicted horizontally on a base. Two vertical rods fixed on a base belonged to the god of
writing. The symbols of Nabû became popular
enough in Late Assyrian times to make it fash-
ionable for men to wear earrings in the shape of
the stylus. Fig. 5(a) reprinted from G. R. Driver,
Semitic Writing (London: Oxford University
Press, 1976), 63, by permission of Oxford University Press; fig. 5(b) reprinted from D. Douglas
van Buren, *Symbols of the Gods in Mesopotamian
Art* (Rome: Pontificium Institutum Biblicum,
1945), 191, by permission of Pontificium Institutum Biblicum.

Hermes, and his Roman counterpart, Mer-
cury.[13]

Extant Egyptian texts portray Thoth
as the supreme intelligence, who during
the Creation uttered words which were
magically transformed into objects of the
material world. As was suggested in the
examples from Mesopotamian mythology,
these utterances also contain no clear differentiation between language and writing.
Borst argues that the failure to distinguish
between the origins of speech and script
is characteristic of many ancient societies,
that most peoples have myths which accept
the magical identity of mythical representation and concrete reality and do not
abstractly separate spoken and written communication.[14] Extant texts from as early
as 2700 B.C. verify that while Egyptian
scribes revered the god Thoth as the patron
of writing, they also associated the "master of papyrus" with the creative powers
of divine speech: "The mighty Great One
is Ptah, who transmitted [life to gods], as
well as (to) their ka's, through his heart, by
which Horus became Ptah, and through his
tongue, by which Thoth became Ptah."[15]

As creator of speech and writing, Thoth
is also the administrative keeper of established order and protector against rebellion: "thou shalt be scribe there and keep in
order those who are in them, *those who may
perform deeds of rebellion . . . against me*."[16]
Like Nabû, Thoth assumed certain calendrical and astronomical attributes of other
gods. He was called the inventor of the arts
and sciences as well as chronologer of the
universe, for which reason he also became
the god of the moon and is often artistically

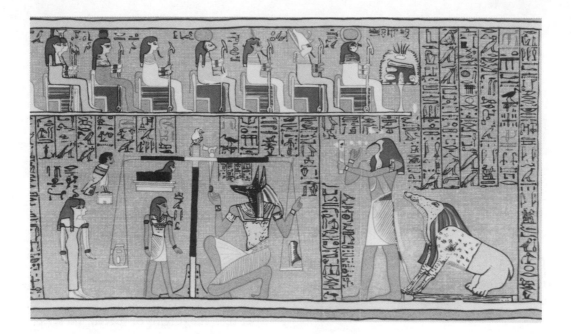

Figure 6 The judgement scene. Here, the deceased is led in and his heart is weighed against "maat," a feather of truth and justice. Ammit, a beast formed of a crocodile, lion, and hippopotamus, waits to devour the heart if it is not found innocent. Thoth (with the Ibis head) records the verdict and Horus presents the deceased to Osiris enthroned between his four sons and two goddesses of "maat." From *The Book of the Dead*, trans. E. A. Wallis Budge (New York: University Books, 1960), 191.

portrayed with a moon crescent. One of Thoth's most prominent functions is illustrated most memorably in the Book of the Dead, where he is portrayed as the scribe of truth and justice in the rite of the weighing of souls (fig. 6).

Other civilizations have produced their own myths about the origins of writing, ranging from Diodorus Siculus's account of Zeus's gift to the muses (*Diodorus of Sicily* 5.74.1–3) to the Chinese legend of the four-eyed dragon god. Common to most of these early records, however, is the basic conviction that writing was sacred and of divine origins. And lest we try to restrict this notion to the earliest nonalphabetic systems of history, we need only consider the legendary accounts Bellamy presents in his chapter on ancient Arabic or the Koran, where Allah is named the creator of writing:

> Read, in the name of thy Lord!
> Who created man from congealed blood!
> Read, for thy Lord is most generous!
> Who taught the pen!
> Taught man what he did not know!
> 96.2–6 [17]

Or, to take a more recent example, consider the native alphabet of the Far East, the Korean Han'gul. Han'gul was purportedly created by King Seijong (1417–50; and his palace scholars?) but was presented as having been born of divine origins: "It is the revelation of Heaven to the mind of the sage King to accomplish through his hand this great task and it is beyond the power of us, his subjects, to fully explain the wonders of its origins and essence." [18]

At the nucleus of this vast array of mythical functions of the Egyptian and Sumerian as well as other deities of writing is a profound sense of the existential importance of writing to political power and order, to justice, and to the preservation of human life and to human destiny. The reverence which Middle Eastern cultures held for the religious and political values of written language represents one of the most immutable factors in the history of writing. Antiquity, as well as all literate societies since, recognized that with the invention of writing, words and ideas were no longer condemned to the brief fate of the spoken word or the short-lived memory of tradition.

Greek and Roman historians on the origins of writing

Even more diverse accounts of the origins of writing have been preserved in the works of Greek and Roman historians, most of which were collected and expounded upon by a few well-known figures, such as Herodotus, Diodorus Siculus, Pliny the Elder, and Tacitus. Characteristic of most of the Greco-Roman accounts are the political and cultural motivations they serve. Prior to Diodorus Siculus's *Historical Library*, Greek history and philosophy provide little information on ancient Greek views of where and when writing came about. Homer knew of a multiplicity of world languages but other than a vague and controversial reference to "grim, deadly signs" written on a folded tablet (*Il.*, 6.168–69), the *Iliad* reveals no knowledge of the origins of writing. Nor does the father of history, Herodotus, address the question, although he does offer the generally ac-

cepted view in Greek antiquity (a view also supported by Cross and Stroud in chapters 5 and 7) that the Phoenicians under Cadmus "brought into Hellas the alphabet, which had hitherto been unknown, as I think, to the Greeks" (*History*, 5.58).[19]

In *Philebus* (18a), Plato mentions that "Theuth" (the Egyptian Thoth) distinguished three classes of phonetic units (vowels, semivowels, and mutes) and designates the learning of these elements as "the art of letters." Nevertheless, Plato is more concerned with the ontological relation of language and knowledge than with the question of origin and in fact opposed writing, which "will create forgetfulness in the learners' souls, because they will not use their memories; they will trust to the eternal written characters and not remember of themselves."[20] Plato's opposition to writing is ironic, for the reasoning processes he sought to instill in his students were dependent on the visual, dissecting mode of thinking that written texts facilitate.

Diodorus Siculus, an ecclectic historian whose work rarely measures up to modern canons of historical accuracy, presents a somewhat amorphous collage of ideas on the origins of writing. If his scattered observations can justifiably be placed in a uniform context, Diodorus seems to express one of the earliest, albeit mythologized, versions of the unidirectional theory of writing. The unidirectional theory holds that writing systems progress from logographic to syllabographic and finally alphabetographic writing but not the reverse. He describes the earliest generations of the human race as bestial beings who gradually developed a conventional, symbolic type of writing and "by agreeing with one another upon symbols for each thing which presented itself to them, made known among themselves the significance which was to be attached to each term" (1.7.6–8.4).[21] Later, Diodorus rebuts Egyptian claims for the priority of their script and civilization by claiming that Zeus gave "the letters" of writing to the Greeks, who regressed into a state of ignorance without writing after the great flood, which destroyed "the majority of mankind" and "all written documents" (5.57.3–4).[22] He also expands the Phoenician tradition (which he places before Homer) with the argument that the Phoenicians learned the alphabet from the Syrians (5.74.1; here the reference is probably to Aramaic).

The natural historian Pliny the Elder (A.D. 23–79) is also aware of the Egyptian and Syrian theories as well as what he calls the Assyrian origin of writing, which may be a reference to cuneiform script (*Nat. Hist.*, 7.56.192). He expands the Phoenician tradition even further with the claim that the Pelasgians imported the Greek alphabet to Latium (7.56.193) and engages in some fanciful speculation about the origins of astronomical mensuration in Babylon in 750,000 B.C. (7.56.193). Pliny, as do most other Roman historians, ignores the important fact, which Rex Wallace points out in chapter 8, that the Etruscans played perhaps the most significant role in the constitution of the Latin alphabet, particularly in the settlements around Rome.

After Pliny the Elder, few additions to the corpus of theories on writing were forthcoming from secular historians and philosophers. Tacitus reiterates earlier theories and modifies Pliny's view of the emergence of the Latin alphabet with an account of the Etrurians' and Aborigines' bringing the alphabet to Italy (*Annals*, 11.14). Regardless of the accomplishments of Roman historiography, the dominating theories during the first millennium A.D. came from the quills of Jewish and Christian theologians and historians.

The Judeo-Christian tradition

At the nucleus of the religious theories about the beginnings of language and writing were the attempts by Jewish and Christian theologians to come to grips with the omnipresent influence of Hellenism. For some, this meant a vigorous and defensive reinterpretation of tradition against Hellenistic influence as in the Book of Jubilees. For others, like Clement of Alexandria, a solution to the conflict between Christianity and pagan thought lay in the fusion of Christian truth and Greek philosophy. The linguistic axis around which both approaches turned was the justification of the monogenetic theory of Hebrew as the original, holy language of the Garden of Eden, the cradle of civilization. Here we can observe the beginning of the tendency in Judeo-Christian tradition to subordinate the distinction between script and speech to the necessity of formal apologetics.

Genesis (2.19–20, Adam's naming of the creatures) has often been cited as the earliest theory of the original language in spite of apparent contradictions in the Old Testament itself (e.g., Ez. 14.3). The author of the Book of Jubilees or The Little Genesis, written between 135 and 105 B.C., rejects Adam as the inventor of writing. For this Pharisaic defender of the priestly code, the Hebrew God had invented writing, and Enoch, the descendant of Adam, "was the first who learned writing and knowledge and wisdom" (4.17).[23] Here, writing takes on a historiographic dimension in that it lends permanence to man's remembrance of the beginning of history and preserves the record of man's covenant with God. After the Flood and division of the earth into three parts, writing was lost and recovered again from the angels by Abram. The esoteric aspects of the Book of Jubilees aside, the concepts of a monogenetic origin of writing and the subsequent tripartite division of land and language (which ultimately derives from Gen. 10.1–29) had monumental influence on historiography as late as the eighteenth century and on cartography until the Renaissance, when Ptolemy's maps were rediscovered (fig. 7). This is not to say that ideas espoused in the Book of Jubilees did not have their detractors. In fact, in the following three centuries the question of the original script assumed the proportions of a complex and heated debate. Cabalistic tradition as represented in the *Sepher Yetzirah* extrapolated Abraham as the inventor of the alphabet. Declarations by Philo of Alexandria (ca. 25 B.C.–ca. A.D. 50) that Moses had learned the alphabet from the Egyptians (Eusebius, *Praep. Ev.* [31d–32a], 1.9) and denigrations by the Roman encyclopedist Aulus Cornelius Celsus (first century A.D.) of the antiquity of Moses' story of the Tower of Babel sparked heated

Figure 7 World map from Isidore of Seville (ca. 560–636), *Etymologiarum*, Augsburg, 1462. Courtesy of the Newberry Library, Chicago.

responses from Clement of Alexandria and his disciple Origen, both of whom represent the culmination of two centuries of apologetics for the young Christian theology.

Speaking for the harmony of philosophy and the Old Testament as a preparation for the Christian faith, Clement tried to justify Hebrew as the original language by using the secular logic he had learned from Greek philosophers. He modified the universalist theory from Greek philosophy and postulated an ideal, perfect language (in this case Hebrew) from which various imperfect, real languages descend. Origen substantiated Alexandrian apologetics by advocating the theory that Moses and the Judaic tradition superseded Greek antiquity (*Contra Celsum*, 4.21). Here again, bear in mind that early apologists were more occupied with philosophical posturing than with the clear distinction between the original language and the first writing system.

The impact of the theological speculation of the Judaic tradition and the Alexandrian school on the following centuries is manifest in the writings of some of the most influential representatives of early Christian theology and philosophy. Saint Jerome (340–420), whose Latin version of the Bible (the Vulgata) remained the official version of the Roman Catholic Church and the source of all vernacular translations until the Reformation, continued the belief in the monogenetic theory as did Saint Augustine (354–430), who wrote that "the Hebrew language always had a literate record of itself" (*Civ. Dei.*, 18.39).[24] There were, of course, independent thinkers such as Boethius (480–525, *De consolatione philosophiae*), who broke through the growing sterility of contemporary thought and reflected on the difficulty of correlating theological postulations with the diversity of languages as a natural condition of man. By the High Middle Ages, however, the monogenetic theory was irreversibly ensconced in the minds of even such thoughtful scholars as Thomas Aquinas and Roger Bacon and would dominate Western thinking on the origins of writing for the next five hundred years. A reevaluation of the monogenetic theory was called for by the humanist Joseph Scaliger (1540–1609), the father of philological text criticism. Scaliger protested for the application of the comparative method and a reconsideration of the Phoenician theory. But Scaliger and other contemporaries of like mind were forced to abdicate in the face of overwhelming religious tradition. The first serious critical opposition to the cradle-of-civilization

theory was voiced by the German philosopher Gottfried Leibniz (1646–1716). Using arguments that foreshadow the momentous advances of nineteenth-century comparative philology, Leibniz proposed abandoning attempts to derive all languages from Hebrew which itself seemed to be a descendant of an "older and richer language."[25]

Western speculation on the origins of the Chinese and Egyptian scripts

Examples of the extent to which theological and philosophical speculation distorted Western perspectives of major writing systems for many centuries exist in abundance in the historical documentation of the origins of the Chinese script and Egyptian hieroglyphics. There are, of course, many more examples for other civilizations, but these two will serve to demonstrate the immense historical barriers that twentieth-century scholars have had to overcome.

It would be fruitless here even to attempt to examine the plethora of descriptions of China in memoirs, diaries, histories, and poetry that reach back at least as far as Claudius Ptolemy's brief notation (ca. A.D. 150) of an unknown land lying east beyond "sina" and "the regions of the Seres" (50.27).[26] Ptolemy's geographical reference to China, if indeed it is such, foreruns the almost exclusively geographical and commercial interest of Europeans in China until the late Middle Ages.[27] Given the strong biblical tradition of the tripartite division of the world in European cartography with Jerusalem at the center and Paradise in the East, where China also lay, the "Empire of Cathay" became a natural point of attraction for the growing numbers of world travelers like Marco Polo (ca. 1254–ca. 1324) and John Marignolli (1290–1355).

By the time Marco Polo set out on his famous journey to the East, Roger Bacon had already recorded one of the earliest Western accounts of Chinese writing: "The people in Cathay to the east write with the same instrument with which painters paint, forming in one character groups of letters, each group representing a sentence. By this method characters are formed with many letters together, whence reasonable and natural characters have been composed of letters and have the meaning of sentences."[28] Bacon's European-oriented perspective of alphabetic writing is repeated in a fourteenth-century document by an Armenian historian who saw a resemblance of Chinese characters to "the Latin letters."[29]

After Jesuit missionaries had become established in China in the sixteenth century, reports began to filter back to Europe which seemed to verify even further the monogenetic canon. Irrefragable evidence of China's link to the Middle East seemed to be at hand in 1625 with the discovery of the so-called Nestorian tablet (after a Christian sect from Mesopotamia and Persia), which contained a mixture of Chinese and Syrian writing. Convinced that the Nestorian reports provided sufficient reason for a new interpretation of an old theory, Georg Horn (1620–70), professor of history at Leiden, proclaimed the Chinese to be descendants of Cain, who had separated from the birthplace of humanity before the Flood.[30] Horn's claims were reaffirmed by many others in the course of the next two hundred years.

Horn's ruminations were essentially nothing new; they simply represent one of many attempts to fit the exciting discoveries being made by world explorers during the European Renaissance into an overworn image from the past. Similar proclamations had also been made after the Spanish discovery of the Mayan civilization. To theologians and scholars of the sixteenth century, the pyramids and Mayan glyphs found on monuments around the Yucatán town "Great Cairo" were proof of the ten lost tribes of Israel and thus of the link of Mayan civilization to the cradle of civilization.[31] And like Roger Bacon, the sixteenth-century Spanish missionary Diego de Landa also tried to understand the elusive Mayan glyphs at least partially in alphabetical terms: "I will set down here an alphabet of these letters since their difficulty does not allow anything more."[32] As Lounsbury expostulates in chapter 12, however, Bishop de Landa may have been closer to the truth than most linguists have believed (fig. 8).

Early Chinese historians, on the other hand, attributed the origins of their script to prehistoric emperors such as Fu-hsi (a name Georg Horn associated with Adam), who as universal ruler laid the foundation for chronology and writing. This view obviously conflicted with the beliefs of the Jesuits and became a contributing factor to the increasing discord that arose after the arrival of the Franciscans and Dominicans

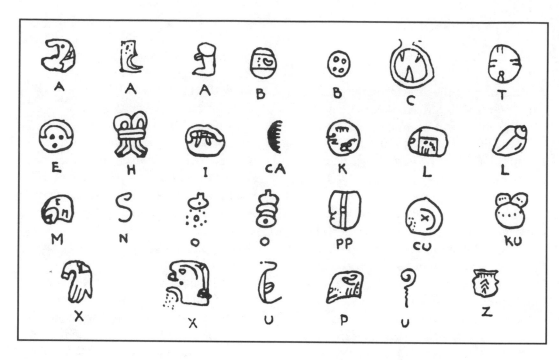

Figure 8 Diego de Landa's alphabet.

in the seventeenth century.[33] Thereafter, numerous internecine religious clashes and disputes with the Chinese led to persecutions and expulsions. Colonial attitudes and the arrival of Protestant missionaries did little to resolve cultural conflicts in the nineteenth century, and by mid-century cultural chauvinism had seriously tainted European research on the origins of Chinese writing. In the 1860s, Terrier de Lacouperie wrote: "They [the Chinese people] cannot conceal the fact that they are themselves intruders in China proper, they have always tried to use big words and large geographical denominations, which blind the unwary readers, to shield their comparatively small beginnings."[34] Even the more cautious contemporary James Legge failed to avoid the theological pitfalls of the monogenetic canon when he asserted that the Chinese were called the "black-haired

people" "to distinguish them from the descendents of Noah, from whom they separated, and who, while they journeyed to the east, moved in an opposite and westward direction."[35]

Keightley's discussion of the origins of Chinese departs sharply from such pre-twentieth-century interpretations. For Keightley, the discovery and decipherment of oracle-bone inscriptions, which had lain undiscovered in the ground for three thousand years, revolutionized our understanding of the origins of the Chinese script. He rejects any genetic connection to Sumerian, Egyptian, or Hittite writing systems (as well as to Neolithic markings on pots at the Yang-Shao site), and in his analysis of archaeological evidence discovered during the twentieth century, he shows why the door has closed permanently on a millennium of philosophical and theological ruminations about the origins of ancient Chinese.

In *The Myth of Egypt and Its Hieroglyphs*,

Erik Iversen has examined more than two thousand years of evidence to show that the Western world's mystical veneration for the wisdom of the Egyptians and their hieroglyphics was based on preconceived notions about the Egyptian mind that began with the Greek classical writers. Iversen notes that "none of the Greek writers had any first hand knowledge of the hieroglyphics" and that the magical identity of myth and reality in Egyptian was foreign to the Greek way of abstract analysis.[36] In an attempt to make the Egyptian view of writing comply with scientific, logical reasoning, the Greeks and early Christian fathers explained hieroglyphics in terms of symbolic and allegorical relationships. Clement of Alexandria (*Stromata*, 5.4.20–21) was the first to distinguish clearly three types of Egyptian writing, namely, hieroglyphic (from ἱερογλυφικα, "sacred carved letters"), for monumental inscriptions; hieratic (from ἱερατικος, "priestly"), a cursive script for secular and occasionally religious texts; and demotic (from δημοτικος, "common," "popular"), for everyday purposes (fig. 9).

As indicated above, Clement understood Egyptian writing to be allegorical. In his *Stromata* he admits of two kinds of hieroglyphics: "Of the symbolic, one kind speaks literally by imitation, and another writes as it were figuratively; and another is quite allegorical, using certain enigmas" (5.4.20).[37] Iversen admits that the Egyptian practice of deriving some of the signs by mythical speculation did influence later interpretations and that an actual allegorical meaning of some of the signs enhanced this aspect of Egyptian writing in Western tradition. This, however, misses the point.

For example, the picture of the "goose" was interpreted allegorically to mean "son" because of the belief that the goose more than any animal loved its offspring.[38] In fact, the goose picture was used to mean "son" because the words for "son" and "goose" are homonymous. That is to say, Egyptian hieroglyphics are, and always were, phonetic.

This crucial point was obscured for almost the next two millennia by the persistence of tradition. Diodorus Siculus offers a fitting example of the beginnings of the Western tradition of allegorical interpretation:

> For their writing does not express the intended concept by means of syllables joined one to another, but by means of the significance of the objects which have been copied and by its figurative meaning which has been impressed upon the memory by practice. For instance, they draw the picture of a hawk, a crocodile, a snake, and of the human body—an eye, a hand, a face, and the like. Now the hawk signifies to them everything which happens swiftly, since this animal is practically the swiftest of winged creatures. (3.4.1–2)[39]

This method of interpretation was applied several centuries later in a book that was to become one of the most influential and unchallenged sources on Egyptian hieroglyphics during the Renaissance: *The Hieroglyphics of Horapollo. Hieroglyphics* is thought to have been written down sometime in the fifth century by a certain

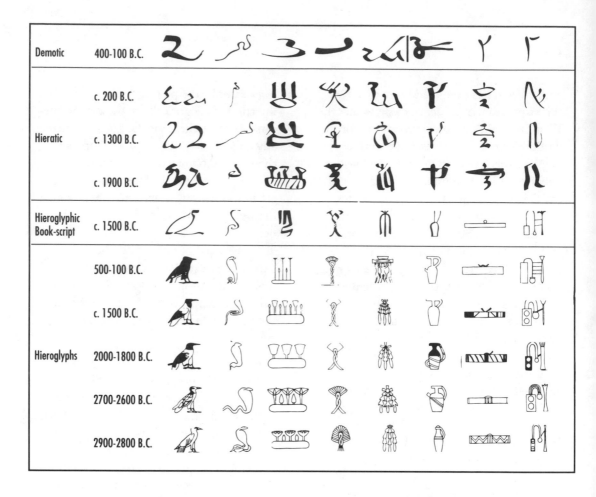

Demotic	400-100 B.C.							
Hieratic	c. 200 B.C.							
	c. 1300 B.C.							
	c. 1900 B.C.							
Hieroglyphic Book-script	c. 1500 B.C.							
Hieroglyphs	500-100 B.C.							
	c. 1500 B.C.							
	2000-1800 B.C.							
	2700-2600 B.C.							
	2900-2800 B.C.							

Figure 9 Development of Egyptian scripts. From Keith Schoville, *Sign, Symbol, Script: An Exhibition on the Origins of Writing and the Alphabet* (Madison: University of Wisconsin, 1984), 27; copyright © 1984 by the Board of Regents of the University of Wisconsin.

Horapollo and translated into Greek perhaps two centuries later. That *Hieroglyphics* strengthened the allegorical relationship between sign and meaning is evidenced by the following explanation of the hawk picture: "When they wish to symbolize a god, or something sublime, or something lowly, or superiority, or victory, or Aries, or Aphrodite, they draw a hawk. A god, because the hawk is fecund or long-lived."[40]

Hieroglyphics gained a permanent niche in European libraries when the Italian humanist Marcilio Ficino (1433–99) published the book at the beginning of the sixteenth century. Ficino's efforts to join together Neoplatonic philosophy, humanism, Christianity, and Egyptian wisdom were driven by a vision he found common to all four: the eternal search for the knowledge and revelation of God. For Ficino, Egyptian hieroglyphics were allegorical, albeit imperfect, revelations of the one God in a pre-Christian civilization.

Although Ficino's grasp of hieroglyphics was erroneous, his work inspired much interest in Horapollo. During the next hundred years some thirty editions, translations, and reprints of *Hieroglyphics* appeared. Little progress was made in changing traditional attitudes toward Egyptian writing, however, until the seventeenth century, when the German scholar Athanasius Kircher (1601–80) established Egyptology as a specific philological discipline and advocated a comparative study of Coptic and hieroglyphics.

Revolutionary changes in Egyptology came with the discovery of the Rosetta stone in 1797 by French military troops during Napoleon's Egyptian campaign (fig. 10). The Rosetta stone bears an inscription in three different scripts: the bottom script is Greek, which could be read; the middle script, hieratic; and the top, hieroglyphic. Copies of the inscriptions were sent to various European scholars for decipherment, but a complete decipherment was not achieved until 1822, when a young French scholar, Jean François Champollion, proved the phonetic character of the inscription and brought to an end yet another long tradition of fallacious speculation.

Nineteenth-century decipherments and archaeological discoveries

As the example of the discovery and decipherment of the Rosetta stone demonstrates, the philological and archaeological research of the nineteenth and early twentieth centuries indeed marks the turning point in our understanding of early writing systems and provides the foundation for the scholarly background of many of the contributions to this volume. The archaeological discoveries and decipherments are far too numerous to be mentioned here, but suffice it to say that the independent decipherments of cuneiform writing by Georg Friedrich Grotefend (1775–1853) and Henry Rawlinson (1810–95), the decipherment of the Decree of Canopus (March 7, 238 B.C.) (second only to the Rosetta stone in its value for the deciphering of ancient Egyptian), the discovery and unraveling of the Hittite texts at Tell el-Amana and Boğazköy, and Arthur Evans's (1857–1941) find at Knossos of tablets containing both Greek and Semitic elements represent inestimable advances in our knowledge of the past and helped usher in the concept of a much more cohesive unity of the Near East and the West.

The history of nineteenth- and twentieth-century efforts to decipher early writing systems is, however, not entirely a success story. Some philological research was beset by failures that led scholars into linguistic blind alleys. The decipherment of Mayan hieroglyphs is a case in point. In chapter 12, Floyd G. Lounsbury takes issue with nineteenth- and twentieth-century conceptions of the earliest decipherment of Mayan hieroglyphs by Diego de Landa, who collected information on Mayan customs and language in a manuscript known as "Relacion de las Cosas de Yucatán." As noted earlier, Landa claimed that Mayan writing was alphabetic. After the much-belated publication of an abridged version of his work in 1864, however, Western scholars gradually abandoned their attempts to read

texts with Landa's alphabet and proclaimed Mayan writing to be nonphonetic. Lounsbury elaborates on the major steps taken to verify the historical relationships between the Mayan script and real persons. He then establishes the linguistic premises for relating calendrical data to syntactic constructions of spoken language and for analyzing the phonetic nature of the hieroglyphs. On the basis of close analyses of several "king" glyphs, he demonstrates how the flexibility of Mayan writing and the rich, combinatory alternatives and equivalences available in the graphic system allowed scribes an unusual linguistic and poetic freedom of virtuosity.

Some of the archaeological discoveries and decipherments of the nineteenth century have revolutionized the Western world's views of the origins of man. To cite just one case, from 1873, when Darwin's theory of evolution was beginning to undermine confidence in the biblical account of the Creation, George Smith discovered the missing eleventh tablet of the Sumerian epic of *Gilgamesh*. The descriptions of the Deluge in this tablet, written down many centuries prior to the corresponding event of the Old Testament, caused a crisis in classical studies of biblical antiquity and catapulted fifteen centuries of recorded history before the civilizations of the Greeks and Hebrews into the con-

Figure 10 The Rosetta stone. From Keith Schoville, *Sign, Symbol, Script: An Exhibition on the Origins of Writing and the Alphabet* (Madison: University of Wisconsin, 1984), 22; copyright © 1984 by the Board of Regents of the University of Wisconsin.

Approximate Dates for the Origins of Major Writing Systems

Plain tokens in the Fertile Crescent	8000–7500 B.C.
Complex tokens in South Mesopotamia	3350 B.C.
Sumerian cuneiform	3200 B.C.
Egyptian hieroglyphics	3050 B.C.
Linear A	1650 B.C.
Old Canaanite alphabet	1500 B.C.
Linear B	1380 B.C.
Chinese	1200 B.C.
Phoenician	1100 B.C.
Old Hebrew	1000 B.C.
Aramaic	11th cent. B.C.
Greek	740 B.C.
Latin	620 B.C.
Runes	25 A.D.
Ogham	200 A.D.
Mayan	292 A.D.
Arabic	328 A.D.

sciousness of modern man.

Some of the chapters in this book also reshape the temporal boundaries of the beginnings of writing (see chart). Applying precise linguistic analysis, Elmer H. Antonsen debunks the long tradition of *mysteria et arcana sapientiae* that once clouded research in runic writing and at one point in early modern Scandinavian history instilled so much fear in scholars that "nobody would admit to any knowledge of runes for fear of being accused of sorcery."[41] Antonsen reevaluates the frontiers of this oldest of Germanic writing systems and emphasizes the necessity of utilizing archaeological dating. He calls for comparisons of not just the shapes of letters but also the linguistic and orthographic features that determine the derivation of an entire writing system. Finally, the theoretic conclusions of Denise Schmandt-Besserat's examination of Mesopotamian tokens complement the historical ramifications of the discovery of the missing Gilgamesh tablet and push back the origins of writing another two thousand years.

The ideas and theories offered in the following chapters on the origins of major writing systems of the world do not, of course, represent the final word on these matters. They do provide the indispensable link between the historical speculations of the past and the direction of research in the future.

······

Notes

1. See David Diringer, *Writing*, Ancient Peoples and Places, 25 (London: Thames and Hudson, 1962), 27–34, and I. J. Gelb, *A Study of Writing*, rev. ed. (Chicago: University of Chicago Press, 1962), 24–59.

2. Diringer, *Writing*, 16.

3. Gelb, *A Study of Writing*, 12; Naomi S. Baron, *Speech, Writing, and Sign: A Functional View of Linguistic Representation* (Bloomington: Indiana University Press, 1981), 152.

4. Baron, *Speech, Writing, and Sign*, 151. To illustrate this often overlooked aspect in the relationship between art and writing Baron also discusses common points of convergence in the Bayeux Tapestry and a fresco cycle. She utilizes in part arguments forged by the eighteenth-century German author and critic Gotthold Lessing in his *Laocoon, or the Boundaries between Painting and Poetry*, where Lessing incisively attacks the late-medieval practice of portraying epic events in tableau paintings.

5. See Alexander Marshak, *The Roots of Civilization* (New York: McGraw-Hill, 1972), 147–68.

6. "The Grammar of Dionysios Thrax," trans. Tomás Davidson, *Journal of Speculative Philosophy* 8 (1873): 328.

7. Diringer, *Writing*, 19.

8. See Walter J. Ong, *Orality and Literacy: The Technologizing of the Word* (London: Methuen, 1982), 78–83 and 89–90.

9. Diringer, *Writing*, 21.

10. Arno Borst, *Der Turmbau von Babel: Geschichte der Meinungen über Ursprung und Vielfalt der Sprachen und Völker* (Stuttgart: Hiersemann, 1957), 1:15–42.

11. Quotation in James Pritchard, *Ancient Near Eastern Texts Relating to the Old Testament*, 3d ed. (Princeton: Princeton University Press, 1969), 575.

12. G. R. Driver, *Semitic Writing: From Pictograph to Alphabet*, new rev. ed. (London: Oxford University Press, 1976), 64.

13. Philo Byblius, a first-century Greek historian of the Phoenicians, put forth the unusual and controversial thesis that a learned historian from the second half of the second millennium B.C., Sanchuniathon of Berytus, had researched the writings of a certain Taautos and recorded in Phoenician that Taautos had reasoned out the invention of letters in order to begin a compilation of historical records (preserved by Eusebius of Caesarea, 264?–339?, in *Praep. Ev.* 1.9.31–32). The fame of his invention then spread throughout Egypt under the name Thöyth and in Alexandria as Thoth, the form generally accepted today. For an in-depth discussion of the name "Thoth," see Otto Eisfeldt, *Taautos und Sanchunjaton* (Berlin: Akademie Verlag, 1952).

14. For a detailed discussion see Arno Borst, *Der Turmbau von Babel* 4:2004–47. See also Erik Iversen, *The Myth of Egypt and Its Hieroglyphs in European Tradition* (Copenhagen: Gec Gad Publishers, 1961), 38–41.

15. Pritchard, *Ancient Near Eastern Texts*, 5. See also Driver, *Semitic Writing*, 70ff., for examples from Babylonian writing which underscore the ambigious relationship between language and writing.

16. Pritchard, *Ancient Near Eastern Texts*, 8.

17. The Qur'an, trans. E. H. Palmer (Delhi: Motilal Banarsidass, 1965), 2:336.

18. King Seijong Memorial Society, *King Seijong the Great* (Seoul: King Seijong Memorial Society, 1970), 60–61.

19. *Herodotus*, trans. A. D. Godley, Loeb Classical Library (Cambridge, Mass.: Harvard University Press, 1957), 3:63.

20. *The Dialogues of Plato*, 4th ed., trans. B. Jowett (Oxford: Clarendon Press, 1955), 3:184.

21. *Diodorus of Sicily*, trans. C. H. Oldfather, Loeb Classical Library (Cambridge, Mass.: Harvard University Press, 1946), 4:29.

22. Ibid., 4:253.

23. *The Old Testament Pseudepigrapha*, vol. 2, ed. James H. Charlesworth (Garden City, N.Y.: Doubleday, 1985), 62.

24. Saint Augustine, *The City of God Against the Pagans*, trans. W. C. Greene, Loeb Classical Library (Cambridge, Mass.: Harvard University Press, 1960), 13.

25. *Leibniz and Ludolf on Things Linguistic: Excerpts from Their Correspondence (1688–1703)*, trans. and ed. J. T. Waterman, University of California Publications in Linguistics, vol. 88 (Berkeley: University of California Press, 1978), 41.

26. *Geography of Claudius Ptolemy*, trans. and ed. E. L. Stevenson (New York: New York Public Library, 1932), 37–38.

27. For a detailed historical account of geographical expeditions to China, see Ferdinand Freiherr von Richthofen, *China: Ergebnisse eigener Reisen*, vol. 2 (Berlin: Dietrich Reimer, 1877).

28. *The Opus Majus of Roger Bacon*, trans. R. B. Burke (New York: Russell and Russell, 1962), 389.

29. *Cathay and the Way Thither, Being a Collection of Medieval Notices of China*, 2d ed., trans. H. Yule (1866; repr., Taipei, 1922), 1:259.

30. See Borst, *Der Turmbau von Babel*, vol. 3, pt. 1, pp. 1304–1308, for additional accounts.

31. *The Discovery of Yucatán by Francisco Hernández de Córdoba: Documents and Narratives Concerning the Discovery and Conquest of Latin America*, trans. and ed. H. R. Wagner, n.s., no. 1 (Berkeley: The Cortez Society, 1942), 59.

32. *Diego de Landa's Account of the Affairs of Yucatán: The Maya*, trans. and ed. A. R. Pagden (Chicago: J. Philip O'Hara, 1975), 125.

33. See Richthofen, *China* 2:627–92, on missionaries and scientists.

34. Terrier de Lacouperie, *The Language of China before the Chinese* (1866; repr., Taipei, 1966), 4.

35. James Legge, "Prologomena," *The Chinese Classics* (Hong Kong, 1865), 3:191.

36. Iversen, *The Myth of Egypt and Its Hieroglyphs*, 41 and 39–40.

37. *The Ante-Nicene Fathers: Translations of the Fathers Down to A.D. 325*, vol. 2, ed. Alexander Roberts and James Donaldson (Grand Rapids, Mich.: B. Eerdmans, 1983), 449.

38. Iversen, *The Myth of Egypt and Its Hieroglyphs*, 48.

39. *Diodorus of Sicily* (1953), 2:97.

40. *The Hieroglyphics of Horapollo*, trans. G. Boas, Bollingen Series, 23 (New York: Pantheon Books, 1950), 59–60.

41. *Ole Worms Correspondence with Icelanders*, ed. J. Benediktsson, Bibliotheca Arnamagnaeana, 7 (Copenhagen: Einar Munksgaard, 1949), xii.

••••••

Further Readings

Baron, Naomi S. *Speech, Writing, and Sign: A Functional View of Linguistic Representation*. Bloomington: Indiana University Press, 1981.

Borst, Arno. *Der Turmbau von Babel: Geschichte der Meinungen über Ursprung und Vielfalt der Sprachen und Völker*. 4 vols. Stuttgart: Hiersemann, 1957–63.

Ceram, C. W., ed. *Hands on the Past*. New York: Knopf, 1966.

Chadwick, Henry. *Early Christian Thought and the Classical Tradition*. New York: Oxford University Press, 1966.

Chappel, Warren. *The Living Alphabet*. Charlottesville: University Press of Virginia, 1980.

Cohen, Marcel. *La grande invention de l'écriture et son évolution*. 3 vols. Paris: C. Klincksieck, 1958.

Denel, Leo. *The Treasures of Time*. Cleveland: World Publishing, 1961.

Diamond, A. S. *The History and Origin of Language*. New York: Philosophical Society, 1959.

Diringer, David. *The Alphabet: A Key to the History of Mankind*. 3d. ed. 2 vols. New York: Funk and Wagnalls, 1968.

———. *Writing*. Ancient Peoples and Places, 25. London: Thames and Hudson, 1962.

Doblhofer, Ernst. *Voices in Stone: The Decipherment of Ancient Scripts and Writings*. Translated by Mervyn Savill. New York: Viking Press, 1961.

Driver, G. R. *Semitic Writing: From Pictograph to Alphabet*. New rev. ed. London: Oxford University Press, 1976.

Gelb, I. J. *A Study of Writing: The Foundations of Grammatology*. Rev. ed. Chicago: University of Chicago Press, 1963.

Gordon, Cyrus. *Forgotten Scripts: How They Were Deciphered and Their Impact on Contemporary Culture*. New York: Basic Books, 1968.

"Human Records: A Survey of Their History from the Beginnings." *Bulletin of the John Rylands Library*. Vol. 27. Ed. Henry Guppy. Manchester, 1942–43.

Iversen, Erik. *The Myth of Egypt and Its Hieroglyphs in European Tradition*. Copenhagen: Gec Gad Publishers, 1961.

Jackson, Donald. *The Story of Writing*. London: Studio Vista and Parker Pen, 1981.

Jensen, Hans. *Sign, Symbol and Script: An Account of Man's Efforts to Write*. Translated by George Unwin. New York: Putnam, 1969.

Marshack, Alexander. *The Roots of Civilization*. New York: McGraw-Hill, 1972.

Nakanishi, Akiri. *Writing Systems of the World: Alphabets, Syllabaries, Pictograms*. Rutland, Vt.: Tuttle, 1982.

Naveh, J. *Early History of the Alphabet*. Leiden: E. J. Brill, 1982.

Ong, Walter J. *Orality and Literacy: The Technologizing of the Word*. London: Methuen, 1982.

Révész, G. *The Origins and Prehistory of Language*. New York: Philosophical Society, 1959.

Sampson, J. *Writing Systems*. Stanford: Stanford University Press, 1985.

Schmitt, Alfred. *Entstehung und Entwicklung von Schriften*. Ed. Claus Haebler. Cologne: Böhlau Verlag, 1980.

Stam, James H. *Inquiries in the Origin of Language: The Fate of a Question*. New York: Harper and Row, 1976.

Wellisch, Hans H. *The Conversion of Scripts: Its Nature, History, and Utilization*. New York: Wiley, 1978.

2

Two Precursors of Writing: Plain and Complex Tokens

......

Denise Schmandt-Besserat

......

Plain and Complex Tokens

Before the Sumerian writing system—the first script ever developed—was invented at the end of the fourth millennium B.C., accounting was practiced in the ancient Middle East by means of small counters.[1] These were small tokens modeled in clay in different shapes, each symbolizing a particular commodity. The token system consisted of two kinds of tokens—"plain" and "complex." The two types were similar in many ways, but each managed to develop a life of its own. They had, for example, different appearances, chronologies, geographic extensions, meanings, and functions (see map). As a result, each type of token gave rise to a different type of sign in the Sumerian script and can be considered as a separate precursor of writing.

The assemblages

Plain and complex tokens were of identical manufacture but can be distinguished either by their shapes or surface treatment (figs. 1 and 2). Plain tokens are characterized both by a simple geometric form and a plain, smooth surface, devoid of any markings. Their shapes include spheres, flat and lenticular disks, cones, tetrahedrons, and cylinders. These forms seem fully arbitrary

and to be dictated only by the concern for making, with the least effort, shapes easy to identify and to duplicate. There is no way of knowing, however, whether they suggested daily life commodities. It is conceivable, for example, that cones depicted pointed vases.

Assemblages of complex tokens include a greater repertory of forms and markings.[2] Among the shapes of complex tokens are biconoids, ovoids, bent coils, rhomboids, parabolas, quadrangles, and triangles, as well as miniature representations of tools, utensils, containers, and animals. Some of these, such as a series of small vessels, required skill to manufacture.

The application of markings to the face of tokens is another distinctive feature of the complex counters. These markings consisted of linear patterns, notches and punctations, traced or impressed with a stylus, with rare examples of appliqué pellets. Markings were applied to the traditional plain token shapes, such as spheres, disks, cones, tetrahedrons, and cylinders (thus converting them into complex tokens) as well as to the typical complex forms, such as biconoids, ovoids, bent coils, triangles, parabolas, rhomboids, and quadrangles.

The fact that both plain and complex tokens belong to the same accounting device is undeniable for several reasons. First, all specimens bear obvious family resemblances, sharing the same size, material, color, and method of manufacture. Second, both plain and complex tokens occur in the same basic shapes, namely, spheres, disks, cones, tetrahedrons, ovoids, and quadrangles, either plain faced or covered with markings. Third, examples of both

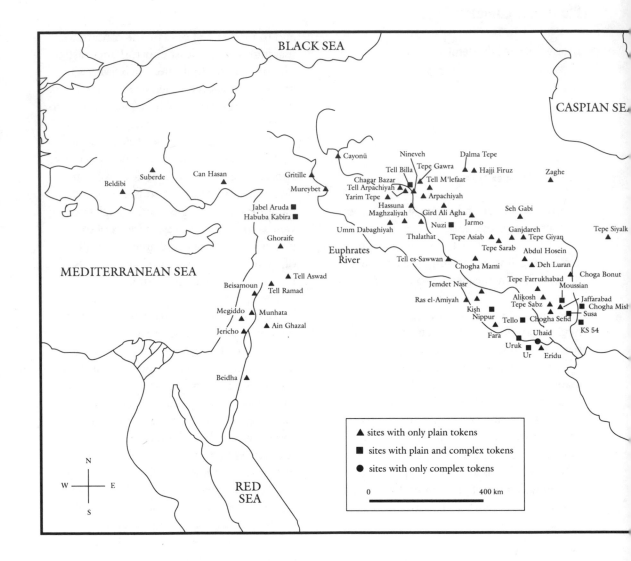

Distribution of Tokens in the Middle East.
From Denise Schmandt-Besserat, "An Ancient
Token System: The Precursor to Numerals and
Writing," *Archaeology* 39 (Nov.–Dec. 1986): 38;
reprinted with permission from *Archaeology*.

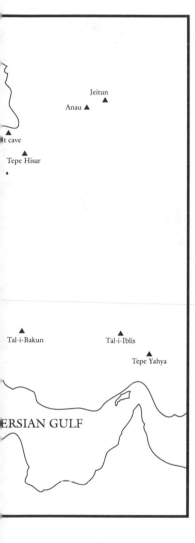

Jeitun ▲

Anau ▲

▲

t cave
▲
Tepe Hisar
▪

Tal-i-Bakun ▲

Tal-i-Iblis ▲

Tepe Yahya ▲

ERSIAN GULF

categories of artifacts start to be perforated at the same time in order to be strung. Fourth, plain and complex types are found together in hoards and, furthermore, may be enclosed together in the same envelope.[3] Fifth, plain and complex tokens were perpetuated by pictographs of the Sumerian script expressing common commodities.

Chronology

Plain tokens made their appearance with the beginning of agriculture; complex tokens, not until the rise of cities. The earliest assemblages of plain tokens have been recovered in the remains of villages of the Fertile Crescent dating to 8000–7500 B.C. These villages, built with round huts typical of the period of transition between hunting-gathering and farming cultures, relied upon grain consumption; they show no obvious evidence for animal domestication. They participated in a trade network, attested by the presence of obsidian tools at each site except one. Among these villages, Tell Aswad I, Tell Mureybet III, and Cheikh Hassan in Syria were fully sedentary settlements and show direct evidence for the cultivation of cereals. On the other hand, Tepe Asiab and Ganj Dareh Tepe E were perhaps no more than semipermanent encampments of hunters and gatherers.[4]

The first occurrence of tokens at Tell Mureybet, in the third level of occupation of the site, is particularly revealing. There were no tokens in Mureybet I and II, when the village economy was based on hunting and gathering but already traded obsidian. Tokens coincide in Mureybet III with such

Figure 1 (Above) Plain tokens from Susa, Iran, late fourth millennium B.C. Courtesy Département des Antiquités Orientales, Musée du Louvre, Paris, France. **Figure 2** (Below) Complex tokens from Susa, Iran, late fourth millennium B.C. Courtesy Département des Antiquités Orientales, Musée du Louvre, Paris, France.

new features as a quantum jump in quantity of cereal pollen in the soil, the first evidence for the cultivation of grain in fields around the site; the construction of rectangular silos; and a substantial increase in the population, which implies a new social structure.[5] Accordingly, the invention of a record-keeping device in the ancient Middle East appears to have little to do with animal domestication and herding. The correlation with trade is also not convincing. Instead, the need for counting and accounting seems to be related, in that part of the world, with an economy based on hoarding and cultivating cereals and the socioeconomic changes that followed agriculture.[6] It seems indeed logical that an economy involving the planning of subsistence over the seasons would require record keeping.

Complex tokens belong to the later part

of the fourth millennium B.C., which is characterized in the ancient Middle East by the urban phenomenon and the rise of the Sumerian temple institution, viewed as the origin of state formation. The first occurrence of complex tokens is best documented in the Sumerian metropolis of Uruk. There, the earliest group was recovered in the ruins of Eanna, the major temple precinct dedicated to the goddess of love, Inanna. They belonged to level VI of the temple, dated to about 3350 B.C., which is also the level when buildings decorated with colorful clay cone mosaics were introduced into the precinct.[7] It is particularly significant that complex tokens coincide with these architectural features because they bring the evidence for the first monumental public buildings, which in turn mark the emergence of Eanna as a predominant economic institution in the ancient Middle East. We have some insights into the economy implemented by the Sumerian temple between 3350 and 3100 B.C. corresponding to levels VI–IV. It was based on the pooling together, management and redistribution, of a substantial surplus produced by the community. Sumerian art has preserved for posterity the representation of processions of individuals delivering their dues to the temple in the form of goods in kind. The En, or chief administrators, are often seen leading the procession, recognizable by such status symbols as a beard, a special headdress and a long garment (fig. 3). Levels VI–IV are also characterized by a profusion of typical vessels such as beveled rim bowls and nose-lugged jars, which are believed to have served as standardized measures for the deliveries of

(a)

(b)

(c)

Figure 3 Representation of the En bringing an offering to the temple (a, b) and presiding over the torture of prisoners (c). From Pierre Amiet, *La Glyptique mesopotamienne archaique* (Paris: Editions du Centre National de la Recherche Scientifique, 1980): figs. 642, 643, and 661.

dues to the temple.[8] There is also evidence for a strengthening in the administration, with an increase in the use of seals, and in particular, with the introduction of cylinder seals. Interestingly, some of these have carvings showing the En presiding over scenes of torture, such as beating, probably inflicted on the first tax delinquents.[9] In this perspective, the quantum jump in the number of token shapes coincides with the establishment of a coercive redistribution economy. The imposition of taxation required an authority and administration to implement it, a system of measures and a precise reckoning device for record keeping, large storage facilities, and a system of penalties for noncompliance. These needs explain, in levels VI–IV of Eanna the first evidence for the En, the cylinder seals, beveled rim bowls, complex tokens, monumental architecture, and the scenes of tortures depicted on seals. The complex tokens can be viewed, therefore, as fulfilling an important function in the collection of taxes, which is crucial to state formation.

Tokens bearing simple markings such as one or two strokes or notches were already present in the earliest token assemblages of the early eighth millennium B.C.[10] Such tokens, however, remained exceedingly rare until the remarkable increase in the number and variety of markings that coincided with the multiplication of token shapes characteristic of the complex tokens. Throughout the fourth millennium B.C., plain tokens continued to exist unchanged. The complex tokens never supplanted the plain ones but, rather, complemented them.

The evolution of a reckoning device can logically be assumed to mirror the socioeconomic development of a society. It is therefore not surprising that the two major events in the development of the token system correspond to the two major economic transformations that occurred in the ancient Middle East: the invention of the counting device coincides with the transition to agriculture, and a quantum jump in the complexity of the system occurs at the rise of the Sumerian temple, which was to lead to state formation.

Geographic distribution

Geographic distribution is a third major difference between plain and complex tokens. Plain counters pervaded small and large settlements of the ancient Middle East, but the complex assemblages occur only in selected fourth-millennium sites.

Plain tokens are reported in practically every site of the eighth millennium to the fourth millennium B.C., excavated from Anatolia to Palestine and from Syria to Iran, showing that during this period of some four thousand years plain tokens were ubiquitous in the region. From settlement to settlement the collections vary only in number, some areas producing a handful of the artifacts and others yielding several hundred and, in one site—Jarmo, Iraq—more than one thousand.[11] Plain tokens seem, therefore, to know no boundaries in the ancient Middle East.

The complex counters, in contrast, have a limited extension; for example, none has been recovered, so far, in Turkey or in Palestine. They seem to be, in fact, a southern Mesopotamian phenomenon, extending only sporadically to isolated sites in the north, no farther than the adjacent Susiana plain toward the east, and to rare sites along the Euphrates River toward the West. In Sumer, complex tokens were used at Uruk, Girsu, Ur, Nippur, and Ubaid. In the north, Tell Billa has yielded a few, but Tepe Gawra none. In Susiana, complex tokens have been found only in Susa, Chogha Mish, Moussian, and KS 54.[12] In Syria they are included in the assemblages of Habuba Kabira, Tell Kannas, and Jebel Aruda. The vast discrepancy in the number of complex tokens recovered at each of these sites may reflect more than archeologists' luck. For example, the main metropolis of Uruk and Susa both yielded large assemblages of about eight hundred tokens each, compared with a single example at Ubaid or Jebel Aruda.

Whereas plain tokens were used in all possible settings, including cities, towns, villages, and even cave dwellings, complex tokens occur mostly in urban centers. Moreover, the sites which produced complex specimens usually share a very particular assemblage consisting of clay cone mosaics for the decoration of public buildings; cylinder seals, with examples carved with such motifs as the En in his typical attire; and pottery vessels among which are beveled rim bowls and incised nose-lugged jars. These features, which are characteristic of Eanna levels VI–IV, were a foreign intrusion in Susiana, Syria, and northern Mesopotamia.[13] The distribution of complex tokens seems, therefore, to identify centers directly under the influence of the Sumerian temple.

Function

Both kinds of counters served the same purpose, namely, they were part of the same mnemonic device used to organize and store economic data. There is indication, however, that each type of token was handled by different hands and, in particular, was stored in different ways. Plain counters were enclosed in hollow spherical envelopes, whereas complex tokens were strung to a solid oblong *bulla* (figs. 4 and 5).

It is not hard to conceive the help provided by tokens which translated economic data into symbols easy to manipulate. One can visualize how counters, representing units of real goods in one-to-one correspondence, were lined up in front of accountants who organized them according to types of goods, producers or recipients, entries or expenditures, or any other criteria. Furthermore, the tokens could be

Figure 4   Envelope with its content of five spheres from Susa, Iran, late fourth millennium B.C. Courtesy Département des Antiquités Orientales, Musée du Louvre, Paris, France.

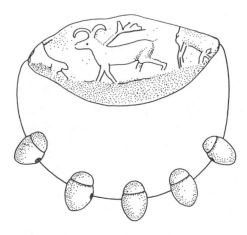

Figure 5 Proposed reconstruction of a string of complex tokens held by a solid oblong *bulla*. Drawing by Ellen Simmons.

arranged into visual patterns, facilitating the estimation and counting of quantities of items at a glance.

Tokens were also used for the reliable storage of data. For example, sets of counters could serve as permanent records for transactions to be completed in the future. This seems to be the case for groups of tokens found enclosed in hollow globular cases covered with seal impressions which, most likely, represented formal agreements —IOUS—kept in temple archives of the fourth millennium B.C. Interestingly, the envelopes predominantly held plain tokens and rarely complex types.

On the other hand, 16 percent of the Uruk counters and 55 percent of those from Susa were perforated, suggesting that some of the complex tokens were strung on a fine tie. This finding, in turn, spread light on the use of the oblong *bullae,* solid oblong blobs of clay impressed with seals. It is likely that the oblong bullae, which at both ends reveal the imprint of a string around which they were originally wrapped, served

to secure the knot and loose ends of the strings holding tokens. More important, they identified the accounts in question by displaying the pertinent seals.

The two devices used to group tokens, envelopes and oblong bullae, were both made of clay and bore seal impressions— in some cases from the same seal. That they held different kinds of tokens, in different ways, suggests that they fulfilled similar, but not identical, functions. There are also multiple examples of perforated plain tokens, and like complex tokens, these too were occasionally kept in envelopes, thus showing a crossover between the storage devices.

Interpretation

The key to cracking the code of the tokens is provided by the Sumerian script which derived from them. It seems that plain and complex tokens referred to different types of goods: the first stood for products of the country, whereas the second represented goods manufactured in urban temple centers.

Bodies of symbols systematized by communication devices exhibit a unique capacity to survive for millennia. Writing systems have the flexibility, for example, of adjusting to new technologies and new cultural needs by modifying the form of signs without altering the meaning. For instance, the letters of our Latin script have retained, for the most part, the value they had in the former Greek and Phoenician alphabets of 2,500 and 3,500 years ago. The Egyptian and Chinese writing systems are other notorious examples of the persistence of symbols through the ages. Some Egyptian signs can be followed, carrying the same meaning, from pre-dynastic three-dimensional amulets to hieroglyphs carved in stone and the cursive hieratic and demotic scripts traced with a brush on papyrus. As I describe below, the same is true for cuneiform writing, which can be traced back in time from the first and second millennium Assyrian and Babylonian syllabaries to Sumerian ideographs of the third millennium B.C. and their token prototypes in the fourth millennium B.C. Only a few tokens can be decoded by following their evolution step by step to the well-understood cuneiform characters of the second millennium B.C. The few scores of examples which can be satisfactorily identified provide an insight, however, into yet another major difference between plain and complex tokens, namely, the kinds of goods represented by each.

The cuneiform and ideographic signs of the second and third millennium B.C. expressing cereals and domesticated animals —the two traditional staples of the ancient Middle East—point to plain tokens as their progenitors. Namely, cones and spheres referred to the two most common Sumerian grain measures, the *ban* and the *bariga,* approximately equivalent to our liter and bushel. Large cones, large spheres, and flat disks were larger capacity units of grain. Furthermore, cylinders and lenticular disks were used as units of animal count with the cylinder standing for one and the lenticular disk for a collection of animals—a flock, perhaps ten.[14]

Complex tokens also find counterparts among Sumerian pictographs indicating animals, but in this case, they include precise reference on sex and age of the creatures. Such disks with various patterns stand, for example, for "one male sheep," "one ewe," "one lamb." [15]

More typically, however, complex tokens can be matched with signs representing finished products.[16] For example, incised cones, ovoids, and rhomboids represented processed foods such as bread, oil, and beer. Biconoids and triangles indicate luxury goods such as perfume and metal. One series of tokens seems particularly significant because the tokens refer to items of the textile industry, important in the early Mesopotamian temple economy. Among them are disks and parabolas with linear markings which signify types of fibers, cloths, and garments; incised cylinders and rectangles stood for strings and mats. Finally, examples of naturalistic tokens clearly represented processed foods, such as trussed ducks, as well as manufactured products, such as tools, weapons, pieces of furniture, and a variety of vessels.

It becomes apparent, therefore, that the token system was used solely for keeping records of commodities. Each category of tokens referred, however, to fundamentally different kinds of goods: plain tokens counted the basic products of the farm, quantities of grain and animals in particular; complex forms were used mostly to calculate goods produced by workshops. This different usage explains the duality of the token system, elucidating, especially, the discrepancy in chronology and geographic distribution. It becomes obvious why the first assemblages of plain tokens coincide with the beginning of farming whereas complex tokens start occurring in the urban period. The different usage also explains why plain tokens were ubiquitous and complex tokens occurred only in selected areas: staples are consumed or accumulated in every possible setting, but industry flourishes in particular circumstances. In the latter case, the typical assemblages of clay cone mosaics, seals, and vessels present in sites yielding complex tokens, envelopes, and oblong bullae make it obvious that the workshops where accounting took place were developed under the auspices of the Sumerian temple. The distribution of complex tokens far afield in Susiana and Syria shows centers of activity of the Sumerian temple outside Sumer. It can be postulated that the system of record keeping with complex and plain tokens, envelopes, oblong bullae, and seals was related to a coercive redistributive economy, as it was in the homeland of Sumer. In this case, however, the amounts of goods in kind required from the foreign centers should be viewed as tribute.

Finally, the different kinds of goods dealt with by the two kinds of tokens explains their different storage in temple archives. In fact they were handled by different hands in different services: the one group belonged to the pens and granaries, whereas the other served the superintendents of workshops.

······

The Introduction of Two Kinds of Signs

The duality of the token system was perpetuated in writing when each kind of counter gave way to different types of signs in the Sumerian script: plain tokens were replaced by impressed markings, whereas complex tokens were reproduced by pictographic signs incised with a stylus.

As I have explained elsewhere, plain tokens can be traced through the various stages of their evolution to writing.[17] In short, the metamorphosis was triggered by the fact that plain tokens, contained in envelopes, were hidden by the thick clay walls of the cases. This led clerks to mark the surface of the envelopes by impressing each token prior to enclosing them inside, thus making visible at all times the number and shapes of the tokens included. The marked envelopes, in turn, promptly led to a further improvement, namely, solid clay tablets in the form of a small cushion, bearing token impressions. In other words, plain tokens were replaced by markings consisting of their negative imprint on a clay tablet (fig. 6).

The repertory of impressed markings on envelopes, as well as those on tablets is limited to a dozen signs, eight of them deriving from plain tokens.[18] They include circular markings of various diameter and depth, standing for the former small and large spheres, the flat and lenticular disks. They also include wedges of different lengths and widths corresponding to the former cylinders, cones and large cones.

The merging of complex tokens with writing was bound to be different, since

Figure 6 Impressed tablet showing one circular marking and two wedges, standing for one large and two small measures of grain, from Susa, Iran, late fourth millennium B.C. Courtesy Département des Antiquités Orientales, Musée du Louvre, Paris, France.

they were generally not held in envelopes and, furthermore, the method of imprinting tokens was not well suited for rendering the outline of the complex token shapes and especially the linear and punched markings they bore. Complex tokens were therefore perpetuated on the tablets by signs written with a stylus.[19] This technique is not surprising, since it made use of the same pointed stylus as was used to trace the markings on their face.

As is the case at each step of the development of the token system, there is some overlap between the methods of rendering the tokens in a graphic form. Tetrahedrons, one of the most usual plain tokens, led, seemingly, to an incised pictograph.[20] On the other hand, there are examples of incised ovoids being impressed on at least two envelopes.[21] Finally there is a unique tablet displaying a composite impressed-incised technique with incised markings applied over the impressions of spheres and triangles.[22]

The new system of notations was infinitely more practical, since the clay tablets displaying neatly aligned signs were far less cumbersome than the loose tokens. It was also more expedient, since impressing or tracing markings was quicker than modeling each individual token. The new formula was so satisfactory that tablets remained in use during the next three millennia in the ancient Middle East, to be displaced only when the Aramaic script, written with a flowing hand on papyrus, provided a yet more efficient system of handling information.

The invention of numerals

Differences far greater than technique existed between the two categories of signs, however. The most significant distinction between the impressed and incised signs lay in the way they expressed plurality, which led to the impressed sign expressing numbers and the incised sign indicating the nature of the items counted.

Like the former tokens, the impressed signs continued to show the number of items counted by repeating the marking in one-to-one correspondence: one, two, or three small measures of grain were indicated by one, two, or three small wedges, and one, two, or three bushels of grain were indicated by one, two, or three circular markings. The same is true for the impressed markings indicating units of animal counts.

On the other hand, incised signs are never found repeated in one-to-one correspondence. Thirty-three jars of oil, for example, were no longer expressed by repeating the sign for a jar of oil thirty-three times. Instead, the pictograph for a jar of oil was preceded by numerals—special signs expressing a number (fig. 7).

In fact, the new signs to express abstract numbers were nothing else than the impressed signs for measures of grain used in a novel fashion. An impressed wedge and an impressed circular sign standing for a small and a large measure of grain came also to signify "one" and "ten." This seems confusing to us but it did not seem to trouble the ancient clerks, who could decide from the context which reading was appropriate. In fact, the system of using identical signs for numbers and measures of grain was perpetuated throughout the Sumerian period without causing any confusion, apparently, among scribes.

Whereas plain and complex tokens differed in the products they represented, the one rural and the other urban, the impressed and incised signs differed in their

Figure 7 Pictographic tablet from Uruk, Iraq, late fourth millennium B.C. The account in the upper central case, for example, shows the sign for sheep and five wedges standing for the abstract numeral 5. Courtesy Vorderasiatisches Museum, Staatliche Museen zu Berlin, East Germany.

usage to a considerably greater degree. The impressed signs conferred a notion of quantity; the incised signs indicated the nature of the item counted. These concepts of quantity and quality, which were fused together in the token system, were abstracted from each other for the first time in writing. This is why an ovoid stood for "one jar of oil" whereas it took two signs to give the same information on the tablets—an impressed sign for "one" and an incised sign for "jar of oil."

The invention of zero and place notation has been heralded as a major accomplishment of the civilized world, but the literature does not treat the advent of abstract numerals because of the common but erroneous assumption that abstract numbers are intuitive to humans. The token system is one piece of artifactual evidence proving that counting, like anything else, is not spontaneous. Instead, counting is cultural and has to be learned. It seems logical to assume that a reckoning device must reflect the various modes of counting of the culture using it, and consequently, two steps of the evolution of counting can be identified in the ancient Middle East. The first step was taken about 8000 B.C., when tokens of various shapes were used to count different merchandise in a one-to-one correspondence. The second major step was the introduction of abstract numerals when impressed signs showing units of grain measures came to indicate, alternatively, abstract numbers.[23] The extraordinary invention of abstract numerals amounted to a revolution in accounting and communication, since it provided, for the first time, a reckoning system applicable to any and every item under the sun. Each numeral stood for the concept of oneness, twoness, threeness, and so on, abstracted from the item counted. This put an end to the cumbersome system necessitating particular symbols for counting different goods. From there on, jars of oil as well as measures of grain or sheep of a flock could be counted with the same symbols. The system did not fully depart at once from the traditional one-to-one correspondence since 1, 2, 3, and so on were expressed by one, two, three wedges and 10, 20, 30, by one, two, three circular signs. Abstract numerals brought about, however, a tremendous economy of notations by replacing ten wedges by one sign for the number ten. As a result, for example, ten jars of oil could be shown by two signs only: "ten" and "jar of oil."

······
Summary

The system of plain tokens which originated at the beginning of agriculture in the ancient Middle East was supplemented by complex tokens at the rise of the Sumerian temple. Plain and complex tokens were counters of the same reckoning device, but each served one branch of the Sumerian economy: plain tokens referred to products of the farm, whereas complex tokens stood for goods manufactured in workshops. For this reason, the two kinds of tokens belonged to different services of the temple administration, where they were kept in a different manner. Plain tokens were stored in globular hollow clay envelopes, while complex tokens were strung together on a tie held by a solid bulla. This, in turn, had major consequences for the origins of Sumerian script. The plain tokens were replaced by impressed markings, but the complex counters gave rise to incised pictographs. The duality of the token system was thus carried over in writing where the split between the two kinds of symbols grew ever wider. The impressed signs evolved to express the quantities of items counted, whereas the incised pictographs indicated the nature of the items counted. The duality of our own writing system which uses numerals (ideographs) and letters (phonetic signs) was presaged in the first reckoning device using tokens. Plain tokens and impressed signs brought about the use of abstract numerals, whereas the complex tokens and, as M. W. Green demonstrates in the following chapter on Sumerian cuneiform, incised pictographs slowly evolved to the acquisition of phonetic values.

••••••

Notes

1. Denise Schmandt-Besserat, "The Origins of Writing," *Written Communication* 3, no. 1 (January 1986): 31–45.

2. Denise Schmandt-Besserat, "An Archaic Recording System in the Uruk-Jemdet Nasr Period," *American Journal of Archaeology* 83 (1979): 19–48.

3. Julius Jordan, *Vorläufiger Bericht über die von der Deutschen Forschungs-gemeinschaft in Uruk-Warka unternommenen Ausgrabungen*, Abhandlungen der Preussischen Akademie der Wissenschaften 2 (Berlin, 1931), 47–48, fig. 41; Denise Schmandt-Besserat, "The Envelopes That Bear the First Writing," *Technology and Culture* 21, no. 3 (1980): 369, fig. 4, Sb 1938.

4. On Tell Aswad I, see Henri de Contenson, "Recherches sur le Néolithique de Syrie (1967–1976)" *Comptes Rendus des Scéances de l'année 1978*, Proceedings of the Académie des Inscriptions et Belles-Lettres (Paris, 1979), 821; Jacques Cauvin, *Les premiers villages de Syrie-Palestine du IXème au VIIème millénaire avant J.C.: Collection de la Maison de l'Orient Méditerranéen Ancien* 4, Série Archéologique 3 (Lyons: Maison de L'Orient, 1978), 74; Robert J. Braidwood, Bruce Howe, and Charles A. Reed, "The Iranian Prehistoric Project," *Science* 133 (1961): 2008; Phillip E. L. Smith, "Garij Dareh Tepe," *Paleorient* 1 (1974): 207–8.

5. Cauvin, *Les premiers villages*, 74, 43, 75; Olivier Aurenche et al., "Chronologie et organization de l'espace dans le Proche-Orient," in *Préhistoire du Levant*, Proceedings of the Colloque CNRS, no. 598 (Lyons: CNRS, 1980), 7–8.

6. Denise Schmandt-Besserat, "The Emergence of Recording," *American Anthropologist* 84, no. 4 (1982): 871–78.

7. Julius Jordan, *Vorläufiger Bericht über die von der Deutschen Forschungs-gemeinschaft in Uruk-Warka unternommenen Ausgrabungen*, Abhandlungen der Preussischen Akademie der Wissenschaften 3 (Berlin, 1932), 19. Denise Schmandt-Besserat "Tokens at Uruk," *Baghdader Mitteilungen* 19, (1988): 1–175.

8. Thomas W. Beale, "Bevelled Rim Bowls and Their Implications for Change and Economic Organization in the Later Fourth Millennium B.C.," *Journal of Near Eastern Studies* 37 (October 1978): 311–12.

9. Mark A. Brandes, *Siegelabrollungen aus den Archaischen Bauschichten in Uruk-Warka*, Freiburger Altorientalische Studien 3 (Wiesbaden: Frank Steiner, 1979), 17–166.

10. Schmandt-Besserat, "Emergence of Recording," 872.

11. Vivian Broman-Morales, "Jarmo Figurines and other Clay Objects," in *Prehistoric Archeology along the Zagros Flanks*, ed. Linda S. Braidwood et al., Oriental Institute Publications 105, (Chicago: University of Chicago Oriental Institute, 1983), 369–426.

12. Denise Schmandt-Besserat, "Tokens at Susa," *Oriens Antiquus* 25, no. 1–2 (1986).

13. Pierre Amiet, "Alternance et Dualité: Essai d'interpretation de l'histoire élamite," *Akkadica* 15 (1979): 6; Eva Strommenger, "Ausgrabungen der Deutschen Orient-Gesellschaft in Habuba Kabira," in *Archaeological Reports from Tabqa Dam Project-Euphrates Valley, Syria*, ed. David Noel Freedman, Annual of the American School of Oriental Research (Cambridge: American School of Oriental Research, 1979), 79.

14. Schmandt-Besserat, "Envelopes," 370–75.

15. Schmandt-Besserat, "An Archaic Recording System," 42; Schmandt-Besserat, "Envelopes," 374–75.

16. Schmandt-Besserat, "An Archaic Recording System," 41–48.

17. Schmandt-Besserat, "Envelopes," 382–85.

18. Denise Schmandt-Besserat, "From Tokens to Tablets: A Re-Evaluation of the So-called Numerical Tablets," *Visible Language* 15 (1981): 331–33.

19. Schmandt-Besserat, "An Archaic Recording System," 41–48.

20. Schmandt-Besserat, "Envelopes," 375.

21. The two artifacts were excavated at Habuba Kabira. Eva Strommenger, "Ausgrabungen in Habuba Kabira und Mumbaqat," *Archiv für Orientforschung* 24 (1973): 170–71.

22. Schmandt-Besserat, "From Tokens to Tablets," 328, fig. 4b.

23. Denise Schmandt-Besserat, "Before Numerals," *Visible Language* 17, (1984): 55–58.

• • • • • •

Further Readings

Amiet, Pierre. *Elam*, pp. 70–71. Auvers sur Oise: Archée Editeur, 1966.

———. *Glyptique Susienne: Mémoires de la délégation archéologique en Iran*, no. 43, 1: 69–70. Paris: Librairie Orientaliste Paul Geuthner, 1972.

Goody, Jack. *The Domestication of the Savage Mind*. Cambridge: Cambridge University Press, 1978.

Schmandt-Besserat, Denise. "Before Numerals." *Visible Language* 18 (1984): 48–60.

———. "The Decipherment of the Earliest Tablets." *Science* 211 (1981): 283–85.

———. "The Earliest Precursor of Writing." *Scientific American*, (June 1978), 50–59.

———. "The Envelopes That Bear the First Writing." *Technology and Culture* 21, no. 3 (1980): 357–85.

———. "From Tokens to Tablets: A Re-Evaluation of the So-called Numerical Tablets." *Visible Language* 15 (1981): 321–44.

———. "The Origins of Writing." *Written Communication* 3, no. 1 (January 1986): 31–45.

———. "Tokens and Counting." *Biblical Archaeologist* (1983): 31–45.

3

Early Cuneiform

. . . . . .

M. W. Green

. . . . . .

Cuneiform was the script used in the ancient world of Mesopotamia. Its name (from the Latin *cuneus,* "wedge") reflects its appearance as triangular wedge-shaped impressions made with a reed stylus on a clay tablet. Invented by the Sumerians about 3200 B.C., the cuneiform script later was adapted for numerous other languages of the ancient Near East, including the Akkadian group (Old Akkadian, Assyrian, Babylonian), Eblaite, Hittite, and Elamite. Cuneiform's history spans nearly three millennia; it continued in use in Mesopotamia through the second century B.C., eventually giving way to the more efficient alphabetic scripts and ink-and-brush media with which it had coexisted for several centuries.

Cuneiform's invention occurred within the framework of a rapidly expanding urban environment, social stratification, technological specialization, the emergence of a politically powerful nobility, large-scale community labor projects and commodity distribution, and intercity and international exchange networks. Writing in Mesopotamia first served to document the affairs of an extensive bureaucratic network controlling labor, materials, and subsistence resources. The invention of cuneiform was a technological innovation designed for clerical function. Its early evolution was utilitarian, directed toward streamlining

the graphic form and the sign repertoire, extending the vocabulary range, and providing scribal training. New applications and writing practices were often compromises between limiting the complexity of the writing system and expanding its capacity to convey information.[1]

As the script became more flexible and more powerful in transcribing messages, its scope branched out from the documentary into the narrative and creative literary spheres. From simple itemizations, texts expanded to poetry and prose, chronicles and epics, and magico-religious and scientific recipes; out of flattened lumps of clay evolved multivolume bilingual dictionaries, archives, antiquarian libraries, and monumental stone stelae and wall reliefs. These were developments spanning millennia; the Archaic period saw the first, immature stages of expansion in various directions.

Some four thousand clay tablets excavated at the ancient Sumerian city of Uruk, a major urban center of the southern Mesopotamian river plain, comprise the earliest known corpus of cuneiform texts. Within this corpus, which is itself thought to span about two centuries, appear the first stages of the paleographic evolution characteristic of cuneiform's continuing development. Comparison with cuneiform graphemes of later historical eras has enabled the decipherment of about 75 percent of these early Archaic period signs, although over the centuries there were major changes both in the shape of the signs and in the repertoire of signs in current use.[2]

The earliest cuneiform signs were pictographic. Many of them are easily recognizable, particularly those which represented an object or animal. The sign for "hand" was a picture of a hand; the sign for "arm" showed the arm from hand to elbow; the sign for "barley" was a stem with two opposing rows of sprouts; for "jar," a neatly drawn jar with neck, rim, and spout shown clearly; "bird," "fish," and "dog" were obvious graphic illustrations. Other signs require some imagination to discover the association between the pictograph and its indicated word, like an arrowhead-shaped sign representing "wine," which may have depicted a bunch of grapes, or the sign for "tree" or "wood," a long, narrow rectangle which might have been intended as a simple log. Still others seem to have been based on an elusive symbolism (fig. 1).[3]

At first the signs were drawn smoothly in the barely moist clay surface with a pointed tool, but soon the technique of impressing the sign's outline into the clay with a narrow reed stylus was adopted.[4] The latter method gave cuneiform its characteristic wedge-shaped appearance and began the process of reducing the original pictorial signs to conventionalized line combinations.

Sign abstraction was a gradual but continuous process. The curved outlines common in the earliest cuneiform signs became straightened; sharp angles and fine details were eliminated. Thus originally circular shapes gradually evolved into squares, and triangular shapes into rectangles, and the facial details of signs representing animals or men disappeared. The beginnings of these and other graphic changes are observable within the Archaic period corpus. In time the cuneiform characters evolved into

Figure 1 Pictographic cuneiform (ca. 3200 B.C.)

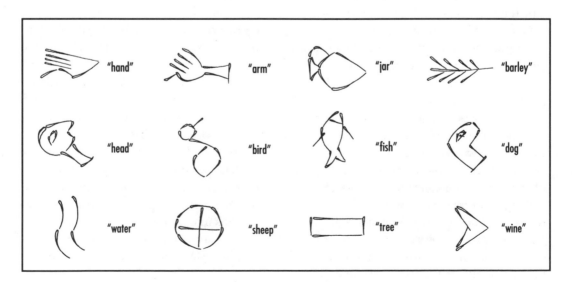

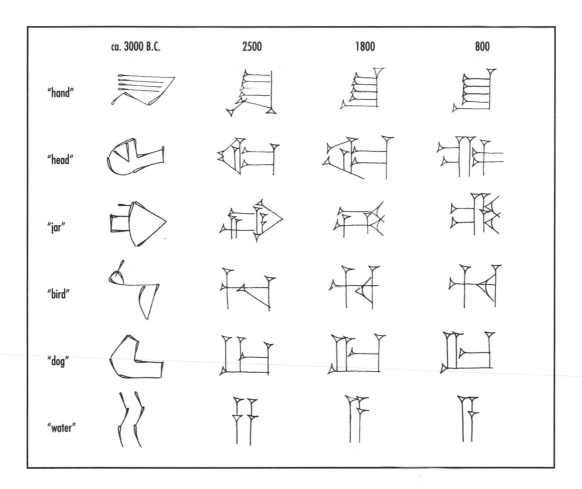

	ca. 3000 B.C.	2500	1800	800
"hand"				
"head"				
"jar"				
"bird"				
"dog"				
"water"				

Figure 2   Graphic evolution of cuneiform

nonpictorial, regular, linear arrangements of wedgelike stylus marks (fig. 2).[5]

Very early in cuneiform's history the number of written characters reached over seven hundred, and the total stayed at that high level through the following centuries. However, the number of fundamental graphic components from which signs were composed was significantly lower. Nearly 60 percent of the sign repertoire in the Archaic period consisted of modifications of other signs. Sometimes decorative elements were added, such as stippling or cross-hatching, but most often new signs were constructed by combining two other signs, the one either abutting the other in a graphic ligature or inscribed within the outline of the other (fig. 3).

As the repertoire of signs stabilized, systematic combination of graphic elements became the predominant technique for internal changes.[6] While new composite signs continued to be introduced, some other distinctive sign forms were reshaped and simplified into apparent ligatures. In the Ar-

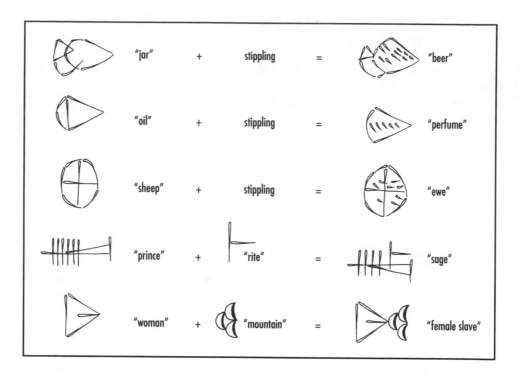

Figure 3 Combination of graphic elements

chaic period composite signs often incorporated semantic mnemonic information, as in the sign for "eat," which was contrived as a ligature of the two signs meaning "head" and "food." As phonetization of the script developed, sign combinations increasingly employed phonetic markers. Eventually, linking of signs in semantic or phonetic units approximated writing of language phrases and, thereafter, with the addition of grammatical indicators, approached sentence structure.[7]

The earliest cuneiform script was logographic, with direct association between written signs and language words. Phonetization, which began during the Archaic period and is clearly evidenced in the Uruk corpus, reflected the predominantly mono-syllabic character of Sumerian vocabulary. Thus individual signs acquired syllabic phonetic values. For example, the sign representing "arrow," the Sumerian word TI, acquired the syllabic value *ti*; as such it could be used to write Sumerian "arrow" or, following the rebus principle, the homophonous Sumerian word TI meaning "life."

Complexity arises from the polyphony of Sumerian cuneiform, whereby a single sign could represent more than one word. Thus the sign for "mouth" could be read in Sumerian variously as KA, "mouth"; ZU_2, "tooth"; DU_{11}, "speak"; INIM, "word"; or GU_3, "voice"; but as a syllabic sign its primary syllabic value became *ka*. On the other hand, homophonies in the Sumerian vocabulary were reflected in the script, as for

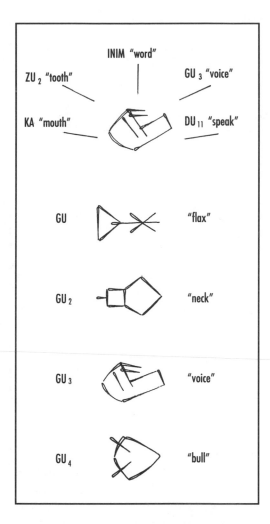

ZU₂ "tooth"   INIM "word"   GU₃ "voice"

KA "mouth"   DU₁₁ "speak"

GU   "flax"

GU₂   "neck"

GU₃   "voice"

GU₄   "bull"

Figure 4   Polyphony and homophony

example in GU, "flax"; "GU₂, "neck"; GU₃, "voice"; and GU₄, "bull"; each represented by a different grapheme (fig. 4).

Transformation of the script from logographic to syllabic proceeded haltingly. Phonetization was productively applied during the Archaic period primarily to construct new graphemes. Expanding the established technique of combining signs to produce a composite grapheme, sign components were selected for their phonetic values. The logogram MEN, for example in GU, "flax"; "GU₂, for ex-

ample, representing the Sumerian word for "crown," was designed as a composite sign using the simple rectangular outline of the sign GA₂ to enclose the sign *en* as a phonetic indicator. Later the sign form was made more explicit by inscribing the signs *me* and *en* together within the GA₂ enclosure.

A variety of composite signs, both semantically and phonetically based, were created using GA₂ and other suitable graphemes with a spacious mid-ground. The choice of the sign serving as carrier seems to have been somewhat free-associative but not entirely random. The signs URU and EŠ₃, representing the Sumerian words for "city" and "shrine," respectively, were often used in composite logograms for city names. A number of logograms were devised using the sign SAG, "head," for terms relating to parts and actions of the head or mouth. Later these same logograms were written instead with the sign KA, "mouth," itself a modification of SAG made by adding a series of short wedge lines to the mouth area of the face depicted by SAG. New phonetically based logograms with KA included EME, "tongue," written as KA + *me;* NUNDUM, "lip," written KA + *nun;* and SU₆, "beard," written KA + *sa* (fig. 5).

An extension of the sign combination technique was the use of supplementary signs to gloss a polyphonous logogram and thereby indicate which of several possible readings was correct in the given context. A phonetically based example from the Archaic period was the use of the syllabic signs *u₂* and/or *ga* as glosses to the logographic

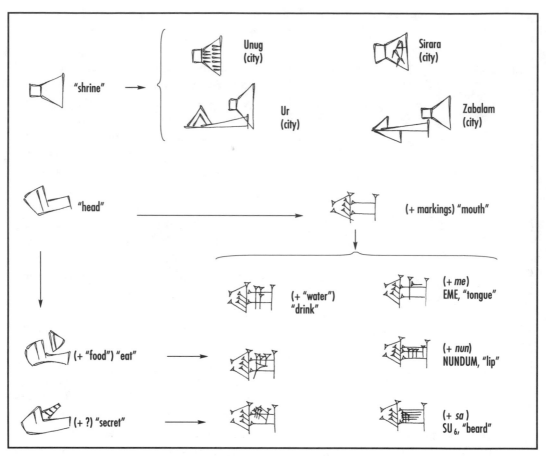

Figure 5 Composite signs

sign NAGA when it was to be read UGA, meaning "raven." Other possible readings for the same signs were NAGA, "soap"; EREŠ₂, a city; or NISABA, the patron goddess of that city. Through long usage the sign complex *u*₂ + NAGA + *ga* became the customary writing for "raven" and, in effect, itself a compound logogram.

In the case of *uga* the original grapheme was conserved as part of the compound unit. In other cases an early logogram was fully replaced by a syllabic spelling. When, for example, the syllabic spelling *ga-ar*₃ for Sumerian GA'AR, "cheese," became

preferred, sometime in the late second millennium, the pictograph which had been in use since the Archaic period was eliminated from the cuneiform sign repertoire.[8] Other Archaic period graphemes for which no later stylized forms have been identified were probably similarly lost through phonetic replacement.

Use of semantic glosses was also initiated during the Archaic period, eventually evolving into a system of determinatives used throughout the history of cuneiform and transferred as well into Akkadian context. Through the use of determinatives, certain common categories of nouns were signalized. When the sign NAGA was to be understood in a given context as the goddess Nisaba, the determinative for divine names, DINGIR, in Sumerian "god(dess)," was added; to mark it as the city Ereš, the geographical determinative KI, "place," was written as a gloss. Mixed semantic and phonetic indicators were used in such writings as u_2 + NAGA + ga + MUŠEN, where u_2 and ga glossed the reading uga and MUŠEN glossed the semantic classification "bird."

Only slowly did glosses and complements come to be distinguished as specialized logograms. In the earliest script, logographic units could be built of two or several components, with the chief criterion for their relative position being a space constraint. Wider, open signs were suitable to enclose inscribed signs, whether as gloss or determinative; narrower signs were combined in direct ligature or as a sign cluster drawn to fit the available space (fig. 6).

Sign units constituted brief words or, later, phrases read as a whole. The visual arrangement of signs within such a unit was not standardized until late in the third millennium, when phrases became lengthier, beginning to approximate speech, and the written sequence of signs began to imi-

Figure 6   Semantic and phonetic indicators

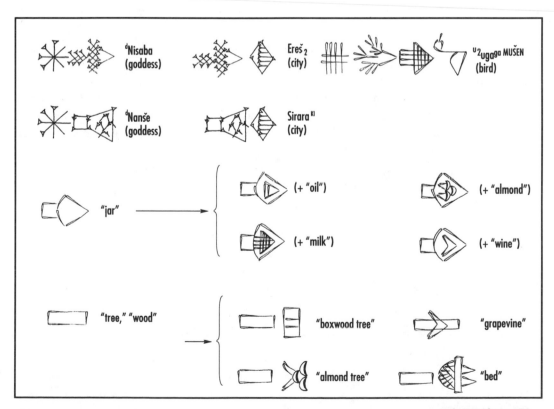

tate sentence structure.[9] Even thereafter, throughout the history of cuneiform, sign sequence in some compound logograms was irregularly written.

The principle of phonetic glosses led to cuneiform's transformation into a logo-syllabic script for writing Sumerian. The Sumerian of the earliest texts was of a highly abstracted and abbreviated form suited to clerical memoranda, largely limited to numerals, nouns, and a few adjectives. As verbs began to be included and memos grew both more elaborate and more precise, glosses began to be used to indicate grammatical forms. Eventually, with the expansion of writing into the realm of narrative, written Sumerian evolved as a mixture of logographic signs used for the nuclear structure and syllabic signs used supplementarily for linguistic detail.[10]

The logosyllabic adaptation of cuneiform to Sumerian reflected the agglutinative structure of that language, wherein grammatical indicators of tense, person, case, and so on, were incorporated as pre-fixes and suffixes to semantic roots. In application to other, nonagglutinative, inflexive languages like Akkadian, Sumerian logograms or "Sumerograms" were used in Akkadian context together with phonetic glosses for linguistic precision. Thus LUGAL-*im*, using the Sumerogram LUGAL, "king," plus the phonetic complement *im*, served to express *šarrim*, the genitive conjugation of Akkadian *šarrum*, "king" (fig. 7).

Although syllabic cuneiform was first used conservatively for constructing new logograms, its utility for writing foreign words, especially personal and geographical names, led to its adoption and transformation by other linguistic cultures.[11] In the process of phonetization, new elements were added to the inherent polyphony of Sumerian cuneiform. A sign used syllabically could represent several phonetically similar syllables. The cuneiform sign with primary syllabic value *ka* could also be read as ga_{14} or qa_3; the signs *bu* and *ab* also had possible values *pu* and *ap*, respectively; *luh*

Figure 7 Logo-syllabic writing

Sumerian	MUŠEN - e	KU_6 - ra	INIM	in -	na -	an -	GI_4 - GI_4	
	("bird") (ergative)	("fish") (dative)	("word")	(conjugation)	(dative)	(3d pers. obj.)	("to return")	
	"the bird replied to the fish"							

Akkadian:	*a* - *na*	LUGAL	- *i*	*aq* - *bu*
	(*ana* "to")	("king")	(1st pers. poss.)	(*qabû* "to speak")
	"I spoke to my king"			

could also be read as *lah* or *rah;* *ig* could also be used for *ik, iq, eg, ek,* or *eq*.[12] Besides this, some signs acquired new syllabic values from the Akkadian translations of their original logographic Sumerian meanings. For example, the sign ab_2, pictographically depicting a cow's head and used for Sumerian AB_2, "cow," acquired an additional syllabic value *lit* from the Akkadian word *littu,* "cow."

Signs which had been devised to represent polysyllabic Sumerian words were largely ignored when cuneiform was adapted for syllabic use in writing other languages. A few polysyllabic logograms were shortened to monosyllables, as the sign $BARA_2$, meaning in Sumerian "throne," became bar_2 and DIRI, Sumerian "extra," became *dir*. For others, an alternative reading was chosen for syllabic use, usually based either on a Sumerian reduction already established or a foreshortened Akkadian translation. The sign KALAG, used for both Sumerian KALAG, "strong," and KAL, "precious," acquired syllabic values *kal* as well as *dan,* from the Akkadian *dannu,* "strong."[13]

Further refinement of syllabic cuneiform occurred in non-Sumerian context. By the late third millennium the Semitic-speaking empires of Ebla and Akkad were using syllabic cuneiform extensively for their own written documents and royal inscriptions. A brief spate of syllabic writing of Sumerian came at the beginning of the second millennium, but except for some dialectical forms, logosyllabic writing remained normative for Sumerian, which survived in an esoteric or scholastic written form even long after the native spoken language

had died out.[14] In non-Sumerian context, logosyllabic writing found profusion in certain specialized Akkadian text genres like onamastic and astronomical texts.[15] Bilingual Sumero-Akkadian dictionaries of the second and first millennia, used for scribal training or as reference works, also were replete with unusual complex logograms and pseudologograms derived from Akkadian.

Paleographic evolution was a utilitarian aspect of textual evolution; record keeping and communication were the driving forces of cuneiform's invention and progressive refinement. The first cuneiform texts were clerical records, highly abbreviated, concise accounts of the inventory or distribution of commodities and animals. Clerical documentation persisted as the prime function of cuneiform for many centuries, during which time both the script and the documentary format evolved.

The antecedents of script, inscribed calculi and engraved seals, employed the clay form and surface as well as distinctive markings or designs in their visual conveyance of record-keeping information.[16] Newly invented cuneiform followed that precedent by incorporating the tool and medium as well as the graphic symbols into the writing system. The use of clay tablets before cuneiform was limited to counting and quantifying by means of coarse markings. The radical innovation of a writing system set improved quality standards for clay tablet production, transformed the markings into an organized system of numerical and metrical notation, and introduced a comprehensive graphic character set.

Pictographs with semantic meaning were

linear in appearance, drawn with a stylus, while numerals were indicated by flat, shallow, circular or semicircular impressions. The size and arrangement of the numerical impressions indicated the unit of measurement. Some of the more than fifty different numerical signs were differentiated by additional wedge lines, and some very few semantic signs included circular or semicircular impressions. These inconsistencies eventually disappeared as cuneiform came to be written exclusively in wedge lines. As a corollary development, the variety of distinctive numerals was severely reduced and some of the inherent metrical units became written with semantic signs. A few numerical signs were transformed into semantic signs. In the Archaic period accounting system, for example, animals or slaves were reckoned with semicircular impressions for units of one and circular impressions for units of ten; to indicate those which had died, a wedge was drawn through the numeral. The semantic sign for "dead" or "die," UG7, evolved from the numeral one with a wedge drawn through it (fig. 8).

Tablet shapes and surfaces, although not directly word associated, were meaningful parts of the Archaic period writing system. The first written texts were small, compact clay tablets no larger than one or two inches square, each bearing a single record or account. As documentation progressed from single entries to the multiple transactions common by the end of the Archaic period, ledger rulings were devised to orga-

Figure 8 Numerical and semantic signs

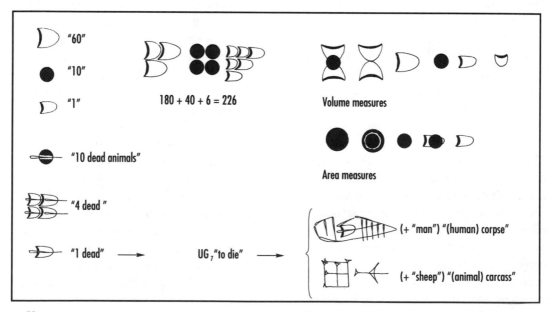

nize the data. Tablets were divided into columns and subcolumns read from left to right and, within these, lines, or "cases," read from top to bottom. Cases could be subdivided horizontally and vertically into subcases, and narrow bands could be inserted as intercolumnar subdivisions.

Specific locations within a case or column, or specific areas of the tablet were reserved for particular types of data: quantities in the upper left corner of a case, titles or names of supervisory personnel at the bottom of a column, transaction descriptions and totals on the reverse of the tablet, and so on. Some of these format guidelines were more flexibly defined than others, and some specialized types of accounts used quite complicated or idiosyncratic formats. Certain textile accounts, for example, allotted the right column on the reverse of the tablet for subtotals and the left column for totals, authorizing officials, and disposition. Herders' reports reckoned adults in column 1 of the obverse and offspring in column 2, with subtotals and totals sequentially on the reverse; field surveyors' documents arranged the data in rows instead of columns; sales contracts entered land areas first in column 1, case 1, followed by individual parcels and payments.[17]

The usual tablet shape was rectangular, somewhat taller than wide, with slightly rounded corners. Some tablets were narrower at the bottom, deformed by the pressure of being held between the fingers of the left hand while written. Occasionally thumb and finger impressions and, very rarely, nail impressions remain from the hand of the scribe.

Tablet size depended mainly on the amount of information to be recorded. From the minimal data of the small early texts, expansion proceeded rapidly. Several records concerning a commodity came to be listed together on a single account tablet and supplementary details were added, such as the occasion for an offering or the site where a transaction took place. By the end of the Archaic period ration lists appeared, written on exceptionally large tablets and packed with sometimes several hundred entries, divided on both the obverse and reverse of the tablet into four or often more columns and multilevel subcolumns and subcases, and naming several levels of personnel from recipient to overseer and supervisor.

Although most Archaic period tablets were approximately palm size, several text categories are, like the ration lists, immediately recognizable from the unusual size and shape of the tablets. The Uruk corpus includes one group of large and thick tablets, coarsely made and easily fragmented, giving calculations for field sowing. Another group of tablets, remarkable for their sharp corners and nearly square shape, deals exclusively with metal implements. Circular, or disk-shaped, tablets were reserved for junior scribes' handwriting practice; advanced students' exercises were usually written on large tablets ruled into several columns with very regularly spaced, narrow lines.[18]

In later times, the information once embodied in the physical characteristics of the tablet was made explicit through written words and phrases. Totals were labeled as such, documents were categorized and

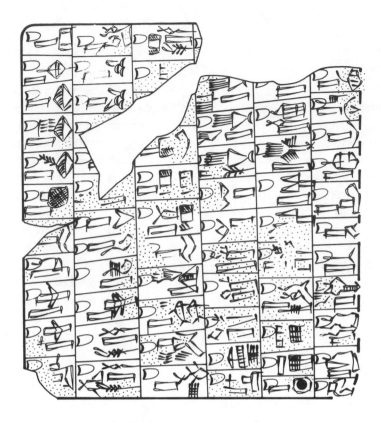

Figure 9 Archaic period list of trees

labeled, administrative procedures were described in verbal phrases. Always remaining tersely formulaic, administrative documentation developed such standard phrases as "so-and-so received it," "from the account of so-and-so," "brought into the granary," "balanced account," "completed court case." As cuneiform grew capable of expressing such details, the ledger formats were simplified into regular, evenly spaced lines and columns, although remnants of the formating technique persisted in certain specialized text genres.

Some 90 percent of the Archaic period Uruk tablets were clerical records; the remaining 10 percent were writing exercises which illustrate teaching techniques for scribal training in cuneiform. These tablets contained practical lists of standard clerical terminology. Their thematic organization of vocabulary items into lexicons of trees and wooden objects, metals and metal implements, birds, fish, garments, and so on, was to become typical of scribal school curriculum for another three thousand years (fig. 9).

The earliest lexical texts had no fixed sequence of listed items, but very soon a structure was imposed and standardized lists were compiled. Duplicate copies by Archaic period scribal students allow the reconstruction of the standard form, and later duplicates of the same list reveal the evolution of individual graphemes and compound logograms.

Thirteen different standard lists are preserved among the approximately four hundred lexical texts in the Uruk corpus, most in multiple copies and one, a list of noble and professional titles, with more than a hundred duplicates. Several editorial stages are represented, from preliminary lexical compilation through standardization and further editorial refinement. Nearly all the known Archaic period lists became part of the traditional school curriculum used for many centuries of scribal training. Duplicates of some of the Archaic period lists were written a thousand years later, with phonetic glosses or Akkadian translations added.[19]

During the third millennium B.C., new lexical compendia were composed on the same principle, and other tutorial devices were introduced, such as sign lists and syllabaries arranged according to grapheme shape. Shortly thereafter, the major Sumerian glossaries were radically revised and updated. Eventually, lexical training included several dozen thematic lists, each containing several hundred entries with Akkadian translations, as well as bilingual lists of legal phrases and grammatical forms, syllabaries, dialectical dictionaries, cosmologies, and explanatory commentaries (fig. 10).[20]

Most of the evolutionary trends of cuneiform can be traced back to preliminary stages in the Archaic period; some find their first traces among the lexical texts of that era. Semantic determinatives, for example, used infrequently in Archaic period clerical records, were a hallmark of the contemporary vocabulary lists, regularly repeated in each successive entry. They were an innovation of the list standardization process, absent from the earliest lists but present in the standard fixed-sequence versions. Strictly phonetic spellings and nuclear sentences are also first recognizable in Archaic period lexical compilations.

The clerical and scholastic spheres served complementary functions within the Archaic period administrative framework.

Figure 10 Bilingual list of trees (first millennium B.C.). After B. Landsberger, *Materialien zum Sumerischen Lexikon*, vol. 5 (Rome: Pontifical Biblical Institute, 1957), 92.

Column 1 (Sumerian)	Column 2 (Akkadian)	
GIŠ-TAŠKARIN	tas-ka-ri-in-nu	"boxwood"
GIŠ-ESI	u_2-šu-u_2	"ebony"
GIŠ-NU$_{11}$	sa-mul-lum	"sandalwood"
GIŠ-ḪA-LU-UB$_2$	ḫa-lu-up-pu	"oak"
GIŠ-ŠA$_3$-KAL	šak-kul-lum	"willow"
GIŠ-ŠA$_3$-KAL-SIG$_7$	ta-ra-du-u_2	(type of willow)

Scribal education provided practical training in cuneiform script and clerical vocabulary. The items which were collected into thematic lists for study and training were those commodities and administrative offices whose transactions and accounts were voluminously recorded in clerical texts. The increasing complexity of bureaucratic record keeping and the increasing flexibility of writing were parallel developments. As levels of accountability for administrative transactions were recorded with ever-greater precision by title, function, and name, new logograms and writing principles were developed to enable such precision. As writing progressed from logographic to logosyllabic, applications began to appear in personal and geographical names of both lexical compendia and clerical records. As in later times, the range of didactic writing skills and vocabulary of the school texts exceeded that of the preserved clerical accounts.

Scribes were professionally trained servants of the local administration, which was an intricate coordination of religious and political authority and a distributive economic system. The writing system, devised for record keeping, provided a management tool for bureaucratic authority and expansion. As cuneiform evolved to approximate spoken language, writing spread to the arenas of propaganda, science, and entertainment. Although literacy remained the skill of a specialized elite, its productivity pervaded public and private life, from monumental inscriptional displays and international diplomacy to private correspondence and contracts, and daily business accounting of commodity exchange and distribution.

......

Notes

1. M. W. Green, "The Construction and Implementation of the Cuneiform Writing System," *Visible Language* 15 (1981): 347ff., 362ff.; I. J. Gelb, *A Study of Writing* (Chicago, 1963), 62ff.

2. The pioneering study of the Archaic period Uruk tablets was made by Adam Falkenstein on the basis of discoveries made during the first three seasons of excavation at that site: *Archaische Texte aus Uruk* (Leipzig, 1936). An updated, comprehensive list of cuneiform signs based on twenty-seven seasons of excavation can be found in M. W. Green and Hans J. Nissen, *Archaische Texte aus Uruk*, vol. 2: *Zeichenliste der archaischen Texte aus Uruk* (Berlin: Gebr. Mann Verlag, 1987).

3. Green, "Construction and Implementation," 356ff.; Gelb, *Study of Writing*, 97.

4. Marvin A. Powell, "Three Problems in the History of Cuneiform Writing: Origins, Direction of Script, Literacy," *Visible Language* 15 (1981): 424ff.; Green, "Construction and Implementation," 358–59.

5. The graphic evolution of cuneiform through three millennia is depicted in extensive detail, with geographical and chronological variants, Sumerian and Akkadian sign values, and abridged French translations, in René Labat, *Manuel d'Epigraphie Akkadienne (Signes, Syllabaire, Idéogrammes)* (Paris, 1976).

6. Gelb, *Study of Writing*, 98–99.

7. M. Civil and R. D. Biggs, "Notes sur des textes sumériens archaïques," *Revue d'Assyriologie et d'Archéologie Orientale* 60 (1966): 12ff.

8. Anton Deimel, "Produkte der Viehsucht und ihre Weiterverarbeitung," *Orientalia* 21 (1926): 12.

9. Robert D. Biggs, "The Abū Ṣalābīkh Tablets: A Preliminary Survey," *Journal of Cuneiform Studies* 20 (1966): 76.

10. The complexity of the Sumerian writing system in expressing phonological and morpholexical information is described with greater detail and insight by

Miguel Civil, "The Sumerian Writing System: Some Problems," *Orientalia*, n.s. 42 (1972): 21ff.

11. Gelb, *Study of Writing*, 194, 196, emphasizes the innovative role of foreign cultures and languages in the evolution of phonetic writing.

12. Differences between the Sumerian and Akkadian phonetic systems are masked by their sharing a writing system and by the centuries-long process of transforming that writing system for Akkadian use. The non-Sumerian phonemes /q/, /ṣ/, and /ṭ/, for example, were present in the Akkadian language, while Sumerian /d^r/, /g^w/, /ḡ/, and /o/ were absent. Recent studies of Sumerian phonology include: Miguel Civil, "The Sumerian Writing System," 21ff., and "From Enki's Headaches to Phonology," *Journal of Near Eastern Studies* 32 (1973): 57ff.; Stephen J. Lieberman, "The Phoneme /o/ in Sumerian," in *Alter Orient und Altes Testament*, vol. 203, *Studies in Honor of Tom B. Jones*, ed. Marvin A. Powell, Jr., and Ronald H. Sack (Neukirchen, 1979), 21ff.

13. For a fascinating analysis of how alternative values are sorted through and selected by a reader of Akkadian cuneiform, see Erica Reiner, "How We Read Cuneiform Texts," *Journal of Cuneiform Studies* 25 (1973): 3ff.

14. Joachim Krecher, "Die sumerischen Texte in 'syllabischer' Orthographie," *Zeitschrift für Assyriologie* 58 (1967): 16ff.

15. Miguel Civil provides sample data on the relative proportions of logograms, syllabic signs, and semantic glosses in a variety of Sumerian and Akkadian texts in "The Sumerian Writing System," 26.

16. Denise Schmandt-Besserat, "The Beginnings of the Use of Clay in Turkey," *Anatolian Studies* 27 (1977): 133ff., and "An Archaic Recording System and the Origin of Writing," *Syro-Mesopotamian Studies* 1 (1977): 31ff.

17. For a general survey and interpretation of Archaic period tablet formats, see Green, "Construction and Implementation," 348ff., 361ff. A detailed study of the formats and data of herders' reports is presented in M. W. Green, "Animal Husbandry at Uruk in the Archaic Period," *Journal of Near Eastern Studies* 39 (1980): 1ff.

18. Round tablets continued to be used for elementary-level scribal training, among other specialized but nonlexical uses; see Robert S. Falkowitz, "Round Old Babylonian School Tablets from Nippur," *Archiv für Orientforschung* 29/30 (1983/84): 18ff.; Giovanni Pettinato, *Analecta Orientalia*, vol. 45, *Texte zur Verwaltung der Landwirtschaft in der Ur-III Zeit: "Die Runde Tafeln"* (Rome, 1969). A standard typology of tablet formats used for lexical exercises in the Old Babylonian scribal schools has been devised by Miguel Civil, *Materials for the Sumerian Lexicon*, vol. 12, *The Series Lú = ša and Related Texts*, 27–28, 151ff.

19. Full editions of the Archaic period lists from Uruk and their later duplicates are to appear in M. W. Green and Hans J. Nissen, *Archaische Texte aus Uruk*, vol. 3, *Lexikalische Listen* (in press). Partial editions highlighting evolutionary stages and glossing practices are presented in M. Civil and R. D. Biggs, "Notes sur des textes sumériens archaïques," 1ff.; M. W. Green, "A Note on an Archaic Period Geographical List from Warka," *Journal of Near Eastern Studies* 36 (1977): 293–294; M. W. Green, "Early Sumerian Tax Collectors," *Journal of Cuneiform Studies* 36 (1984): 93ff.; Miguel Civil, "Early Dynastic Spellings," *Oriens Antiquus* 22 (1983): 1ff.

20. An excellent survey of Mesopotamian lexical compilations is M. Civil, "Lexicography," in *Sumerological Studies in Honor of Thorkild Jacobsen on his Seventieth Birthday, June 7, 1974*, ed. Stephen J. Lieberman (Chicago, 1976), 123–57.

······

Further Readings

Falkenstein, Adam. *Archaische Texte aus Uruk*. Leipzig: Harassowitz, 1936.

Gelb, I. J. *A Study of Writing*. Chicago: University of Chicago Press, 1963.

Green, M. W. "The Construction and Implementation of the Cuneiform Writing System." *Visible Language* 15 (1981): 345–72.

Green, M. W., and Hans J. Nissen. *Archaische Texte aus Uruk*. Vol. 2, *Zeichenliste*. Berlin: Gebruder Mann, 1987.

Labat, René. *Manuel d'Epigraphie Akkadienne (Signes, Syllabaire, Idéogrammes)*. Paris: Geuthner, 1976.

4

The Origin of Egyptian Hieroglyphs
......

Henry George Fischer

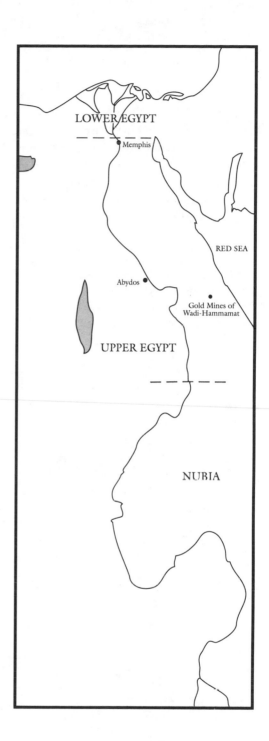

......

The Archaic period of Egypt, which embraced the first two dynasties (3050 B.C.–2670 B.C.) as well as a few earlier kings, ushered in a number of momentous advances in art, architecture, technology, and administration. The most important of the technological advances was the creation of a phonetic system of writing, the exact nature of which eluded historians, philosophers, and scholars until the decipherments of the French philologist Champollion in the early nineteenth century (see chapter 1). In this chapter I consider the beginnings of writing in Egypt both chronologically and in terms of influence from Mesopotamia, indicating how much is known and how much still remains unknown, or uncertain, about our interpretation of the early evidence, much of which is neither as homogeneous nor as complete as that available for early Sumerian.

The first evidence of phonetic writing in Egypt apparently coincides with the unification of the country under a divine king, who was identified with the god Horus. Of the several early kings whose names have been preserved from contemporary evidence, Narmer (ca. 3000 B.C.) is generally taken to be the one who completed this consolidation, as shown on his well-known cosmetic palette from Hieraconpolis, the reverse of which displays a semianthropo-

morphic emblem of the northern marsh-
land, surmounted by the Horus-falcon, one
human arm extended to hold a rope that is
attached to the nose of its captive (fig. 1[a]).
The king, wearing the crown of Upper
Egypt, holds a more naturalistic representation of a captive labeled W^c-$š$ representing

Figure 1 Ceremonial palette of Narmer: (a) re-
verse; (b) obverse. After J. E. Quibell, "Slate
Palette from Hieraconpolis," in *Zeitschrift für
Ägyptische Sprache* 36 (1898), pls. 12, 13.

either the name of a chieftain ($W^c š$) or a
district—"Harpoon-lake" (or "Canal").[1]
Since each Egyptian king began his reign
with a symbolic reenactment of the union
of Upper and Lower Egypt, this evidence
is hardly conclusive, however. Produce of
some kind, deriving from Upper and Lower
Egypt, is mentioned on jar inscriptions of
the earlier king generally identified as Ka
(fig. 2), and it therefore seems likely that
he too exercised control over the southern
and northern realms. The same conclusion
is even more likely in the case of Scorpion,[2]

(a)

(b)

(a)

(b)

Figure 2 Pottery inscriptions of (a) Ka, and (b) Aha. Fig. 2(a) after W. M. F. Petrie, *Abydos*, vol. 1 (London, 1902), pls. 2 (16), 3 (27); fig. 2(b) after W. B. Emery, *Tomb of Hor Aha* (Cairo, 1939), pls. 14 (bis) (2), 21 (158).

and it would also be true of the Horus Ro (or Iry), if the name has been identified correctly.[3] Possibly the latter is simply to be read *Ḥr(w)*[4] (Horus), in which event most of the occurrences would be analogous to a number of cases where the *serekh,* a paneled façade that normally frames the name of the king, is surmounted with a Horus-falcon, but evidently contains no name at all.[5]

To clarify the chronological references in the following pages, one may divide the Archaic period into four periods as follows:

– The earliest rulers (ca. 3050–3000 B.C.): Ro/Iry(?), Ka (or Zekhen),[6] Scorpion
– Early Dyn. I (ca. 3000–2850 B.C.): (1) Narmer (or Mery-Nar),[7] (2) Aha, (3) Djer, (4) Djet
– Late Dyn. I (ca. 2850–2750 B.C.): (5) Den, (6) Anedjib, (7) Semerkhet, (8) Qa-a
– Dyn. II (ca. 2750–2670 B.C.): concluded with Peribsen and Khasekhem/Khasekhemwy

It should be noted that the reading of several of these names is much more problematic than is indicated by the parenthetical alternatives, which represent only a few of those that have been suggested.[8] "Scorpion," of course, circumvents any reading at all, and simply describes a sign.[9]

The emergence of writing in Egypt also coincides with a period of intense contact with Mesopotamia, and of very definite influence from Sumer and Elam.[10] While Egyptologists have sometimes discounted the impact of that influence, there can be no doubt that it was profound and catalytic.[11] The contact from Mesopotamia was direct, almost certainly by ship, around the Arabian coast to the Red Sea and thence probably overland, through the Wadi Hammamat. Not only were goods imported, but ideas as well. The clearest example of such a borrowing is the cylinder seal (see chapter 2).[12] It was greatly exploited in the first dynasties and throughout the ensuing period of the Old Kingdom, although it almost immediately acquired a completely Egyptian character, as a vehicle for the newly devised hieroglyphs. Several very distinctive Mesopotamian motifs appear on decorated objects of this time, as exemplified by the cosmetic palette of Narmer, the obverse of which shows a pair of serpo-felines, their necks intertwined around the cup in which eye paint was prepared (fig. 1[b]).[13] It is also difficult to gainsay Henri Frankfort's argument for the Sumerian origin of a type of paneled brick architecture which makes its first appearance in Egypt with the earliest kings and which appears in the serekh that displays their names.[14] All this influence stems from a period when the Sumerians had gradually evolved a system of writing to the point that they could record the distribution of goods and compile lexical lists. No such period of incubation can convincingly be demonstrated for phonetic writing in Egypt.

Meager as it is, the first evidence, from the reign of Ka, shows the two most essential ingredients—monoconsonantal and biconsonantal signs—as well as a sign that represents a complete triconsonantal word. Inscribed in ink on jars of funerary offerings (see fig. 2[a]), they refer to some sort of produce called "*ip* of Upper Egypt" and "*ḥmn* of Lower Egypt," these two realms being read *Šmꜥ(w)* and *Mḥ(w)*.[15] Although the precise meaning of *ip* and *ḥmn* is unknown, very similar labels are known on jars bearing the name of Aha, where *ip* is replaced by *inw* and *ḥmn* by *iwt* (fig. 2[b]).[16] These examples also illustrate the normal orientation of the hieroglyphic system, in which the signs face rightward and are read toward the left.

If it seems apparent that the idea of writing was borrowed from the Sumerians, by whom the Egyptians were so profoundly influenced in other ways,[17] it is equally clear that the Egyptian system was very different both in form and in the use to which it was put. Sumerian writing, like that of Egypt, originally employed pictographs that not only represented the thing depicted

but were also used purely phonetically, by the rebus principle, to spell out words that could not be expressed by a concrete image (see chapter 1). But the earliest Sumerian pictographs give only the most rudimentary impression of what is depicted, and the initial forms soon became less recognizable (see chapter 3). Egyptian hieroglyphs were not only much more clearly representational but acquired an even greater degree of naturalism, which persisted for well over three millennia, down to their replacement by the essentially Greek alphabet imposed by Christianity. This degree of naturalism is understandable, since larger-scale representations and hieroglyphs of identical style supplemented each other in a complementary relationship. In Mesopotamia, on the other hand, inscriptions were not combined with representations until the second dynastic period, corresponding to the Egyptian Third Dynasty, and were combined in this manner only rarely before the period that followed.[18] Moreover, as a relief plaque of Urnanshe shows, the Sumerian script was then imposed directly upon two-dimensional figures—a practice that is completely at variance with the complementary use of inscriptions on Egyptian reliefs.[19]

The representational character of the hieroglyphs is underscored by the fact, already demonstrated, that a more cursive style of writing, written with brush and ink, was evidently in use as early as hieroglyphs. Evolution in the interest of greater speed and efficiency was channeled along this separate but parallel track, leaving the hieroglyphs themselves relatively immune to change. As the difference between the hieroglyphic and cursive scripts increased (the latter termed "hieratic" by the Greeks), a semicursive style was added in the Old Kingdom, and yet another in the Middle Kingdom; these were adopted for special situations, such as the heading of a hieratic text, the whole of a formal religious text, or for certain materials, such as wood or metal, which lent themselves to incised characters.[20]

Another very fundamental departure from the Sumerian system stems from the Egyptians' much more approximate use of the rebus principle, which required only the agreement of consonants, and in which weak consonants were often disregarded.[21] In view of the fact that Egyptian belongs to the Hamito-Semitic (Afro-Asiatic) family of languages, which characteristically has triconsonantal roots, John D. Ray has suggested that the disregard of vowels resulted from a tendency to write words of a single root with a single sign.[22] While this tendency is valid enough, it does not apply to the monoconsonantal signs, which are much in evidence from the outset. An equally striking feature of the Hamito-Semitic group of languages in question is the variability of vowels and shift of accent in different grammatical forms, including —in some cases—the plural; this is illustrated by a word like 𓄿𓃀𓏏 [23] $\exists ht$, "field," in which the vocalic shift is displayed by Coptic *yōhe*, pl. *yahū* (the final *t* having been lost). The avoidance of such changes is probably to be attributed to a predilection for the characteristic and permanent aspect of things that is so evident in Egyptian art, including the forms of the hieroglyphs themselves. The monoconsonantal

signs in particular sometimes derive from words that have been stripped of weaker consonants to a considerable degree: for example, 𓏭 (*j*), which Jürgen Osing reconstructs as *waɜjá. ˇt*.[24] There was evidently a concerted effort to make the repertory of monoconsonantal signs as complete as possible; several of them (𓇌, 𓊪, 𓈖, 𓂋, 𓏏, 𓍿, 𓏭 :) *i̯, p, n, r, t, č, j* occur in the very few words left by Narmer and his predecessors; most of the rest are attested by the stelae of subsidiary burials around the tomb of Djer, early in the First Dynasty, and nearly all twenty-four are known to have been in use by the end of the dynasty.[25] Biconsonantal and triconsonantal signs are likewise known from the First Dynasty and earlier, as well as a characteristic repetition of the final consonant (the "phonetic complement"), which marks yet another difference from Sumerian: for example, 𓋹𓏤 (*ʿnḫ*), 𓌀𓏤 (*w3s*), 𓏠𓈖 (*mn*), 𓌶 (*mr*), 𓊵 (*ḥtp*), 𓋴𓂧 (*šd*), the third from the reign of Aha,[26] the fifth from the reign of Djer, the rest from that of Den. This peculiarity was very probably an original feature of the system.

From the very beginning the monoconsonantal signs were indispensable in writing words that could not otherwise be expressed; by the reign of Djer they were used for grammatical adjuncts such as suffix-pronouns and finally, at least by the end of the Second Dynasty, they were employed for writing prepositions such as the dative *n*, "to, for" (see figs. 6 and 7).[27] The Egyptian script continued to make much use of them for these purposes; they served to write some of the commonest words in the language; in addition to nearly half of the simple prepositions, these include *rn,* "name"; *rḫ,* "know"; *snb,* "be healthy"; *ḫt,* "thing"; *ḏd,* "say"— none of which required a determinative (a classifying element, see chapter 1) in the Old Kingdom, nor did the gods Ptah, and Re, in theophoric personal names. Many more examples could be added that, from the Old Kingdom onward, regularly added the determinative, for example, the verb *spḫ,* "lasso," or the noun *nỉꜣ,* "ibex." These examples show the function of the final ideographic element, which may be generic (the rope of the first example,) or specific (the ibex in the second case,). In the Old Kingdom, and to a lesser degree thereafter, such determinatives might be eliminated if an adjacent representation served the same purpose.[28] Thus the importance of the monoconsonantal signs should not be underestimated, even though they remained but one element of a fairly complex orthography.

While hieroglyphic inscriptions of the first two dynasties show far fewer determinatives than were employed in the Old Kingdom and later (ca. 2670 B.C. onward), more extensive use was made of them than in the Sumerian script of the corresponding periods (see Margaret W. Green's discussion of glosses and determinatives in cuneiform, chapter 3).[29] From the very beginning the presence of large-scale figures frequently served that purpose. The same is true of the stelae of nonroyal persons, where smaller figures, usually at the end of the name, might be regarded as hieroglyphic determinatives;[30] no such deter-

minatives occur after such names in other contexts, however. The term is more legitimately applied in the case of those determinatives that frame one or more other signs to categorize them as a royal name (the serekh), a fortress (, buttressed wall), a settlement or vineyard (, fenced enclosure), or a building ( ). The hieroglyph for "town" ( ) was probably also used as a determinative from the reign of Djer onward.[31] In some cases, such as the use of , it is not certain that this element was not read as a separate word, as also in the case of the land-sign ( ), which appears after the names of Libya, Asia, and Nubia.[32] The same question is raised by the names of boats, such as the one mentioned on the Narmer Palette (fig. 1b). A more certain example is again to be found in the pair of legs that is appended to signs that are thus categorized as verbs of motion, and notably *ỉnỉ,* "bring") and *ỉỉ,* "come"), both attested in the First Dynasty, and *šmỉ,* "go"), which is known from the Second Dynasty. On the other hand, two similar composites and are probably an amalgam of + , + , "produce of Upper/Lower Egypt."[33]

Meaningful composites of this sort are characteristic of the early use of hieroglyphs. They are scarcely known in Sumerian, which may, however, show a simple fusion such as (*lu + gal,* "king"; lit., "great man"). A complex Egyptian example of the First Dynasty is shown at the left in figure 3. As just noted, the royal name is enclosed by the serekh, which is surmounted by a falcon designating Horus. The king is "the Horus Aha," and the mace and shield that express the word *ꜣḥꜥ,* "fighter," are

Figure 3 Wooden label of Aha. After Petrie, *RT* 2, pl. ɪɪ (ɪ).

gripped by the claws of the bird. This idea is repeated by adding a second pair of arms to the serekh, one brandishing a mace to deliver the coup de grace to a kneeling captive, who is held by the other hand. The captive is labeled "Nubia."[34] Although composite signs continued in use during the Old Kingdom and later, hieroglyphs were generally presented in a discrete sequence of phonetic and ideographic elements, and this in turn facilitated the complementary relationship of representations and inscriptions that was fully realized only after the Archaic period. Even when two signs were combined, the components and their relationship remained clearly recognizable.[35] Devices such as the aforementioned ⚒ were therefore avoided; had they not been, the script might well have proliferated along the lines of Chinese. In the event, rather than the thousands of characters required to write Chinese, scarcely more than four hundred were needed by the Egyptians down to the end of the Pharaonic period

in 342 B.C., and the meaning of many of these was self-evident.[36] With the passage of time, hieratic gradually required somewhat greater effort to learn, as the signs became more abstract and more frequently ligatured, but it remained a fairly exact cursive equivalent of the hieroglyphic script.

The repertory of signs shows remarkably little resemblance to early Sumerian pictographs. Some of the signs may well derive from native preliterate emblems or devices, such as ⌇ (the *wȝs*-scepter), scratched on a black-topped pot from Naqada,[37] or an even earlier pot, mounted on human feet, that is strangely similar to the sign 𐦀, mentioned earlier.[38] The impressive variety of predynastic pot marks has, in fact, persuaded some to regard them as an early form of writing, but the evidence strains credulity.[39] Furthermore, as Alexander Scharff has pointed out, a number of other hieroglyphs depict objects that clearly belong to the end of the predynastic period.[40] They include implements such as ⌇ (the piriform mace), 𐦀 (dagger), ⌐ (flint knife), ⌾, ⌀, 𐦀, ○ (vessels), as well as the serekh,

Figure 4 Ceremonial macehead of Narmer (right end omitted). After J. E. Quibell, *Hierakonpolis*, vol. 1 (London, 1900), pl. 26B.

representing paneled brickwork.

In view of all that has been said thus far, we may go a step further. Since the hieroglyphic system does not seem to have undergone a long period of incubation, it may well have been conceived by a single individual. One is reminded of more recent inventors of scripts quite different from those that inspired them. Among these are Sequoya, who invented a syllabary for Cherokee, and King Njoya, who invented a system of about one thousand stylized hieroglyphs, partly ideographic and partly syllabic, for Bamun; the latter is particularly interesting because it was swiftly refined, between 1900 and 1918, to an almost completely phonetic system of only seventy signs.[41]

Unlike Sequoya and King Njoya, however, the hypothetical inventor of Egyptian writing was evidently a talented draftsman; in designing the hieroglyphic system he simultaneously created a new style of art, a style that aimed to present forms with the utmost clarity, often combining a multiplicity of points of view for that purpose. It has already been noted that instead of becoming unrecognizable abstractions, as in the case of Sumerian, these forms became more naturalistic and precise; a good example is provided by the swaybacked falcon that surmounts the serekh of the earliest kings, which began to acquire a straighter back in the reign of Aha and assumed a much more elegant and convincing appearance in the reigns of his successors. The interrelationship of art and writing is also demonstrated by the fact that, in the Old Kingdom, the same verb, *zš3*, was used both for "write" and "paint," although a special term, *zš3 qdw*, "scribe of contours," usually distinguished the draftsman.[42] While the limitations of space preclude a more detailed exposé of this aspect of the subject, it may be said that in no other civilization have art and writing been so completely amalgamated.

The surviving evidence for the first use of writing in Egypt may be summarized as follows, with reference to the preceding or following figures:

1. Ceremonial objects, such as the cosmetic palette of Narmer (fig. 1) and the mace-heads of Narmer (fig. 4) and Scorpion.
2. Stelae marking the tombs of kings, a single queen, lesser persons, and pet dogs.
3. Labels attached to goods placed in royal tombs, some dated by events of a specific regnal year (figs. 3, 8).
4. Seals and sealings of kings, queens, and officials (figs. 6, 7).
5. Inscriptions on vessels of pottery or stone, usually identifying the owner and/ or contents (fig. 2).

Figure 5 Wooden label of Den. After Petrie, *RT* I, pl. 15 (16).

The first class of inscriptions includes the best known of all Archaic monuments, the Narmer Palette, the obverse of which well exemplifies the complementary use of hieroglyphs and larger figures. While it is relatively understandable, it once again illustrates how many details of reading and interpretation remain uncertain in the early inscriptions. At the top the royal serekh, containing the king's name, is flanked by the emblem of the goddess Bat (the feminine of "soul"), a human-faced fetish with bovine ears and horns, possibly borrowed from Mesopotamia.[43] In the first of the three main registers the image of the king now serves as determinative, instead of the serekh, for the two signs that spell out his name. He is preceded by an official,

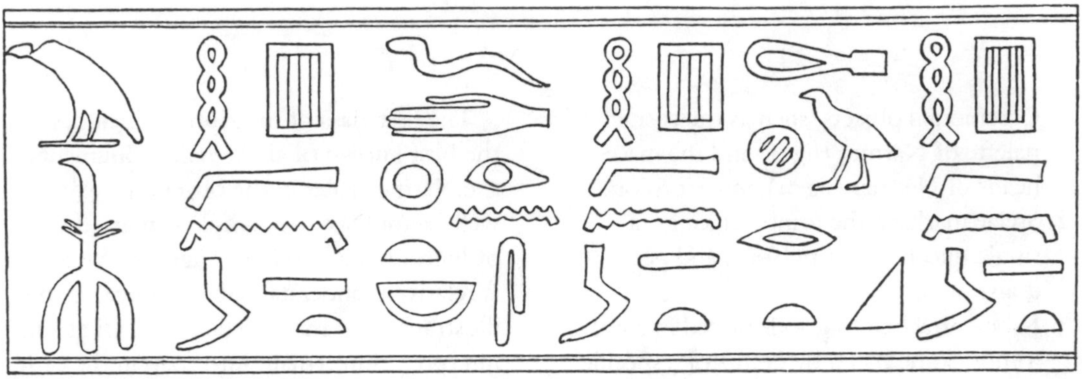

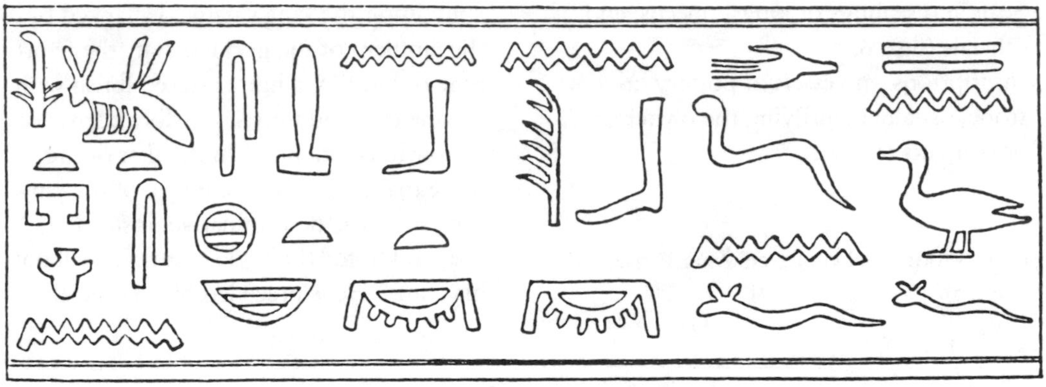

Figure 6 Seal impression of Queen Ny-maat-Hep. After Petrie, *RT* 2, pl. 24 (210).
Figure 7 Seal impression of Peribsen. After Petrie, *RT* 2, pl. 22 (190), with correction of a sign by Kaplony, *IÄF*, fig. 368.

clad in a short leopard skin, whose title has been variously interpreted as *č(ꜣ) t(y),* "vizier,"[44] and *(ꜣ)čt,* "tutor,"[45] and bearers of three standards that are familiar from Fifth Dynasty representations of royal ceremonies (ca. 2450 B.C.). The designation of the attendant who follows the king, carrying sandals and a handled vessel, is even more perplexing; it has been explained by Schott as *wdpw Ḥrw,* "butler of Horus,"[46] while Helck has suggested that it may represent *wdpw nčr,* "butler of the god," which is known from the aforementioned ceremonies.[47] Since the starlike rosette reappears before the name of Scorpion on his ceremonial macehead, it is generally agreed that it must refer to the king.[48] There is also the tempting but dubious possibility that it might derive from the Sumerian sign for "god" (✱).[49] The procession of king and attendants moves away from a rectangle at the left, which Schott plausibly explains as a house determinative, enclosing a sign for robing, the whole meaning "robing house" (later written , with the house determinative at the end).[50] Their destination is the heap of decapitated enemies shown at the right, supplemented by hieroglyphs identifying the place, "the great door," and the boat, "Horus the Harpooner," which has transported the bodies. The connection between the bodies and the hieroglyphs requires the latter to be reversed (reading left to right)—the first and most essential manifestation of a logic of orientation that was to be elaborated in all kinds of ways in the course of pharaonic history.[51] The lowermost register displays a bull, doubtless another avatar of the king, who was later known as "the victorious bull" (*k3 nḫt*), simultaneously breaking open a settlement and trampling its inhabitants; the hieroglyph identifying the place looks like a bag or garment, but has not been explained. The three rectangles near it doubtless represent scattered bricks.

The evidence of cursive writing in the final category of uses (5), dating back to the very earliest rulers, strongly indicates the loss of much more perishable documents, on papyrus or leather, and the remaining

Figure 8 Ivory label, reign of Aha. After J. de Morgan, *Recherches sur les origines de l'Egypte*, vol. 2 (Paris, 1897), p. 167, fig. 554.

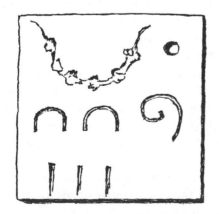

evidence suggests what the content of such documents might have been. There were certainly accounts of booty seized in successful encounters with the neighboring regions to the east, west, and south, for the macehead of Narmer (fig. 4) shows an approximate tally, which includes examples of the entire system of higher numbers: millions, hundred thousands, ten thousands, and thousands. This gives a total of 120,000 prisoners, 400,000 cattle, and 1,422,000 goats.[52] They are brought into the presence of the king, behind whom stand the two attendants shown on the Narmer Palette. The smaller numbers—hundreds, tens, and units—are attested on ivory labels from the reign of Narmer's successor, Aha; the example in figure 8 evidently records "123 beads." From the tomb of Djet, two reigns later, an obscure enumeration of alabaster objects,[53] dashed off in ink on the bottom of a stone dish (fig. 9), confirms that inventories were made,[54] and we can be fairly sure that they were made on papyrus by this time, for a small inscribed roll of that material is known from the following reign, that of Den.[55]

To judge from the Palermo Stone and other fragments of a hieroglyphic copy of annals from the first five dynasties, the Nile levels of virtually every regnal year were also systematically recorded.[56] The first evidence of such annals is to be found in the third class of evidence, the labels, which designate the regnal years of the First Dynasty by events, including—as on the Palermo Stone—the "fashioning" (𓐍) of the statues of various gods. Thus, in figure 3, the "fashioning of [a statue of]

Figure 9 Accounts on base of dish from tomb of Djet. After Petrie, *RT* 1, pl. 19 (11).

Anubis" is mentioned in connection with the name of a building. From the reign of Den until the end of the dynasty the sign for "year" (⸕) was placed at the right side of such labels, and there is no doubt that it is to be understood in the earlier cases. The labels of Den's reign still pose many problems, but their content is clearer than that in earlier examples, and we begin to find an increasing number of elements that are familiar from later inscriptions. The one shown in figure 5 characteristically devotes half of the available space to the events of the regnal year, beginning in the top register with a coronation or royal jubilee (the king running). The next register begins with the "opening" (⏝) of a settlement and the "smiting" (⏞) of its inhabitants, whose name has been thought to contain an early example of three strokes indicating the plural; it seems likely, however, that these represent scattered bricks (cf. fig. 1b).[57] The rest of this section is difficult to interpret

except for a mention of the king's other name, Khasty (⬚). On the left side of the label is the serekh of Den, behind which is the name of a high official "the Treasurer of the King of Lower Egypt Hemaka." Below this is a designation of the product to which the label was evidently affixed; it begins with an obscure phrase, then "the best of olive oil, 1200." The column of signs at the left is again obscure, but may designate the workshop of "the king's mansion" in which the oil was prepared, and the title and name of the supervising official.[58]

Unfortunately the use of such labels seems to have been discontinued after the First Dynasty; from then on, throughout the Second Dynasty, we must rely primarily on seal impressions for most of our information, except for a few entries from the Palermo Stone. But even from so unpromising a source we begin to recognize not only a greater number of familiar titles but some longer phrases such as the epithet of Queen Ny-maat-Hep (see fig. 6) "who says anything and one does [it] for her," which is also known in slightly different form from the furniture of Queen Hetep-heres at the beginning of the Fourth Dynasty.[59] This sealing dates to the end of the Second Dynasty, while that of a slightly earlier king provides our earliest evidence of a sentence that is completely written out (fig. 7): "The Ombite (Seth); he has united(?) the Two Lands for his son, the King of Upper and Lower Egypt Peribsen."[60] The first of the seals was made for a "sealer of the shipyard," the second for "the sealing of everything of gold."

For the first narrative of any length we must wait until the end of the Third

Dynasty, the biographical inscription of Metjen (ca. 2600 B.C.); it is very simply phrased, but it shows a more abundant use of determinatives, which now regularly take the form of separate signs, placed at the ends of words.[61] Among the more plentiful evidence from the later dynasties of the Old Kingdom (Fourth to Eighth), which includes more extensive biographies, hieroglyphic copies of decrees, funerary contracts and testaments, as well as hieratic letters and temple accounts, there is a single hieroglyphic copy of a contract for the purchase of property—a tomb.[62] Although little hieratic evidence of such transactions has come to light, this document proves beyond any doubt that the Egyptians recorded economic transactions just as did the Sumerians, and emphasizes once again how heavily the loss of perishable papyrus must be weighed against the abundance of virtually indestructible clay tablets.[63]

A discussion of the development of the ancient Egyptian writing systems after the Archaic period would vastly exceed the scope of this chapter. Suffice it merely to indicate that both the hieroglyphs and the cursive writing systems continued to flourish and undergo orthographic and representational changes even beyond the period of cultural stagnation, which was accelerated by the Assyrian and Persian conquests in the seventh and sixth centuries B.C. The ultimate fate of hieroglyphic writing came with the advance of Christianity, which brought to Egypt an alphabet derived primarily from Greek, used for the writing down of the latest stage of the Egyptian language, generally referred to as Coptic.

After the advent of Christianity there still remained a few scattered areas in the Roman Empire where cultic interests in the hieroglyphs continued to exist, but for most of the world and for most of history this unique writing system remained an isolated mystery with many unsolved riddles —a mystery which, to be sure, claimed the attention of the classical world and Renaissance Europe, leading to the creation of many pseudohieroglyphic inscriptions.[64] But writing in the proper sense of the word did not become one of the major cultural exports of Egypt. Aside from the influence of the hieroglyphs and the acrophonic principle on the Old Canaanite pictographic alphabet, which Frank Moore Cross analyzes in the next chapter, and the Egyptian derivation of a few letters in the Coptic alphabet, the hieroglyphic writing system played only a small role in the further evolution of world scripts.

......

Notes

The following abbreviations are used:

Hemaka   W. B. Emery, *Tomb of Hemaka* (Cairo: Government Press, Bulâq, 1938)

IÄF   Peter Kaplony, *Die Inschriften der Ägyptischen Frühzeit* (Wiesbaden: Otto Harrassowitz, 1963)

LÄ   Otto Helck, *Lexikon der Ägyptologie*, vol. 4 (Wiesbaden: Otto Harrassowitz, 1982), vol. 5 (Wiesbaden: Otto Harrassowitz, 1984)

RT   W. M. F. Petrie, *Royal Tombs of the Earliest Dynasties*, vols. 1 and 2 (London: Egypt Exploration Fund, 1900–1)

Schott, *Hieroglyphen*   Siegfried Schott, *Hieroglyphen: Abhandlungen der Akademie der Wissenschaften und der*

Literatur in Mainz, Geistes und sozialwiss. Kl. no. 24 (Wiesbaden: F. Steiner, 1950)

1. Schott, *Hieroglyphen*, 22, follows Sethe in misreading the second sign as "province," while Alan H. Gardiner, in "Egyptian Hieroglyphic Writing," *Journal of Egyptian Archaeology* 2 (1915): 74, thinks it may be a completely phonetic writing of a personal name, as does Werner Kaiser in "Einige Bemerkungen zur ägyptischen Frühzeit," *Zeitschrift für Ägyptische Sprache und Altertumskunde* 91 [1964]: 89. The vanquished enemies at the bottom of the palette are also labeled; the sign at the right, representing a papyrus with split stem (Ludwig Keimer, "Altägyptische Naturgeschichte," *Kêmi* 2 [1929]: 100), cannot represent "2000" (Ruth Amiran, "Note on One Sign in the Narmer Palette," *Journal of the American Research Center in Egypt* 7 [1968]: 127), but its meaning remains doubtful, as does its connection with the fortress-enclosure at the left. Some have conjectured, however, that the two signs may refer to Sais and Memphis (see H. W. Müller, "Gedanken zur Entstehung, Interpretation und Rekonstruktion ältester ägyptischer Monumentalarchitektur," in *Ägypten: Dauer und Wandel*, Deutsches Archäologisches Institut, Abteilung Kairo, Sonderschrift 18 [Mainz: Philipp von Zabern, 1985], 11 n. 30).

2. A. J. Arkell, "Was King Scorpion Menes?" *Antiquity* 37 (1963): 31–35; the fragmentary maceheads of this king show him wearing both the Upper and Lower Egyptian crown.

3. W. Kaiser and Günter Dreyer, "Umm el-Qaab," *Mitteilungen des Deutschen Archäologischen Instituts, Abteilung Kairo* 38 (1982): 232–35.

4. The reading *Ḥr(w)* is suggested by the jar inscriptions. See Kaiser and Dreyer, "Umm el Qaab," 234, fig. 10 c–d, which may belong to the "Horus Ka." A similar writing of "The Horus Nar(mer)" may be recognized in Dows Dunham, *Zawiyet el-Aryan* (Boston: Museum of Fine Arts, 1978), 26 and pl. 16a; for the rounded form of the sign beneath the falcon see *RT* 1, pl. 44, and Kaiser and Dreyer, "Umm el-Qaab," p. 263, fig. 14 (16, 18, 20), from Abusir El-Meleq.

5. H. G. Fischer, "A Fragment of Late Predynastic Egyptian Relief from the Eastern Delta," *Artibus Asiae* 2 (1958): 84–85; "Varia Aegyptiaca: 8, A First Dynasty Wine Jar from the Eastern Delta," *Journal of the American Research Center in Egypt* 2 (1963): 44–47; W. Kaiser, "Einige Bemerkungen zur ägyptischen Frühzeit," *Zeitschrift für Ägyptische Sprache und Altertumskunde* 91 (1964): 113–15; Kaiser and Dreyer, "Umm el-Qaab," 262–67.

6. The alternative "Zekhen" is suggested by the fact that the sign read as Ka may be placed at the bottom of the *serekh* or inverted; see P. Kaplony, "Sechs Königsnamen der 1. Dynastie in neuer Deutung," *Orientalia Suecana* 7 (1958): 54–57.

7. G. Godron, "A propos du nom royal 𓉻 ," *Annales du Service des Antiquités de l'Egypte* 49 (1949): 217–20. Schenkel, *LÄ* 5:723, offers the unlikely translation "Schlimmer Wels."

8. Alternative readings for Djet are assembled by I. E. S. Edwards in *The Cambridge Ancient History*, vol. 1, 3d ed. (Cambridge: Cambridge University Press, 1971), 24 n. 6, and for Den by E. S. Meltzer, "Horus DN 'Cutter,' Severer (of Heads)?" *Journal of Near Eastern Studies* 31 (1972): 338–39. Alternatives for other First Dynasty names are proposed by Kaplony, "Sechs Königsnamen," including the improbable substitution of *Sḥtj* for Djer, which appears throughout his *IÄF*.

9. Some possible readings are Selqet, Selqety, Djaret, Djarety.

10. As summarized by Henri Frankfort, *The Birth of Civilization in the Near East* (Bloomington: Indiana University Press, 1951), appendix; also Edwards, *Cambridge Ancient History*, 41–45.

11. See, in particular, Helene Kantor's rebuttal of Helck in *Chronologies in Old World Archaeology*, ed. Robert W. Ehrich (Chicago: University of Chicago Press, 1965), 11–14. Helck has, in the meantime ("Gedanken zum Ursprung der ägyptischen Schrift," *Mélanges Gamal Eddin Mokhtar*, vol. 1 [Cairo: Institut Français d'Archéologie Orientale, 1985], 395–408), pushed his idea of trade links with Syria a great deal farther, arguing that that region and Lower Egypt had a language in common, different from that of Upper Egypt, and a culture that produced the first hieroglyphic writing (on perishable material of which nothing remains). It is conjectured that unfamiliar forms and orthography in some of the earliest inscriptions

from Abydos are to be explained by the adoption of this protohieroglyphic system by the Upper Egyptians when they conquered the Delta. The same argument is taken up again in Helck's *Untersuchungen zur Thinitenzeit* (Wiesbaden: Otto Harrassowitz, 1987), 138–43. Many of the archaic inscriptions are discussed, but the volume has appeared too late to make much use of it in the following pages.

12. Most recently discussed by M. R. Boehmer, "Das Rollsiegel im prädynastischen Ägypten," *Archäologischer Anzeiger*, 1974–75, pp. 495–514; he considers the oldest examples to be imports from Elam.

13. The connection was first pointed out by L. Heuzey in *Comptes Rendus à l'Académie des Inscriptions et Belles-Lettres* 27 (1899): 66, and by A. E. P. Weigall, citing Newberry, in "Miscellaneous Notes: 3. The Long-Necked Lions of Archaic Times," *ASAE* 11 (1910): 170–71. See also A. Scharff, "Neues zur Frage der ältesten ägyptisch-babylonischen Kulturbeziehungen," *Zeitschrift für Ägyptische Sprache und Altertumskunde* 71 (1935): 98. Mesopotamian influence evidently continued as late as the reign of Den, as may be seen from some inlaid gaming disks illustrated in *Hemaka*, pl. 12C, D, E; these show inlays of diamonds and concentric circles closely set in deep channels; cf. the early Sumerian example cited in n. 49 below.

14. H. Frankfort, "The Origin of Monumental Architecture in Egypt," *American Journal of Semitic Languages* 58 (1941): 329–58. See Jeffrey Spencer, *Brick Architecture in Ancient Egypt* (Warminster, Engl.: Aris and Phillips, 1979), 6, 15, and, for the *serekh*-sign, Michael Atzler, "Einige Erwägungen zum *srḫ*," *Oriens* (Leiden) 23–24 (1974): 406–32.

15. Kaplony, *IÄF*, 999, proposes to read *ḫn* instead of *ḫmn*.

16. 'Inw and *iwt* also occur on wooden labels of this and the next reign: *RT* 2, pl. 10 (2) (Aha); *Hemaka*, 35, fig. 8 (Djer); W. B. Emery, *Great Tombs of the First Dynasty*, vol. 3 (London: Egypt Exploration Society, 1958), pl. 107 (Den).

17. Still doubted, however, by Schenkel (*LÄ* 5, col. 726), who prefers to leave the question open, and by Helck, "Gedanken zum Ursprung."

18. See Henri Frankfort, *Cylinder Seals* (London: Macmillan, 1939), 55.

19. The plaque is in the Louvre; Henri Frankfort, *The Art and Architecture of the Ancient Orient* (Harmondsworth: Penguin Books, 1954), pl. 33B.

20. Ricardo Caminos and H. G. Fischer, *Ancient Egyptian Epigraphy and Palaeography* (New York: Metropolitan Museum of Art, 1976), 40–42.

21. This point is scarcely affected by I. J. Gelb's theory that the phonetic signs represent a syllabary with interchangeable vowels (which, in the case of monoconsonantal signs, might precede or follow); contested by S. Schott in "Abhängigkeit und Einwirkung," *Handbuch der Orientalistik* 1: *Ägyptologie*, ed. H. Kees, pt. 1, *Ägyptische Schrift und Sprache* (Leiden: E. J. Brill, 1959), 32–36, but defended, in part, by W. Schenkel, "Rebus-, Buchstabiersilben- und Konsonantenschrift," *Göttinger Miszellen* 52 (1981): 83–95.

22. John D. Ray, "The Emergence of Writing in Egypt," *World Archaeology* 17 (1986): 313.

23. It should be recalled that the normal orientation of hieroglyphs shows the signs facing right, reading right to left, although they were reversed in certain situations. The signs quoted here are reversed so as to conform to our orientation of reading.

24. Jürgen Osing, *Die Nominalbildung des Ägyptischen* (Mainz: Philipp von Zabern, 1976), 168, 669, 758–59.

25. *RT* 2, pls. 26–27; cf. J. L. de Cenival, in *Naissance de l'écriture: Cunéiformes et hiéroglyphes*, ed. Béatrice André-Leickman and Christiane Ziegler (Paris: Editions de la Réunion des musées nationaux, 1982).

26. *RT* 2, pl. 13 (93); an equally early example is possibly to be seen in ☒ on the protodynastic palette shown by Schott, *Hieroglyphen*, pl. 3 (fig. 6), but this may represent *ḫprr*, "beetle," rather than *ḫpr,* and Helck, "Gedanken zum Ursprung" interprets the bettle as a frog. A likelier one is probably to be found in the supposed "Horus Ro" (☒), for which see n. 4 above; also the similar example read *wr* by Schott, *Hieroglyphen*, 119, and Fischer, "The Evolution of Composite Hieroglyphs," *Metropolitan Museum Journal* 12 (1977): 7, which may well represent the same word.

27. Suffix-pronouns: *RT* 2, pl. 26 (63); the feminine name *Ḥtp.f.*

28. H. G. Fischer, *Egyptian Studies*, vol. 2 (New York: Metropolitan Museum of Art, 1977), 3–4.

29. In practice, however, the early historical texts of Sumer make much less use of determinatives than the lexical lists suggest.

30. The predominance of a terminal female figure, whereas no "determinative" is present in a great many other cases, is perhaps explained by Old Kingdom usage, for which see Fischer, "Redundant Determinatives in the Old Kingdom," *Metropolitan Museum Journal* 8 (1973): 7–25.

31. The clearest example is dated to Anedjib: P. Lacau and J.-Ph. Lauer, *Pyramide à Degrès*, vol. 4 (Cairo: Institut Français d'Archéologie Orientale, 1959), pl. 7; for earlier occurrences of the sign (Djer and Djet), see *RT* 2, pl. 16 (114); *RT* 1, pl. 18 (6); the latter is read *nḥb* (el Kab) by Kaplony, *IÄF*, 765.

32. Accepted as determinatives by Schott, *Hieroglyphen*, 123.

33. For all of these see Fischer, "Evolution of Composite Hieroglyphs," 7.

34. Correctly interpreted by Schott, *Hieroglyphen*, 29 and pl. 7 (fig. 13); the alternative proposed by E. J. Brovarski in "Hor-aha and the Nubians," *Serapis* 4 (1977–78): 1–2, is untenable.

35. Fischer, "Evolution of Composite Hieroglyphs," 7–18.

36. The characters greatly proliferated during the Graeco-Roman period in the cryptographic orthography devised by the priesthood.

37. W. M. F. Petrie, *Naqada* (London, 1896), pl. 52 (62).

38. Fischer, *L'écriture et l'art de l'Égypte ancienne* (Paris: Presses universitaires de France, 1986), 44 n. 63.

39. William S. Arnett, *The Predynastic Origin of Egyptian Hieroglyphs* (Washington, D.C.: University Press of America, 1982); well evaluated by Ray, "Emergence of Writing," 309.

40. Alexander Scharff, *Archäologische Beiträge zur Frage der Entstehung der Hieroglyphenschrift (Sitzungsberichte der Bayrischen Akademie der Wissenschaften, Phil.-hist. Abt.* 1942, Heft 3, Munich); W. Westendorf, "Die Anfänge der Altägyptischen Hieroglyphen," *Frühe Schriftzeugnisse der Menschheit* (Göttingen: Joachim Jungius-Gesellschaft der Wissenschaften Hamburg, 1969), 85, puts more emphasis on the earlier origin of some of the signs and believes, contrary to my next point, in a gradual evolution of writing in Egypt, which has its roots in religious iconography.

41. David Diringer, *The Alphabet* (London: Hutchinson, 1968), 107–109 (Bamun), 128–30 (Cherokee); Hans Jensen, *Sign, Symbol and Script* (London: George Allen and Unwin, 1970), 218–21 (Bamun), 241–43 (Cherokee).

42. For the transliteration of *zš₃* see Gardiner, "Egyptian Hieroglyphic Writing," 65 n. 1.

43. See Fischer, "The Ancient Egyptian Attitude towards the Monstrous," in Anne E. Farkas, Prudence O. Harper, and Evelyn B. Harrison, eds., *Monsters and Demons in the Ancient and Medieval World: Papers Presented in Honor of Edith Porada* (Mainz: Philipp von Zabern, 1987), 15 and n. 20.

44. Schott, *Hieroglyphen*, 23; Schenkel, *LÄ* 5, col. 723.

45. H. Kees, in *Zeitschrift für Ägyptische Sprache und Altertumskunde* 82 (1957): 58–62; I. E. S. Edwards, *Cambridge Ancient History*, vol. 1, p. 37.

46. Schott, *Hieroglyphen*, 25; cf. Schenkel, *LÄ* 5, col. 723.

47. Wolfgang Helck, *Untersuchungen zu den Beamtentiteln* (Glückstadt: J. J. Augustin, 1954), 94 (in the discussions mentioned in n. 11 above, he believes the sign to be indecipherable). The reading *wdpw* is based on the form and orientation of this sign on the Scorpion macehead; others have interpreted it as *ḥm*, "priest."

48. Kaplony, *IÄF*, 994, following others, thinks the rosette may represent the ⌇-plant (*nswt*, "king") as seen from above. For another early example of this sign in a similar context, see Bruce Williams, "The Lost Pharaohs of Nubia," *Archaeology* 33/5 (Oct. 1980): 16–18.

49. S. Curto concludes this in "Annotazioni su geroglifica arcaici," *Zeitschrift für Ägyptische Sprache und Altertumskunde* 94 (1967): 22–24. It should be noted that a similar rosette is a common and early Meso-

potamian motif (e.g., W. Orthmann, ed., *Der Alte Orient: Propyläen Kunstgeschichte*, vol. 14 [Berlin: Propyläen Verlag, 1975], pl. 10). But there is no evidence that the Sumerians associated this with the sign for "god."

50. Schott, *Hieroglyphen*, 23, 123.

51. Fischer, *Egyptian Studies* 2:15 and passim.

52. See G. Godron, "Deux notes d'épigraphie thinite," *Revue d'Egyptologie* 8 (1951): 99, who prefers to read "1,822,000 large and small cattle."

53. For the inverted *śz*-sign in "alabaster" see *IÄF*, 283.

54. Other examples of this kind, less securely dated, are published by P. Lacau and J.-Ph. Lauer, *Pyramide à Degrès*, vol. 5 (Cairo: Institut Français d'Archéologie Orientale, 1965), 22–24; see also the measurements on pp. 24–31.

55. *Hemaka*, 41. The hieroglyph showing the scribal kit seems first to be known from the reign of Semerkhet (*RT* 1, pls. 31 [43], 36 [43]). The hieroglyph representing a sealed roll of papyrus is known from the reign of Sekhemib, in the next dynasty (*RT* 2, pl. 21 [164]).

56. For references concerning the Palermo Stone and other fragments, see Helck in *IÄ* 4, cols. 652–54.

57. Raymond Faulkner, *Plural and Dual in Old Egyptian* (Brussels: Edition de la Fondation Egyptologique Reine Élisabeth, 1929), 21. In a second case (*RT* 1: 21 [28]) the plural strokes may represent the number 3, since the reading of the preceding sign remains uncertain.

58. A similar tablet is described by de Cenival in *Naissance de l'écriture*, 66.

59. H. Junker suggests, as an alternative translation, "of whom one relates all the good things she has done" ("Die Grabungen der Universität Kairo auf dem Pyramidenfeld von Giza," *Mitteilungen des Deutschen Archäologischen Instituts, Abteilung Kairo* 3 [1932]: 138–39), but this fits the earlier version less well, since the adjective "good" is omitted.

60. The questionable word, *d(m)j*, is more usually taken as a reversed writing of *jd*; for the rest, see Kaplony, *IÄF*, 1143, and Edwards, *Cambridge Ancient History*, vol. 1, p. 31.

61. For references see B. Porter and R. L. B. Moss, *Topographical Bibliography of Ancient Egyptian Texts . . . ,*

vol. 3: *Memphis*, 2d ed., revised by J. Málek (Oxford: Oxford University Press, 1974–81), 493–94.

62. For references see ibid., 25; here called a purchase of a house; for the interpretation of "house" as "tomb," see Fischer, "Notes on the Mo'alla Inscriptions and Some Contemporaneous Texts," *Wiener Zeitschrift für die Kunde des Morgenlandes* 57 (1961): 62–63.

63. For some comparable (although less complete) records on papyrus, see Paule Posener-Kriéger, "Le Prix des étoffes," in *Festschrift Elmar Edel*, ed. Manfred Görg and Edgar Pusch (Bamberg: Manfred Görg, 1979), 318–31.

64. See Erik Iversen, *The Myth of Egypt and Its Hieroglyphs* (Copenhagen: Gec Gad Publishers, 1961).

· · · · · ·

Further Readings

André-Leickman, Béatrice, and Christiane Ziegler, eds. *Naissance de l'écriture: Cunéiformes et hiéroglyphes.* Catalogue of an exhibition at the Grand Palais, Paris, May 7–August 9, 1982. Profusely illustrated, with extensive commentaries and discussions by many scholars.

Edgerton, William F. "Egyptian Phonetic Writing, from its Invention to the Close of the Nineteenth Dynasty." *Journal of the American Oriental Society* 60 (1940): 473–506.

Fischer, Henry George. *L'écriture et l'art de l'Égypte ancienne.* Essais et Conférences, Collège de France. Paris: Presses Universitaires de France, 1986.

Helck, Wolfgang. *Untersuchungen zur Thinitenzeit.* Wiesbaden: Otto Harrassowitz, 1987. Incorporates his controversial views on the Lower Egyptian origin of hieroglyphic scripts, as well as the systematic survey of the early inscriptions.

Iversen, Erik. *The Myth of Egypt and Its Hieroglyphs in European Tradition.* Copenhagen: Gec Gad Publishers, 1961.

Kaplony, Peter. *Die Inschriften der Ägyptischen Frühzeit,* 3 vols. Ägyptologische Abhandlungen 8. Wiesbaden: Otto Harrassowitz, 1963. Deals primarily with seals and stelae, much less systematically with the other classes of inscriptions. Recommended for specialists equipped to evaluate the conclusions. Accompanied by a large, though not complete, corpus of facsimiles.

Klasens, Adolf. "Een Grafsteen uit de Eerste Dynastie." *Oudheidkundige Mededelingen uit het Rijksmuseum van Oudheden te Leiden* 37 (1956): 12–34. Includes an additional compendium of 144 names on private stelae, nearly all dating to the First Dynasty.

Petrie, Hilda. *Egyptian Hieroglyphs of the First and Second Dynasties*. London: Quaritch, 1927. Much could now be added to this compilation, but it is still useful.

Ray, John D. "The Emergence of Writing in Egypt." *World Archaeology* 17/3 (1986): 307–16.

Scharff, Alexander. *Archäologische Beiträge zur Frage der Entstehung der Hieroglyphenschrift. Sitzungsberichte der Bayerischen Akademie der Wissenschaften, Phil.-hist. Abt.*, no. 3. Munich, 1942.

Schott, Siegfried. "Die Erfindung der ägyptischen Schrift" and "Das Schriftsystem und seine Durchbildung." In *Handbuch der Orientalistik*, part 1: *Der Nahe und der Mittlere Osten*, vol. 1: *Ägyptologie*, section 1: *Ägyptische Schrift und Sprache*, 18–21, 22–31. Leiden: E. J. Brill 1959.

————. *Hieroglyphen: Untersuchungen zum Ursprung der Schrift*. Abhandlungen der Akademie der Wissenschaften und der Literatur in Mainz, Geistes und sozialwissenschaftliche Klasse, 1950, no. 24. Wiesbaden: F. Steiner, 1951. Still the best introduction to the subject.

Sethe, Kurt. *Vom Bilde zum Buchstaben. Die Entstehungsgeschichte der Schrift*. With a contribution by Siegfried Schott. Untersuchungen zur Geschichte und Altertumskunde Ägyptens 12. Leipzig: J. C. Hinrichs, 1939. Mainly of interest because of the terminal remarks of Schott.

Weill, Raymond. *Les origines de l'Egypte pharaonique*. Vol. 1: *La IIe et la IIIe Dynasties*. Paris: E. Leroux, 1908. Though out of date, this work still contains some useful data.

————. *Recherches sur la Ire dynastie et les temps pré-pharaoniques*. Parts 1 and 2. Bibliothèque d'Etude, vol. 38. Cairo: Institut Français d'Archéologie Orientale, 1961. Published eleven years after the author's death and about twenty years after completion of the manuscript, this is in any case a less useful book than its predecessor.

5

The Invention and Development of the Alphabet

· · · · · ·

Frank Moore Cross

· · · · · ·

The invention of the alphabet was a singular event in human history, occurring probably in the eighteenth century B.C., relatively late in the flowering of the old, high civilizations of the ancient Near East. Earlier, at least five major writing systems, complex and beautiful, were developed in the Mediterranean and Oriental world, each apparently independently of the others. The alphabet was invented only once. All alphabetic writing derives ultimately from an Old Canaanite alphabet and its immediate descendant, the Early Linear Phoenician alphabet. As we shall see, the invention of the alphabet was a revolutionary as well as unique gift to human civilization.

The ancient Near East spawned a number of writing systems. The earliest was the Sumerian, which appeared in Mesopotamia a century or two before 3000 B.C., about the same time as the Sumerian city-states. Shortly later, Egyptian hieroglyphic writing appears—about 3000 B.C. Some have suggested that Egyptian writing arose under the stimulus of Sumerian writing—there *were* early influences of Mesopotamia upon the emerging Egyptian civilization—but if this is so, the only element of influence was the idea of writing in pictographs. As Henry George Fischer demonstrated in the preceding chapter, Egyptian hieroglyphics show no perceptible influence of the actual Sumerian system. Both systems originate in pictographs, which represented words, and very early developed into true writing, word-syllabic in character: signs representing both words and syllables were combined in writing. These two systems of writing, described in the preceding chapters, and others which followed (Proto-Elamite, ca. 3000; Proto-Indic, ca. 2200; Cretan, ca. 2000; Hittite, ca. 1500; Chinese, ca. 1500), were enormously complex and cumbersome means of writing. The Egyptian sign list includes more than four hundred signs, and though all these signs were not in simultaneous use, it is a formidable task to learn even those in common use in a single period. Sumerian writing, pictographs, and abstract signs, which simplified into cuneiform, signs made of complexes of wedges made with a stylus on clay, has a sign list of about six hundred signs (more in the Archaic period) of which some three hundred were in ordinary use in a given era. Moreover, most of these signs had multiple values, logographic and syllabic.

Given such great complexity, only a scholar with years of arduous training and high intellect learned to read and write with facility. Inevitably literacy remained the exclusive possession of a small, powerful elite. Ordinarily, members of this elite were royal and priestly functionaries, attached to the crown and temple. In effect, writing was a monopoly of the court.

The invention of the alphabet provided a new system of writing of breathtaking simplicity. The early alphabet used only twenty-seven or twenty-eight signs and was soon simplified (ca. 1250 B.C.) to twenty-two signs. Each sign represented a single consonantal phoneme. The system was completely phonetic. Although the notation of vocalic phonemes did not exist in the earliest alphabet, a peculiarity of the West Semitic languages—all syllables begin with a consonant—permitted the system to function efficiently. A person could now learn to read and write in a matter of days or weeks.

The weight of the impact of the alphabet on the evolution of human civilization is difficult to exaggerate. Literacy spread rapidly and broadly (in centuries rather than millennia), and with it came the democratization of culture. With the invention and development of the older, complex writing systems, the ancient world very slowly entered a transition from a wholly orally transmitted culture to a culture which supplemented the oral means of transmission of learning and literature with writing. But with the coming of the alphabet, societies, still dominantly oral in literary composition, using memory for storage of learning, quickly, in some few centuries, completed a revolutionary transformation to dominantly written means to preserve and transmit culture. In Assyria a king brags that he can read cuneiform; in Israel a soldier complains bitterly when his commander suggests that he is not fully literate.

Most obviously, alphabetic writing made possible an immediate expansion of the possibilities for accumulating knowledge, preserving it, and widely dispersing it. It multiplied the sources of learning and literature.

Further, the new mode of writing gave rise ultimately to new modes of viewing culture and new ways of thinking. Writing froze oral communication and made it visible, so to speak, to be examined and reexamined at leisure. *Alphabetic* writing vastly facilitated such reflective scrutiny. A text could be deliberately studied, by rich or poor, prophet or poet, lawyer or priest, and with such study arose new possibilities for critical and logical analysis.[1]

The older elitist and relatively static and hierarchical societies of the Near East gave way to new, dynamic societies, alphabetic societies which reached their pinnacle in the ancient world in Israel and Greece: egalitarian Israel with its prophetic critique of state and church, democratic Greece with its gift to humanity of logical thought and skepticism.

How did the alphabet come into being? How did it spread? The first notices concerning the origin of the alphabet are found in classical sources. Herodotus in a famous passage speaks of "these Phoenicians who came with Cadmus . . . brought into Hellas the alphabet, which had hitherto been unknown, as I think, to the Greeks."[2] Herodotus calls the alphabet *kadmēia grammata* and *grammata phoinikēia,* "Cadmean characters" and "Phoenician characters." Herodotus's account is a compound of myth and legend, but the tradition he received, that the Greeks acquired the alphabet through Phoenician mediation, is historically sound. An interesting footnote may be added. A recently published archaic Greek inscription from Crete (predating Herodotus) uses the terms *poinikazen,* "to write," and *poinikastas,* "scribe." Both terms

Figure 1 An Old Canaanite inscription from Serābîṭ el-Khâdem in Sinai. The lower line reads *lbᶜlt,* "To the (Divine) Lady," an epithet of Asherah. Courtesy of G. Gerster and J. Naveh.

derive from *(grammata) phoinikēia,* "Phoenician [letters]."[3]

The modern era of the study of alphabetic origins began with the discovery of the proto-Sinaitic inscriptions by Sir Flinders Petrie in 1905. Petrie, excavating at Serābîṭ el-Khâdem in the Sinai Peninsula, found a dozen short texts inscribed in an unknown pictographic script. He

dated them to about 1500 B.C., a date long disputed but now confirmed as almost certainly correct. Harvard expeditions in 1927, 1930, and 1935 greatly expanded the corpus of proto-Sinaitic texts, and a few more have been found in recent years.

The first tentative steps toward decipherment were taken by Sir Alan Gardiner in 1915.[4] The distribution of signs made evident that the inscriptions were alphabetic, and Gardiner noted a recurrent series of signs: loop of rope—house—eye—loop of rope—cross (fig. 1). Gardiner recognized that, if the signs followed an acrophonic principle, their Canaanite value would be: *lb'lt* [*la-ba'lati*], "[dedicated] to the Lady." Ba'lat was a favorite epithet of the great Canaanite goddess Asherah. Since in Egypto-Canaanite syncretism Ba'lat was identified with Ḥathor, the Egyptian goddess whose temple dominated Serābît el-Khâdem, the reading was highly suitable.

Gardiner propounded a theory that the Old Canaanite alphabet, as we now call it, was acrophonically devised under the inspiration of Egyptian hieroglyphic writing. By acrophony we mean the principle of representing a sound by a picture of an object whose name begins with the sound to be represented: an apple for *a*, a ball for *b*, a cat for *c*, and so on. It was well known that the *names* of the letters in Phoenician and in Hebrew, derived from Phoenician, were acrophonic: *'alp ('aleph)*, "ox"; *bêt*, "house"; *gaml (gimel)*, "throwstick"; and so on. However, the question was, were the names primary, part of the invention of the alphabet, or secondary, mnemonic devices?

Gardiner's partial decipherment, and many attempts to extend it, were hotly debated, and nearly forty years passed before sufficient data were accumulated to settle the basic questions of how the alphabet was devised. Even today, the early pictographic alphabet and its small corpus of texts is not fully deciphered.[5] Some twenty signs can be traced from pictograph to Linear Phoenician letter. Old Canaanite possessed some twenty-seven or twenty-eight consonantal phonemes which required notation, and in addition, for some letters, alternate pictographs were used in different scribal traditions, for example, fish, *dag*, for *d*, and door, *dalt* or *dilt*, for *d* (fig. 2).

In the years that followed there was a steady accumulation of early alphabetic inscriptions, which now can be classified under two headings.

1. Old Canaanite inscriptions, transparently pictographic in origin, found in Syria-Palestine. The proto-Sinaitic inscriptions belong to this group.
2. Linear Phoenician inscriptions, easily read, an alphabetic script which is ancestral to the Old Hebrew, Aramaic, and Greek scripts (fig. 3).

Arbitrarily we use the term "Canaanite" of a people of homogeneous culture and speaking a related group of dialects who lived in Syria-Palestine before 1200 B.C. The name "Canaan," known from biblical usage, stems from the Egyptian province of Canaan, which included Lebanon and Cis-Jordan (modern Israel) in the Late Bronze Age. After the cataclysm which engulfed the Levant about 1200, the remnant of the Canaanites, whose centers were now restricted to the Lebanese coast and the coast of northern Palestine, we now call "Phoenicians" after their Greek name, "the Purple (Dye) People." The Phoenicians' ancestors were Canaanites.

The Old Canaanite inscriptions in pictographic alphabetic signs date from the seventeenth to the twelfth century B.C. The invention of the system probably took place in the eighteenth century, early in the age of the Hyksos.

Inscriptions in Early Linear Phoenician form a series beginning in the eleventh century B.C. Actually, the chronology of

Figure 2 Text 358 from Serābît el-Khâdem. It reads vertically ʾd ḏ ʿlm "(Divine) Father, lord of eternity." Courtesy of Anson Rainey and Carl Rassmussen.

the Linear Phoenician was settled only in the late 1940s and early 1950s. The precise relationship between the Old Canaanite alphabet and the Early Linear Phoenician script remained uncertain until 1953, when a group of inscribed arrowheads was found near Bethlehem at ʾEl-Khaḏr. These inscriptions, from the end of the twelfth century (ca. 1100) B.C., proved to be missing links in the history of the alphabet. Five exist; three were published in 1954, and two, lost in the hands of private collectors for a quarter century, were published in 1980 (fig. 4).[6]

The ʾEl-Khaḏr arrowheads come precisely from the time when the Old Canaanite pictographs were evolving into the Early Linear Phoenician alphabet. We were fortunate that each contained virtually the same short inscription, an inscription we could decipher with certitude: ḥṣ ʿbdlbʾt [bn ʿnt], "arrowhead of ʿabdlabîʾt [son of] Bin-ʿAnat." Both names are known from texts of this general period and evidently were popular names. Shamgar Ben Anat, bearing the same patronymic, was the famous warrior celebrated in the Song of Deborah (Judg. 5:6).

We now recognized clearly for the first time certain features of the two styles of alphabetic writing. The Old Canaanite was multidirectional: written horizontally from right to left, or from left to right, and vertically. Boustrophedon writing ("as the ox plows") was also used. In Linear Phoenician the direction was fixed: right-to-left, horizontal writing was standardized, and the stance of letters became fixed. In the older Canaanite system, letters (picto-

1500	13th	qw	1200	bs	12th	1100	11th Century byba	nora	Crete	Greek	1000

Figure 3 (Left) A script chart of Old Canaanite and Early Linear Phoenician from ca. 1500 to 1000 B.C. The next-to-last column gives archaic forms of Greek letters from a later date. Courtesy of the Harvard Semitic Museum and F. M. Cross. **Figure 4** (Below) Inscribed arrowheads of ca. 1100 B.C. from 'El-Khaḍr. Courtesy of the Harvard Semitic Museum and F. M. Cross.

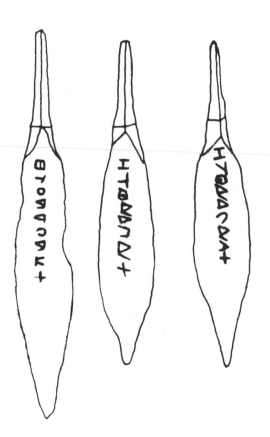

graphs) faced away from the direction of writing. The Greek script was borrowed before the time when the standardization of direction and stance took place. Hence early Greek writing was multidirectional. Later, horizontal writing became standard, but the direction of writing was from left to right. Generally therefore Greek (and Roman) letters face in the opposite direction from Phoenician and Hebrew.

The discovery of the 'El-Khaḍr arrowheads led quickly to the decipherment of a late thirteenth-century ewer from Lachish, and indeed to new readings of the proto-Sinaitic texts. And in 1977 and 1981 two additional twelfth-century inscriptions were published, one from Qubur Walaydah, one from 'Izbet Ṣarṭah in Israel further illustrating and adding detail to our knowledge of the evolutionary transition from the Old Canaanite to the Linear Phoenician stage of the early alphabet (fig. 5).[7]

Two other recent discoveries from the Old Canaanite phase of alphabet merit mention. In 1983 a fragmentary, but readily decipherable, epigraph was found by David Ussishkin in his excavations at Lachish. It is written in boustrophedon style and dates to the end of the Late Bronze Age (thirteenth century B.C.).[8] In the excavations of Gezer, Joe D. Seger recovered a group of jars inscribed with Old Canaanite signs. The importance of the discovery lies in the fact that the jars can be precisely dated by context and by typology to the late sixteenth century B.C., the oldest securely dated material in the Old Canaanite corpus.[9]

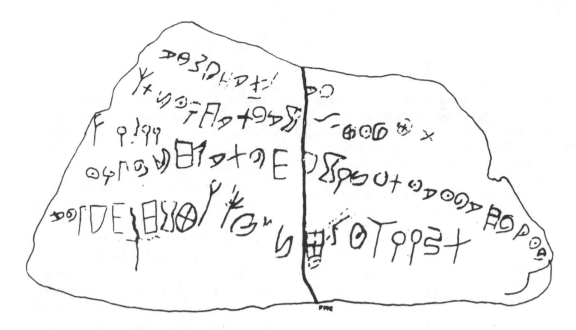

Figure 5 An ostracon from 'Izbet Ṣarṭah dating to the twelfth century B.C. The final line is an abecedary. Courtesy of the Harvard Semitic Museum and F. M. Cross.

Meanwhile, other important discoveries bearing on alphabetic origins were being made. Beginning in 1929 a series of magnificent epigraphic discoveries was made in Ugarit, modern Ras eš-Šamrah on the coast of Syria. The main group of texts contains epic and mythological works inscribed in a cuneiform alphabet in an early Canaanite dialect of the fourteenth century B.C. This alphabet has commonly been called the Ugaritic alphabet. However, it is now clear that the Ugaritic system is only one variant of a more widely used cuneiform alphabet found in ancient Syria, Lebanon, and Palestine—indeed one exemplar has been dug up on Cyprus—and should be called the Canaanite cuneiform alphabet. The standard Ugaritic alphabet, consisting of some twenty-nine signs or graphemes (ignoring some biforms), was

in use in the fourteenth–thirteenth centuries B.C. in Ugarit and its environs. A "reduced" Canaanite cuneiform alphabet of some twenty-two signs is known by its appearance in a few exemplars from Ugaritic and is represented by individual finds from Syria-Palestine and Cyprus, probably all dating to the thirteenth–twelfth centuries B.C. Both probably derive from a common Canaanite cuneiform alphabet of some twenty-seven graphemes. The reduced set of graphemes reflects the broad merging of phonemes in (southern) Canaanite dialects, probably in the course of the thirteenth century. The Old Canaanite alphabetic signs give evidence of the same reduction in the same period.

There can be no doubt that the Canaanite cuneiform alphabet was developed under the inspiration of the Old Canaanite pictographic alphabet. Had there been any doubt, it was resolved by the discovery at Ugarit of abecedaries first published in 1957.[10] One group of abecedaries simply lists alphabetic signs, following the same order that survives in Hebrew, Aramaic, and Greek. Another abecedary, unfortunately broken, lists the signs of the cuneiform alphabet in order and adds a column of Babylonian syllabic signs, which permit us to reconstruct the names of the letters of the alphabet in the fourteenth century B.C. The names, beginning ʾalp, bêt, gaml, are ancestral to the later Phoenician and Greek names (fig. 6).

The pictographic alphabet was devised under indirect influence of Egyptian hieroglyphic writing. Many of the pictographs are transparently derived from hieroglyphic models.[11] Moreover, Egyptian writing has the peculiarity of giving notation only to the consonants in words and syllables. This peculiarity, not found in other contemporary syllabaries, survives in the Canaanite and Phoenician alphabets. In fact, Egyptian

possessed what we call a pseudoalphabet: signs representing a consonant (and any vowel). However, Egyptian scribes used such signs always in conjunction with biliteral and triliteral signs so that Egyptian remained always a word-syllabic system in actual use. For example, the title of the pharaoh, "king of Upper and Lower Egypt," literally "he who belongs to the sedge [symbol of Upper Egypt] and bee [symbol of Lower Egypt]," was written n-sw-bỉt, with a monoliteral, biliteral, and triliteral sign (hieroglyph). Theoretically it could have been written n-s-w-b-ỉ-t—the signs were available—but the Egyptian scribe, bound by tradition, would have considered such alphabetic writing barbaric if he thought of it at all. The pseudoalphabet never functioned as a true alphabet. The Canaanite system came into being when it was seen that one could write using a single sign to represent a single consonant. Vowels were left without denotation. Such a system was well suited to West Semitic: each syllable in these languages begins with a consonant, and the vocalic structure is simple. Part of the invention was to devise pictographs

Figure 6 An abecedary in Canaanite cuneiform script from Ugarit (fourteenth century B.C.). The sequence of signs is as follows: ʾa b g ḫ d h w z ḥ ṭ y k š l m ḏ n ẓ s ʿ p ṣ q r ṯ ġ t ʾi ʾu ś. Courtesy of the Harvard Semitic Museum and F. M. Cross.

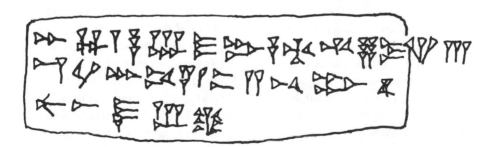

representing consonantal phonemes on the acrophonic principle; part was to set the signs in a fixed order with fixed names, an order that survives to this day. The beauty of the invention is, of course, its simplicity, a simplicity, however, which required an extraordinary feat of abstraction.

As we have observed, the Canaanite and Phoenician alphabets are incomplete in their notation of language. No signs were devised to mark vowels. In the course of the eleventh century B.C., the Aramaeans, upon borrowing the Early Linear Phoenician alphabet, devised a rudimentary system of denoting certain vowels. This system of so-called *matres lectionis* spread to Israel by the early ninth century B.C. Consonants, *h, w,* and *y* were commandeered, so to speak, to represent final vowels, *w* to mark *ū, y* to mark *ī,* and *h* to note final *ā, ē,* and *ō.* Sporadically, internal vowels, *ū* and *ī* were denoted by *w* and *y.* In Hebrew a full notation of long and short vowels evolved only in the Middle Ages between the seventh and ninth centuries with the use of sublinear or supralinear symbols (vowel points).

The first full system of signs for vowels was developed by the Greeks. The Phoenician system was most awkward for the writing of Greek. It contained many signs for consonants which did not exist in Greek, and it had no means to denote syllables in Greek beginning with a vowel. The alphabet was quickly modified, therefore, and signs, consonantal in Phoenician, were co-opted for vowels in Greek: for example, the glottal stop, Phoenician *ʾalp,* became utilized to represent the vowel *a;* the Phoe-nician *ḥet,* a strong voiceless laryngeal un-known in Greek, became a sign for *ē* (*ēta*); a voiced laryngeal *ʿayn* was utilized for Greek *o* (*omicron*).

The antiquity of the borrowing of the Greek alphabet has been the subject of much debate. Until very recently there was a consensus that the borrowing of the Greek alphabet took place in the late ninth or in the eighth century B.C. However, with our present knowledge of the evolution of the Old Canaanite and Linear Phoenician scripts, Semitic epigraphists have rec-ognized that the Greek script stems from an archetype of the Phoenician script no later than the eleventh century B.C., at the time of the transition from Old Canaanite to Early Linear Phoenician (see fig. 3).[12] Evidently it was little used until the late ninth or early eighth century, in the interval being adapted to make a more efficient vehicle for recording the Greek tongue (fig. 7).

The Old South Arabic script, or rather, the Proto-Arabic script ancestral to Old South Arabic, was borrowed about 1300 B.C., late in the period of Old Canaan-ite but when multidirectional writing still prevailed. The Ethiopic script was derived from Old South Arabic. The Aramaeans borrowed the Linear Phoenician alphabet no later than the eleventh century. The Old Hebrew script diverged from Phoenician only in the tenth century, in the time of David and Solomon, and its most charac-teristic features as a national script evolved in the course of the ninth century B.C.

The Aramaic script has a remarkable history. Initially a script used by the Ara-maean city-states of Syria, it later became the official script used for diplomacy and

Figure 7 An Old Greek inscription from Thera. It is inscribed from right to left: *BIAIOS,* a proper name. Courtesy of the Harvard Semitic Museum and F. M. Cross.

commerce in the chancelleries of the Neo-Assyrian empire, the Babylonian empire, and the Persian empire. In Persian times (late sixth century to 332 B.C.) Imperial, or Official, Aramaic and its elegant cursive script was in use from Anatolia in the northwest to Egypt in the southwest, and from the Levantine coast on the west to Persia.

With the breakup of the Persian empire and the arrival of Alexander and the Hellenistic Age in the Near East, national scripts began quickly to evolve from the Aramaic cursive hand of the Late Persian chancelleries.

The modern Hebrew script actually derives from the Jewish national script of the Roman era, which in turn is a derivative of the chancellery hand of the Late Persian empire. The Old Hebrew script, derived directly from Linear Phoenician, was little

used after the fall of the First Temple and the Babylonian Exile (sixth century B.C.). It appears on Judaean coins and inscriptions particularly in eras of national revival, for example in the time of the Maccabaean Revolt, and during the First and Second Jewish Revolts against Rome. It was occasionally used to pen biblical manuscripts. The Palaeo-Hebrew script disappears from use in the Jewish community entirely in the second century of the common era and survived to modern times only in the sectarian Samaritan community (fig. 8).

Among the Nabataeans, whose commercial kingdom flourished in northern Arabia and in Transjordan, a national script evolved, stemming, like the Jewish character, from the Aramaic hand of the Late Persian empire. A cursive form of Nabataean is the immediate ancestor of the modern Arabic script.

In the east a number of local scripts developed from the older Imperial Aramaic script in the course of the Hellenistic

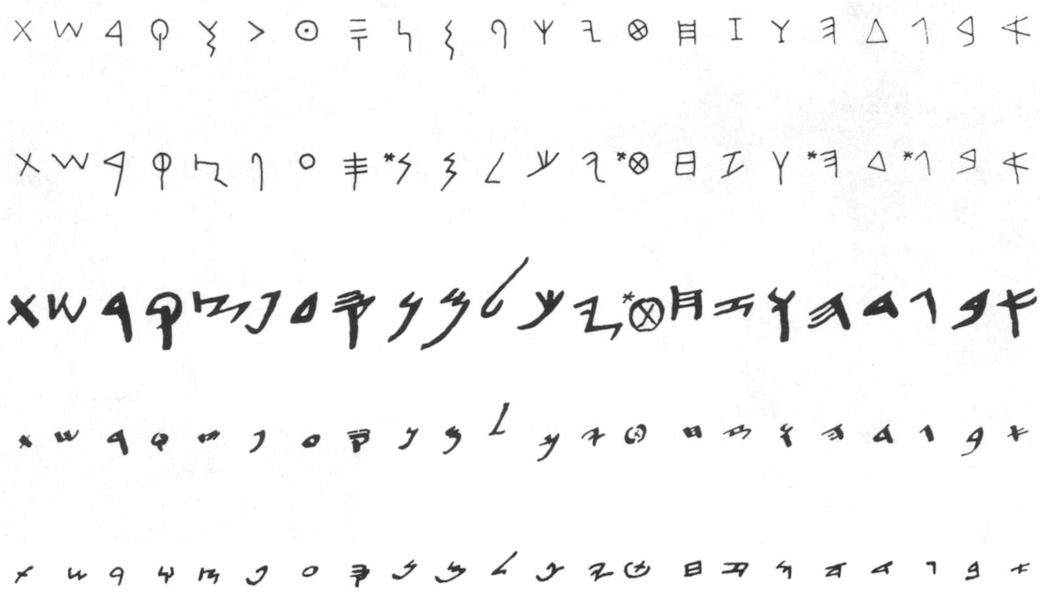

Figure 8 The development of the Old Hebrew script from the tenth to the first century B.C. *Line 1:* an exemplar of the Linear Phoenician script from which the Aramaean and Hebrew scripts were derived; *line 2:* the script of the Gezer Calendar (tenth century B.C.); *line 3:* an elegant Hebrew cursive of ca. 770 B.C.; *line 4:* the script of the Lachish Letters (ca. 600 B.C.); *line 5:* the script of the Leviticus Scroll from Qumrân, Cave II (first century B.C.). Courtesy of the Harvard Semitic Museum and F. M. Cross.

and Roman eras: Palmyrene and Syriac in northern Syria and the Upper Euphrates, Syriac surviving to modern times in the Syrian church; the script of the kingdom of Aśoka in northwest India (third century B.C.); and late Iranian scripts of Parthian and Sassanian times before their replacement by Arabic with the Muslim conquest.

A final, brief word may be said about writing materials used by ancient scribes

who wrote in early alphabetic scripts. Aside from inscriptions engraved on stone or metal, usually monumental texts, and, in the case of the cuneiform alphabet, imprinted on clay tablets with a stylus, a technique borrowed from older cuneiform writing, most alphabetic writing was painted or penned in carbon-black ink on papyrus, leather, or pottery. Papyrus was a favorite writing material for formal purposes: literary works, legal documents, and the like. Made from the inner fibers of the papyrus plant, it was tough and durable. The manufacture of papyrus appears to have been a monopoly of Egypt but was imported throughout the Near East. One of the earliest transshipment depots was Byblos on the Phoenician coast, and the Greek word for papyrus, and hence for book, was *biblos,* derived from the name of the Phoenician emporium. Broken sherds of pottery, *ostraca,* were very widely used for everyday purposes: lists and accounts and letters. Ostraca cost nothing, and, unlike papyrus

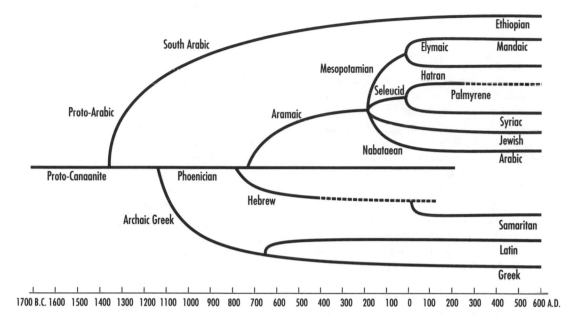

Figure 9 A family tree of early alphabetic scripts. Courtesy of J. Naveh.

or leather, are almost as indestructible as clay tablets in the tells of the ancient Near East. Few papyrus or leather documents survive from ancient times apart from those preserved in the dry sands of Egypt. We know of the intensive use of papyrus in Syria-Palestine chiefly from the imprint of papyrus fibers on the back of clay bullae used to seal ancient documents and from a few rag-tag pieces found in dry caves of the Jordan valley. However, ostraca survive in large numbers, to be found by the archaeologist and to be read by the delighted epigraphist (fig. 9).

· · · · · ·

Notes

An abbreviated version of this essay appeared in *Ebla to Damascus: Art and Archaeology of Ancient Syria*, ed. Harvey Weiss (Washington, D.C.: Smithsonian Institution, 1985), 271–78.

1. Cf. Jack Goody's discussion, "Literacy, Criticism, and the Growth of Knowledge," in his *The Domestication of the Savage Mind* (Cambridge: Cambridge University Press, 1977), 36–51.

2. *Herodotus*, trans. A. D. Godley, Loeb Classical Library (Cambridge, Mass.: Harvard University Press, 1960), 29.

3. L. H. Jeffery and Anna Morpurto-Davies, "POINI-KASTAS and POINIKAZEN: BM 1969. 4-2.I, a New Archaic Inscription from Crete," *Kadmos* 9 (1970): 118–54.

4. "The Egyptian Origin of the Semitic Alphabet," *Journal of Egyptian Archaeology* 3 (1916): 1–16. This paper, originally read in 1915, did not appear until 1917 (delayed publication).

5. A major advance was made by W. F. Albright in his monograph *The Proto-Sinaitic Inscriptions and Their Decipherment* (Cambridge, Mass.: Harvard University Press, 1955). Minor advances have followed, but for the most part based on Albright's work.

6. See F. M. Cross, "Newly-Found Inscriptions in Old Canaanite and Early Phoenician Scripts," *Bulletin of the American Schools of Oriental Research* 238 (1980): 1–18, and bibliography, 19–20.

7. For bibliography, see ibid.

8. D. Ussishkin, "Excavation at Lachish 1978–1983: Second Preliminary Report," *Tel Aviv* 10 (1983): 97–175; and F. M. Cross, "An Old Canaanite Inscription Recently Found at Lachish," *Tel Aviv* 11 (1984): 71–76.

9. Joe D. Seger, "The Gezer Jar Signs: New Evidence of the Earliest Alphabet," in *The Word of the Lord Shall Go Forth*, David Noel Freedman Festschrift, ed. C. L. Myers and M. O'Conner (Winona Lake, Ind.: American Schools of Oriental Research, 1983), 477–95.

10. C. Virolleaud, *Le Palais royal d'Ugarit*, vol. 2 (Paris: Imprimerie nationale, 1957), 199–203; see also F. M. Cross and T. O. Lambdin, "A Ugaritic Abecedary and the Origins of the Proto-Canaanite Alphabet," *Bulletin of the American Schools of Oriental Research* 160 (1960): 21–26.

11. A number of scholars, most recently G. E. Mendenhall, have argued that the Old Canaanite pictographs were derived from a Canaanite syllabary, represented by the so-called Byblian pseudohieroglyphs, which was in turn inspired by Egyptian hieroglyphic writing. While it is clear that Byblian syllabic was in fact inspired by Egyptian, the link between the Byblian syllabary and Old Canaanite pictographic writing is less than clear, and the question must remain sub judice. See M. Dunand, *Byblia Grammata* (Beirut: Direction des Antiquités, 1945), 71–200; and G. E. Mendenhall, *The Syllabic Inscriptions from Byblos* (Beirut: American University of Beirut, 1985). For a defense of the direct linkage between Old Canaanite alphabetic signs and Egyptian hieroglyphic signs, see the forthcoming monograph of Gordon J. Hamilton, *The Development of the Early Alphabet*.

12. See the important study of J. Naveh, "Some Semitic Epigraphical Considerations on the Antiquity of the Greek Alphabet," *American Journal of Archaeology* 77 (1973): 1–8; and his more recent discussion in his volume *Early History of the Alphabet* (Jerusalem: Magnes Press, 1982), 175–86; P. Kyle McCarter, *The Antiquity of the Greek Alphabet and Early Phoenician Scripts* (Missoula, Mont.: Scholars Press for the Harvard Semitic Museum, 1975); and F. M. Cross, "Early Alphabetic Scripts," in *Symposia Celebrating the Seventy-fifth Anniversary of the Founding of the American Schools of Oriental Research*, ed. F. M. Cross (Cambridge: American Schools of Oriental Research, 1979), 105–23.

. . . . . .

Further Readings

Albright, W. F. *The Proto-Sinaitic Inscriptions and Their Decipherment*, Harvard Theological Studies 22. Cambridge, Mass.: Harvard University Press, 1966.

Cross, F. M. "The Development of the Jewish Scripts." In *The Bible and the Ancient Near East: Essays in Honor of W. F. Albright*, ed. G. Ernest Wright, pp. 133–202. New York: Doubleday, 1962.

———. "Newly Found Inscriptions in Old Canaanite and Early Phoenician Scripts." *Bulletin of the American Schools of Oriental Research* 238 (1980): 1–20.

———. "The Origin and Early Evolution of the Alphabet." *Eretz Israel* 8, The Sukenik Volume (1967): 8*–24*.

———. "Early Alphabetic Scripts." In *Symposia Celebrating the Seventy-fifth Anniversary of the Founding of the American Schools of Oriental Research*, ed. F. M. Cross, pp. 97–123. Cambridge: American Schools of Oriental Research, 1979.

Driver, G. R. *Semitic Writing: From Pictograph to Alphabet*. Rev. ed. Oxford: Oxford University Press, 1954.

Gelb, I. J. *A Study of Writing*. Rev. ed. Chicago: University of Chicago Press, 1963.

Jeffery, L. H. *The Local Scripts of Archaic Greece*. Oxford: Clarendon Press, 1961.

McCarter, P. K. Jr. *The Antiquity of the Greek Alphabet and the Early Phoenician Scripts*, Harvard Semitic Monographs 9. Missoula, Mont.: Scholars Press, 1975.

Naveh, J. *The Development of the Aramaic Script*. Jerusalem: Israel Academy of Sciences and Humanities, 1970.

———. *Early History of the Alphabet*. Leiden: E. J. Brill, 1982.

———. "Some Semitic Epigraphical Considerations on the Antiquity of the Greek Alphabet." *American Journal of Archaeology* 77 (1973): 1–8.

Peckham, B. *The Development of the Late Phoenician Scripts*, Harvard Semitic Studies 20. Cambridge, Mass.: Harvard University Press, 1968.

6

The Arabic Alphabet
······
James A. Bellamy

······

The latest chapter in the long history of the linear Canaanite alphabet and its descendants is still being written today. Those of us who use the Latin, Greek, or Cyrillic alphabets to write our language are heirs to this tradition, now more than three thousand years old. There are, however, other alphabets used by people who are closer kin to the Canaanites than we are, who speak Semitic languages, and some of whom, at least, are the direct descendants of those early pioneers in literacy who bestowed on mankind the inestimable benefit of alphabetic writing. The Hebrew alphabet is used in Israel and elsewhere for writing the Hebrew language; Syriac maintains its existence for texts sacred to many Syrian Christians; Geez, the ancient language of Abyssinia, and Amharic and Tigre, the main Semitic languages of modern Ethiopia, are written in a special syllabary that derives ultimately from the Canaanite. But by far the most widely used of the Semitic alphabets today is that of the Arabs. Next to the Roman alphabet, it is of all the descendants of the Canaanite the most widely diffused and is used by the greatest number of people.

The wide diffusion of the Arabic script was brought about by the Arab conquests that followed upon the revelation of the new religion of Islam in the early years

of the seventh century A.D. In about 610, Muhammad, the prophet of Islam, began to receive revelations and soon thereafter began to propagate the new religion in his native town of Mecca, which was a commercial city and pilgrimage center for pagan Arabs in the Ḥijāz, that part of Arabia that lies along the Red Sea coast. Unsuccessful at first, he migrated to Medina, some distance north of Mecca, in 622, the year from which the Muslim era is dated. In Medina he became leader of the community, and by the time of his death in 632, he had subdued much of the Arabian peninsula, the population of which eventually converted to Islam.

The revelations that the prophet received were in the Arabic language, and sometime during the 650s, they were compiled and published in a definitive edition by order of the caliph Uthman; this edition of the Koran, the sacred scriptures of Islam, is the one that is still in use today. After the death of Muhammad, the Muslims embarked on a series of conquests, in which they subjugated the Near East and Egypt, eventually extending their rule to Spain in the west, central Asia, and parts of India to the east. Even after the military conquests came to an end, Muslim traders and missionaries extended the sphere of Islam as far east as Malaysia, Indonesia, and the Philippines. This movement has not yet ceased. Islam is still progressing in sub-Saharan Africa, and there are many Muslim immigrants, as well as new converts, in Europe and North and South America.

Wherever the Muslims went they took the Koran with them. Because of the sacred scriptures and other writings of a religious nature, and because writing was necessary for the governing of a huge empire, Islamic culture, starting from very small beginnings, had within a couple of centuries become one of the most literate cultures in the world. Another result of the conquests was that many non-Arabs converted to Islam; some of these new converts abandoned their native language and adopted Arabic. Even where this did not happen, they usually adopted the Arabic alphabet to write their own languages. The Arabic alphabet has been used, for example, to write Turkish, Persian, Urdu, Malay, and even Ukrainian and Polish. In recent times it has suffered some setbacks: Turkey adopted the Latin alphabet in 1928, as did the people of newly independent Malaysia and Indonesia more recently, and the Muslim peoples of the Soviet Union now use varieties of the Cyrillic alphabet. However, the Persians, Afghans, Pakistanis, and many others still use the Arabic and there is little likelihood that they will ever change.

The Arabic alphabet, like its ancestor the Canaanite, is written from right to left, but this is almost the only point the two have in common. In the course of their evolution, the Arabic letters have altered to such an extent that they no longer bear any resemblance to the forms they originally had in the Canaanite. In Canaanite each letter is isolated from its neighbors, and so has only one form. In Arabic, however, twenty-two of the twenty-eight letters have four forms each: isolated, final, initial, and medial. The isolated and final forms resemble each other closely and are distinguished from the

others by a flourish at the end which runs along the line of writing or descends below it. The forms of the initial and medial letters are much reduced, in some cases to such an extent that there is not much resemblance between them and the isolated and final forms. This reduction, which was carried to the extreme in Arabic, had already occurred in some forms of the Aramaic alphabet because of the evolution of a cursive hand in which many letters are ligatured to each other along a base line. Six letters of the Arabic, however, never developed initial and medial forms; these letters, wherever they occur, even in the middle of a word, are always followed by a space.

The Arabic alphabet contains only the twenty-eight consonants, although the language has six vowels, three short and three long. There are also two diphthongs, *aw* and *ay*, which can be regarded as combinations of the short vowel *a* plus a following consonant. As with some other Semitic alphabets, Arabic, even in its earliest stage, made use of certain consonants to indicate the long vowels: alif (the glottal stop) for long *ā*, *w* for long *ū*, and *y* for long *ī*. Signs for the short vowels were not invented till later times, after the advent of Islam. These will be discussed in more detail below.

The Arabic alphabet developed out of a form of the Aramaic alphabet, which had only twenty-two letters. Moreover, the development of the ligatured cursive form of Arabic still further reduced the number of basic elements; if we consider only the initial and medial forms, there are only fifteen basic elements which must be used to represent the twenty-eight consonants of Arabic.

The expedient devised by the Arabs to obviate this dilemma was to distinguish between consonants having the same basic element by a dot, or dots, placed above or below the letter. For example, initial and medial *n, t, th, b,* and *y* are all written alike, but *n, t,* and *th* have one, two, and three dots, respectively, placed above the letters, and *b* and *y* are written with one and two dots below. These dots are always used today in printed texts, but in the Middle Ages they were often omitted from manuscripts, especially when the sense was clear from the context. The earliest Arabic papyrus so far discovered, which is dated in the month of Jumādā I, 22 (April 643), contains a few pointed letters, so the practice is quite old, going back to pre-Islamic times, although the dots were used only sporadically.[1]

The use of the dots, however, even in principle, did not meet with everyone's approval. In particular, copyists rejected them at the outset for copying the Koran, where they might have been most helpful in establishing a commonly accepted text. The definitive edition of the Koran, which was produced in the 650s, had no diacritics even though, as we have seen, their use is attested as early as 643. It has been suggested that they were not used in order to avoid controversy among the companions of the prophet, who may have had their own favorite readings. Since there are many variants in the Koranic text, and they have never caused serious controversy among the readers and copyists, this argument is not convincing. I think rather that the Koranic text was copied "stenographically" without any dots at the prophet's dictation, and

when an official edition became necessary, the editors merely wrote down what they had before them. Whatever the reason, the earliest Korans in the so-called Kūfic hand —an early Muslim script used for monuments, Korans, and only occasionally other books—do not distinguish the ambivalent consonants.

As one would expect, the Arabs, when they adopted the Aramaic alphabet, also took over many of the Aramaic names of the letters, some with slight modifications. Wāw, zāy, kāf, mīm, nūn, shīn, are the same in both Arabic and Aramaic; jīm is shortened from gimel, lām from lāmedh, dāl from dāleth, and ṣād from ṣādhē. But the Arabs had to invent new names for the letters that did not exist in Aramaic. In some cases they modified an existing name by changing the initial consonant to correspond to the sound of the letter; for example, the sound *ḍ*, which does not occur in Aramaic but is written like a ṣād with a dot over it in Arabic, becomes ḍād. In other cases, a completely new name was invented, consisting of the initial letter followed by *-āʾ*, and this form in some instances was extended to letters that did occur in Aramaic; for example, rāʾ (Aramaic rēsh), ṭāʾ (Aramaic ṭēth).

The order of the letters in the new alphabet was also changed to bring together groups of letters similar in form, though the order is not uniform throughout the Arab world. Even today in Northwest Africa the order of the letters differs somewhat from that employed in the Near East. The old Aramaic order was retained, however, when the letters were used as numerals. Here the Arabs were fortunate, since the six new letters made it possible to extend the numerical value of the letters up to 1,000, whereas the twenty-two letters of the Aramaic go only as high as 400.

The last phase of the development of the Arabic alphabet, which saw the invention of the signs for short vowels, geminate consonants, and absence of vocalization, began sometime in the latter part of the sixth century, at about the same time systems of vocalization were being worked out for Hebrew and Syriac. Curiously, the signs for short vowels in Arabic arose in the Kūfic tradition of copying the Koran, the same tradition which had rejected initially the distinguishing of consonants by diacritics.

There are two systems of noting the short vowels. The oldest is a system of dots, usually written in colored ink so as not to give the impression that they form part of the original text. One dot above the line indicates *a,* one dot below, *i,* and a dot on the line represents *u.* By doubling the dots at the end of nouns and adjectives, one gets *-an, -in,* and *-un,* which are the case endings, plus the final *n,* which is the sign of indeterminateness. The system, though attractive aesthetically, is cumbersome and does not show all the essential features of the text. So about a hundred years later, a new system was adopted, which is the one still in use today. The dots representing *a* and *i* were replaced by short diagonal lines, and the *u* is represented by a small *w* written above the consonant. As before, the final *-n* is noted by doubling the sign. Special signs were invented to mark double consonants and consonants that have no vowels. The

old system continued in use for Koranic manuscripts, but the later Kufic Korans employ the new vowels, and ultimately Korans came to be written fully pointed, with the new system of vocalization. When fully pointed and vocalized, the Arabic alphabet provides a nearly perfect phonemic transcription of the sounds of the classical Arabic language. It has thus avoided the problems of irregular spellings that afflict languages such as English and French, in which the development of the script has not kept pace with that of the language.

Figure 1 illustrates in a modern printed text the end-product of this development into a cursive, fully pointed and vocalized hand. This is the first chapter of the Koran in the Egyptian edition, and since this edition is the one most widely circulated, the typeface employed in it is the best known throughout the Islamic world. Other printed books and newspapers use typefaces resembling this one, but few are as elegant; moreover, the vowels are usually omitted from such works but are always printed in the text of the Koran. This text comes to terms with modernity by using all the diacritics to distinguish consonants—a complete change from the earliest practice —but makes one concession to archaism in the voweling. Long *ā* is often not written with the alif, but to avoid misreading, a short alif is written above the consonant.

The history of the Arabic alphabet, however, does not begin with Islam. Literacy in the Arabian peninsula can be traced back at least as far as the sixth century B.C. In the southwestern corner of the peninsula —the Arabia Felix of the ancient geog-

بِسْمِ اللَّهِ الرَّحْمَنِ الرَّحِيمِ ۝ ١

الْحَمْدُ لِلَّهِ رَبِّ الْعَالَمِينَ ۝ ٢ الرَّحْمَنِ الرَّحِيمِ ۝ ٣

مَالِكِ يَوْمِ الدِّينِ ۝ ٤ إِيَّاكَ نَعْبُدُ وَإِيَّاكَ

نَسْتَعِينُ ۝ ٥ اهْدِنَا الصِّرَاطَ الْمُسْتَقِيمَ ۝ ٦

صِرَاطَ الَّذِينَ أَنْعَمْتَ عَلَيْهِمْ غَيْرِ الْمَغْضُوبِ

عَلَيْهِمْ وَلَا الضَّالِّينَ ۝ ٧

Figure 1   The Koran, Surah I. Rev. ed. (Cairo: Dār al-Kutub al-Miṣrīyah, 1371/1952).

raphers—there arose one after the other in antiquity several powerful kingdoms. They were wealthy because of the trade routes that passed through their territory and for their production of frankincense and myrrh. The people were great traders, as well as agriculturalists, and established trading colonies along the trade routes far to the north. These people did not speak Arabic but a group of related languages that are collectively referred to as Old South Arabic. They were literate and have left innumerable inscriptions in a handsome monumental script, the ancestor of which may have branched off from the Canaanite as early as the fourteenth century B.C. These inscriptions date approximately from the sixth century B.C., or perhaps even earlier, to the sixth century A.D., a period of at least twelve hundred years. The South Arabic alphabet spread ultimately to Africa, where it formed the basis of the Ethiopic syllabary, and northward along the trade routes, where it gave rise to several

alphabets which were used in writing languages closely related to Arabic, the most important of which we know as Thamudic, Lihyanic, and Safaitic.

These languages are referred to as Old North Arabic, but it should not be assumed that Arabic is a descendant of any one of them. They, together with Arabic, seem rather to form a bundle of closely related northern Arabian dialects, which were probably to a great extent mutually intelligible. The longest lived was the Thamudic, of which the oldest inscriptions may possibly go back to the sixth century B.C., while the latest are from the fourth century A.D. They are found mostly in the land of Midian and in the old oasis settlements of northern Arabia, Tabūk, Taimāʾ, Madāʾin Ṣāliḥ, and others. Lihyanic inscriptions are found in the oasis of Dedān, today called al-ʿUlā, in northwestern Arabia, and the oldest of them may go back to the fifth or sixth centuries B.C. They come to an end in the first century B.C. A huge number of inscriptions, upward of fifteen thousand, have been found in Safaitic, which are mostly concentrated in the Ṣafāʾ, a volcanic area some 100 kilometers east of Damascus, but which are also found as far south as the borders of Saudi Arabia and eastward to Durah-Europus on the middle Euphrates. The Safaitic inscriptions date from the first century B.C. to the fourth century A.D.

With a few exceptions, notably in Lihyanic, the Old North Arabic inscriptions are very short and do not convey much information. They are often quite personal; they contain appeals to divinities for help, expressions of love, grief at someone's passing, and short notes, such as So-and-so pastured his camels or flocks here. Taken together, these inscriptions suggest that for hundreds of years before Islam there was a considerable amount of literacy in the Arabian peninsula among people who were related to, if not identical with, the ancestors of the present-day Arabs.

The Arabs themselves are referred to in cuneiform documents as early as the ninth century B.C. From time immemorial, it seems, the Arabian peninsula was inhabited by Arabic-speaking bedouins, who eventually penetrated into the Syrian desert, extending themselves northward as far as the Fertile Crescent. They were not literate, however, and left no record of themselves, so most of what we know about them comes from the Greek and Roman historians and geographers. As the southern Arabian civilization declined, many southerners migrated northward, where they eventually mingled with the northern Arabs and adopted their language. The southerners in their homeland had been sedentary agriculturalists and they had a tendency to settle in the towns and oases; a notable example was Medina, the second home of the prophet Muhammad, which was settled by southern Arabs along with a colony of Arabicized Jews, who, however, retained their knowledge of Hebrew and Aramaic.

An important landmark in the history of the Arabic alphabet was the establishment, in the second century B.C., of the powerful Nabataean Arab kingdom in an area stretching from the northern Hijāz north-

ward into present-day Jordan and westward into the Negev and Sinai. The capital city of the Nabataeans was Petra, in southern Jordan, the "rose-red city, half as old as time," and at the height of their power, they were even in control of Damascus. Their prosperity, like that of the southern Arabians before them, depended on trade, and like them and the speakers of Old North Arabic, they were literate. Arabic was not, however, their official language; instead they used a dialect of Aramaic, which they wrote in a special Nabataean national alphabet. A late form of the Nabataean alphabet, found in the Sinai Peninsula and hence called Sinaitic, is believed by many scholars to be the immediate ancestor of the Arabic alphabet.

We know that the Nabataeans were Arabs because of the personal names which occur in the hundreds of Nabataean inscriptions that have been found and because of isolated Arabic words and phrases that occur, especially in later times, scattered through the Aramaic texts. The Nabataean kingdom endured until A.D. 106, when the region was conquered by the Romans, who incorporated it into the Roman province of Arabia. Nabataean inscriptions, however, are found as late as the fourth century.

When the Arabs began to write Arabic, they did not as yet have an alphabet of their own, so perforce they had to use those that had been devised for other languages. Just as the Greeks borrowed the Phoenician alphabet, the Romans the Greek, and all peoples of western Europe the Latin, so too the Arabs borrowed the writing systems that they knew. A number of inscriptions in Arabic have been found written in the

South Arabic, Lihyanic, and Nabataean alphabets.

The longest and most important pre-Islamic Arabic inscription written in a non-Arabic alphabet is a famous epitaph that was discovered in Namārah, about 100 kilometers southeast of Damascus in the year 1901. The epitaph, except for a couple of Aramaic loanwords, is completely in Arabic but is written in the Nabataean alphabet. Luckily for palaeographers and historians, it is dated in the year A.D. 328 and is the tombstone of a known historical figure, Imruʾ ul-Qays, son of ʿAmr, who, according to the Arab historians, was the second king of the Lakhmid dynasty of al-Ḥīrah.[2] The Lakhmids were one of the groups of southern Arabs referred to above which migrated north. They eventually established themselves in al-Ḥīrah, a city on the Euphrates, where they became vassals and wardens of the marches to the Sassanid rulers of Persia.

Since no earlier inscriptions in the Arabic alphabet have been discovered, most of those epigraphists who accept the Nabataean origin of the Arabic have taken the date of 328 as an approximate terminus post quem for the appearance of the Arabic and have assumed that the latter part of the fourth century was the period in which the Arabic alphabet was formed. A linear progression has been assumed from Nabataean, to late Nabataean from the Sinai Peninsula, to the Namārah inscription, to the pre-Islamic Arabic inscriptions, to the early Kufic monumental script. This view is not accepted by everyone today.

When the Arabs set about fashioning their own alphabet, they modeled it on some form of the Aramaic alphabet. This may seem a bit curious, since, as noted above, the Aramaic alphabet contains only twenty-two consonants, whereas Arabic requires twenty-eight. The Arabs, if they had been willing to make the effort, could have derived their alphabet from the Old South Arabic, or one of its offshoots, all of which have the full complement of Semitic consonants, and so spared themselves the problem of ambivalent letters. However, such was the influence of Aramaic culture, which the Arabs had, to some extent at least, adopted, that they rejected the Thamudic and Safaitic, which were still being written in the fourth century in the region where the early Arabic inscriptions appear, and followed the Aramaic forms that must have been more familiar to them.

When we look at the early Arabic inscriptions, two features stand out most remarkably. The first is their rarity, and the second is the fact that the letterforms seem to have matured early, there being very little development detectable after the oldest inscriptions. Between the three hundred years that separate the Namārah inscription of 328 and the earliest Arabic papyrus of 643, the whole history of early Arabic epigraphy is represented in only five inscriptions. This is especially striking if we contrast it with the innumerable Syriac, Greek, and Latin inscriptions that are found in the same region. It can only mean that writing in Arabic remained a rare and unusual practice even after the Arabs had developed their own alphabet.

The oldest inscription in the Arabic alphabet was found in the Nabataean temple of Allāt, a pagan Arab goddess, in the land of

Figure 2 Inscription from Jabal Ramm, late fourth century. The oldest Arabic inscription so far discovered. From *Revue biblique* 45 (1936), 91.

Midian on Jabal Ramm, about fifty kilometers east of the Jordanian port of Aqabah. In figure 2 the three horizontal lines are Arabic; the writing along the left margin which turns in between the second and third lines of the Arabic is Thamudic. The inscription was first dated about 300, which may be a bit early, but it probably does date from sometime during the fourth century. It was first edited by H. Grimme, and recently a revised edition has been made by the present writer.[3] The inscription is a boast made by an energetic man who went out into the world and made money; this he announces to all those who are so world-weary that they cannot do likewise.

The next oldest is a trilingual Greek, Syriac, Arabic inscription on the lintel of a martyrium in Zebed, a town in northern Syria near Aleppo, which is dated in the year 512. The Arabic part consists of personal names.[4]

The third inscription is undated but comes probably from the fifth century (fig. 3). It was discovered by Enno Littmann in a church in Umm al-Jimāl, a town in northern Jordan, and is sometimes referred to as Umm al-Jimāl II, to distinguish it from an earlier inscription (ca. 250),

found in the same place, which is a Nabataean epitaph of the tutor of an Arab king. It was first edited by Littmann, and a new revised edition has been made by the present writer.[5] The inscription is a monument raised in honor (or memory) of a certain Ulayh, son of ʿUbaydah, who was the secretary of a Roman cohort, which was presumably stationed in the region.

The fourth inscription was discovered in 1965 at Jabal Usays near the Ṣafāʾ, about 100 kilometers east of Damascus. It is dated in the year 528, and in it a certain Ibrāhīm, son of Mughīrah, records that in that year he was dispatched on a military expedition by a king named al-Ḥārith.[6] This can refer only to al-Ḥārith, son of Jabalah, king of the Ghassanid Arabs, who were vassals of the Byzantines. He is known to have defeated the Lakhmids in battle in the same year.

The fifth and last pre-Islamic Arabic inscription in the Arabic alphabet is from a martyrium in Ḥarrān in the Lejā district, south of Damascus (fig. 4). On it a certain Sharāḥīl, son of Ẓālim, records that he built the martyrium in the year 568, a year after the destruction of the town of Khaybar in northern Arabia.[7]

Figure 3 Inscription from Umm al-Jimāl, Fifth century. From *Zeitschrift für Semitistik und verwandte Gebiete* 7 (1929), 198.

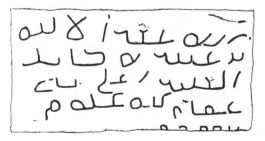

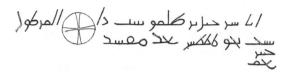

Figure 4 Inscription from Ḥarrān, dated A.D. 568. From P. Schroeder, "Epigraphisches aus Syrien," *Zeitschrift der deutschen morgenländischen Gesellschaft* 38 (1884) pl. 1, opp. p. 530.

Anyone who takes a close look at these inscriptions and compares them with the sample of the Koran in figure 1 will discern a great many letterforms that have not changed at all, or very little, in the sixteen hundred years that have elapsed since the earliest one was written. Although at first sight the differences may appear to be great, most of the letters can readily be identified by anyone familiar only with the modern Arabic printed characters.

We can further detect in these old inscriptions the forerunners—but not necessarily the immediate ancestors—of the two major types of hand that we find in later Muslim epigraphy: a cursive style, as in Umm al-Jimāl II, and a more regular and carefully executed monumental style, as in the inscription in Ḥarrān. The latter foreshadows the script called Kufic, which was mentioned earlier. The cursive style developed many different forms, though all closely related, which are found in the hundreds of thousands of Arabic manuscripts that have survived from the Middle Ages.

The derivation of the Arabic alphabet has in recent years become a matter of controversy among scholars. While everyone agrees that it derives ultimately from some form of the Aramaic alphabet, some hold that it stems from the Nabataean, while another group believes that it comes from the Syriac. The latter view is the older, going back to the eighteenth and early nineteenth centuries. But with the publication of the Sinaitic and Nabataean inscriptions in the nineteenth century, this view was abandoned, and since that time most scholars have followed the lead of Theodor Nöldeke, who proposed the Nabataean origin in 1865. However, in 1966 J. Starcky sought to revive the theory of Syriac origins. His view is that the Arabic alphabet derives not from the Syriac of Syria, where most of the pre-Islamic Arabic inscriptions have been found, but from an assumed cursive variety of Syriac, which he believes was used in the chancellery of the Lakhmid kings of al-Ḥīrah.[8]

Our sources contain two sorts of evidence that adherents of both the Nabataean and Syriac theories have appealed to. The first—and most important—is the resemblance of the Arabic letters to the earlier Nabataean and Syriac. Both Starcky and A. Grohmann, who has attempted the most detailed refutation of the Syriac theory, discuss the individual letters in some detail, pointing out the similarities between the letters in the pre-Islamic Arabic inscriptions and those of the Nabataean or Syriac, as the case may be.[9] Here I cannot illustrate their arguments, since I do not assume that the reader knows any of the alphabets involved, but I suggest that anyone interested in following up this part of the controversy consult the sources referred to.[10] I note here only that such resemblances do not tell the whole tale; since both Nabataean and Syriac descend from a common source, one should expect to find similar letters in all three alphabets.

The second sort of evidence is the accounts that later Arab historians give of the origins of their writing system. These are to a great extent legendary, and often contradictory, but legends sometimes contain a grain of truth, though we can reject out of hand those that ascribe the invention of the Arabic alphabet to Adam or Ishmael. It is certain, however, that writing in Arabic was practiced, at least to a certain extent, in al-Ḥīrah and elsewhere during the sixth century. The names of members of a family of scribes in the service of the Lakhmid kings have been preserved in the Arabic sources, together with some details of the biographies of several of them. An inscription from a monastery near al-Ḥīrah from the same period is cited in a later geographic work.[11] Finally, the histories contain several incidental allusions to writing in Mecca and Medina as well.[12] As late as the ninth century, there was preserved in the library of the caliph Ma'mūn a document in the hand of the prophet's grandfather 'Abd al-Muṭṭalib referring to a debt owed to him by a man of Ṣan'ā' in the Yemen. The handwriting is said to have resembled the "handwriting of women" (khaṭṭ al-nisā').[13]

But the accounts of the actual formation and diffusion of the Arabic script are fraught with uncertainties. According to one story, the Arabic script was invented on the basis of the Syriac by three men of the Arab tribe of Ṭayy, named Murāmir, Aslam, and 'Amir. They then taught it to the people of al-Anbār, a city on the Euphrates, who in turn taught it to the people

of al-Ḥīrah. A certain Bishr, son of 'Abd al-Malik, is said to have learned the script in al-Ḥīrah, and to have later gone to Mecca, where he taught it to leaders of the Banū Umayyah and 'Abd Shams, two of the leading tribes of that city. Another version of the same account connects Bishr directly with the three inventors, and still another leaves him out altogether and states that Ḥarb, son of Umayyah, a leader of the Umayyads, learned the script from Aslam, here only an intermediary, who had it from the inventor Murāmir.[14] Some of the details of the story are completely lacking in credibility. Murāmir, for example, is said to have invented the basic forms of the letters; Aslam, the ligatures; and 'Amir, the diacritical dots.[15]

Another legend, which is much shorter, states that the Arabic script was invented by the kings of Midian, which lies in the area at one time ruled by the Nabataeans. Their names happen to be identical with the words in a mnemonic phrase for memorizing the Arabic letters in the Aramaic order, which, as noted above, continued in use when the letters were used as numbers. After completing these, the kings added the six letters which occur in Arabic but not in Aramaic, which they called the rawādif, "followers." The last bit of information is interesting, since it preserves an early technical term of the Arabic writing system. Furthermore, the story was obviously made up by someone who really knew the Aramaic alphabet, which is not necessarily true of the first account. The same can be said of the man who puts a Syriac/Arabic pun in the mouth of Abraham, who addresses his son Ishmael, whose children were half

Arab. He says to him, "*ʾuʿrub*," from Syriac *ʿrōb*, meaning "mingle," which contains the same consonants as the Arabic word for Arab.[16]

All that these accounts really tell us is that in the eighth century the Arabs, or at least some of them, thought that their writing system derived from the Syriac, and that it had originated in Iraq or Midian. The common insistence on Syriac origins is probably due to the fact that Syriac at the time was still a well-known language, spoken by many people both in Iraq and Syria. Doubtless many Arabs could use the language as well. On the other hand, the memory of the great Nabataean Arab kingdom had long since faded; later Arab historians make no mention of it, and even the word "Nabataean" changes its meaning. In classical Arabic it came to be applied to peasant tillers of the soil and is a term of contempt.

An attempt to synthesize the accounts summarized above was made by Nabia Abbott, who wrote before the new theory of Syriac origins was proposed. She accepts the Nabataean origin of the Arabic alphabet and believes it arose in Syria, in the region that includes Namārah, Umm al-Jimāl, Ḥarrān, and Jabal Usays, from whence it spread in two directions simultaneously; first, northward to Zebed and then down the Euphrates to al-Anbār and al-Ḥīrah, and second, southward to Midian. Afterward the two lines converge. The Iraqi branch comes across the desert to Dūmat al-Jandal, and then southward to Medina; the Syrian branch also ends up in Medina via Tabūk and Madāʾin Ṣāliḥ. The two traditions, now united, go south to Mecca.[17]

There is nothing inherently impossible in Abbott's reconstruction; indeed, one would expect that a system of writing, arising in one locality, would spread in more than one direction. The problem is that there is no inscriptional material that gives support to it. The inscriptions found in Syria and Midian are no proof that the Arabic alphabet really *originated* in Syria, nor is the inscription from Zebed proof that it originated in Syria and reached Iraq by way of the northern Euphrates. So Abbott's reconstruction of events is really only a reconciliation of conflicting legends, no one of which may, strictly speaking, be true. An even more serious problem confronts the proponents of the Iraqi-Syriac theory; no inscriptions from this period, either in Arabic or Syriac, have been found in al-Ḥīrah or its vicinity.

Today, scholars—especially those who hold the Iraqi-Syriac position—tend to see in the development of the Arabic script a more complicated process than has heretofore been realized. No longer do we accept the simple progression from Nabataean to Kufic. In the words of J. Ryckmans, the development "must not be considered as a linear progression in one direction (from Nabataean to Kūfic), but as a sum of various trials, influences, innovations, and dead ends in a discontinuous cultural milieu. In this perspective, the al-Namārah inscription appears no more as a first link, but as one of several dead ends in the history of the early transcription of Arabic."[18]

Such in general terms is the status today of the vexed question of the origin of the Arabic alphabet. The resolution of the question in a manner that will satisfy every-

one must await the discovery of new inscriptional data. Since new inscriptions in
the other languages of pre-Islamic Arabia
are being found and published with increasing regularity, one can hope that the
missing link, if there is one, between Nabataean and Arabic or Syriac and Arabic may
some day be discovered.

······

Notes

1. See Nabia Abbott, *The Rise of the North Arabic Script
and Its Kurʾanic Development* (Chicago: University of
Chicago Press, 1939), 38.

2. For the latest on the Namārah inscription, see
J. Bellamy, "A New Reading of the Namārah Inscription," *Journal of the American Oriental Society* 105, no. 1
(1985): 31–51.

3. H. Grimme, "A propos de quelques grafittes du
temple de Ramm," *Revue Biblique* 45 (1936): 90–95;
J. Bellamy, "Two Pre-Islamic Arabic Inscriptions Revised: Jabal Ramm and Umm al-Jimāl," *Journal of the
American Oriental Society* 108, no. 3 (1988): 369–78.

4. A. Grohmann, *Arabische Paläographie, vol. 2, Das
Das Schriftwesen. Die Lapidarschrift* (Wien: Hermann
Böhlaus, 1971), ii, 14 n. 1, and pl. 2.

5. E. Littman, *Arabic Inscriptions* Syria: Publications of
the Princeton University Archaeological Expeditions
to Syria in 1904–5 and 1909. Division IV: Semitic Inscriptions; Section D: Arabic Inscriptions. (Leyden:
E. J. Brill, 1949), 1–3; E. Littmann, "Die vorislamisch-
arabische Inschrift aus Umm iǧ-Ǧimâl," *Zeitschrift für
Semitistik und verwandte Gebiete* 7 (1929): 197–204; Bellamy, "Two Pre-Islamic Arabic Inscriptions Revised,"
369–78.

6. Grohmann, *Arabische Paläographie* 2:15–16, 15 n. 2.

7. Ibid., 17.

8. J. Starcky, "Petra et la Nabatène," *Dictionnaire de
la Bible. Supplément*, vol. 7 (Paris: Letouzey and Ané,
1966), cols. 932–34.

9. Grohmann, *Arabische Paläographie*, 2:12–20.

10. The reader should also consult the tables of letters found in Grohmann, *Arabische Paläographie*, and
Abbott, *North Arabic Script*, and for the Syriac especially, the table by J. Euting, published in Theodor
Nöldeke's *Kurzgefasste Syrische Grammatik*, ed. A. Schall
(Darmstadt: Wissenschaftliche Buchgesellschaft,
1966).

11. For text and translation, see G. Rothstein, *Die
Dynastie der Lahmiden in al-Hira* (Berlin: Reuther und
Reichert, 1899), 23–24 n. 2.

12. Abbott, *North Arabic Script*, 9.

13. Ibn al-Nadīm, *Kitāb al-Fihrist*, ed. G. Flugel (Halle,
1872), 5. Since the women's hand is not elsewhere mentioned, Abbott, *North Arabic Script*, 9 n. 53, suggests
emending to read *khaṭṭ al-nassākh*, "copyist's hand."
I would prefer to read *khaṭṭ al-bannāʾ*, "builder's
hand," assuming that it resembled the script in the
pre-Islamic inscription of Ḥarrān (A.D. 568; see fig. 4).
ʿAbd al-Muṭṭalib was still living in that year.

14. Abbott, *North Arabic Script*, 6–7.

15. Ibn al-Nadīm, *Kitāb al-Fihrist*, 4–5.

16. Ibid., 5.

17. Abbott, *North Arabic Script*, 2 (map).

18. J. Ryckmans, "Alphabets, Scripts and Languages
in Pre-Islamic Arabian Epigraphical Evidence," *Studies
in the History of Arabia*, vol. 2, *Pre-Islamic Arabia*
(Riyadh: King Saud University Press), 77.

······

Further Readings

Abbott, Nabia. *Grundriss der Arabischen Philologie*.
Vol. 1: *Sprachwissenschaft*. Edited by Wolfdietrich
Fischer. Wiesbaden: Dr. Ludwig Reichert Verlag,
1982.

———. *The Rise of the North Arabic Script and Its
Kurʾanic Development*. Chicago: University of Chicago Press, 1939.

Grohmann, A. *Arabische Paläographie. vol. 2, Das
Schriftwesen. Die Lapidarschrift*. Wien: Hermann
Böhlaus Nachf., 1971.

Sourdel-Thomine, J., Ali Alparslan, and M. Abdul-
lah Chaghatai. "Khaṭṭ" *Encyclopaedia of Islam*. 2d ed.
Vol. 4, fasc. 77–78, pp. 1113–28. Leiden: E. J. Brill,
1978.

7

The Art of Writing in Ancient Greece

······

Ronald S. Stroud

······

At the beginning of her influential book *The Local Scripts of Archaic Greece*, L. H. Jeffery has placed the following brief motto quoted in Greek from the historian Diodoros of Sicily, "What man, indeed, can compose a fitting hymn of praise for the learning of letters? For it is by such knowledge alone that the dead are carried in the memory of the living."[1] Diodoros observes that while it is true that nature is the cause of life, the cause of the good life is education, which is based upon reading and writing. To illustrate the importance placed on the learning of letters by the Greeks at an early stage in their history he cites a law of the sixth century B.C. enacted by the Sicilian legislator Charondas: the sons of all citizens were required to learn how to read and write and the city was to provide the salaries of the teachers. The fruits of this early and continuous concern with reading and writing among the Greeks are their great masterpieces of literature, history, and philosophy that still form an essential part of Western culture. For the survival of these works we are indebted to hundreds of nameless scribes who diligently copied and handed down manuscript texts through the Middle Ages into the Renaissance. Most of them lived far from the centers of Greek civilization and wrote in scripts that would have seemed strange to

Euripides and Plato. To study the development of writing among the ancient Greeks themselves we must turn to contemporary inscribed objects, to clay tablets, painted pottery, stone pillars, and the like. It is from such surviving physical remains that we will briefly explore how the Greeks began to learn how to read and write and how they came to exploit this versatile civilizing instrument.

The earliest examples of writing so far discovered in Greek lands come from the island of Crete. It was to the site of Knossos that the famous British archaeologist Sir Arthur Evans came in 1900 in search of evidence for the writing system employed by the Cretans in prehistoric times. In large-scale excavations over several decades Evans not only found plentiful evidence of Cretan writing, but he also uncovered a whole new civilization. Knossos, home of the legendary King Minos, was revealed as the site of a large and elaborate palace, a veritable labyrinth of elegantly decorated reception halls, throne rooms, shrines, storage magazines, and living quarters, standing to a minimum height of four stories and occupying an area of more than six acres. Subsequent excavations by French, Italian, and Greek archaeologists have revealed other palaces, at Phaistos, Agia Triada, Mallia, Kato Zakro, as well as a host of smaller settlements of Minoan culture. The Cretan palaces flourished in the middle and late Bronze Age, about 1900–1400 B.C.

Three different varieties of writing are represented among the objects that have survived from Minoan Crete. The earliest is a form of pictographic writing some-

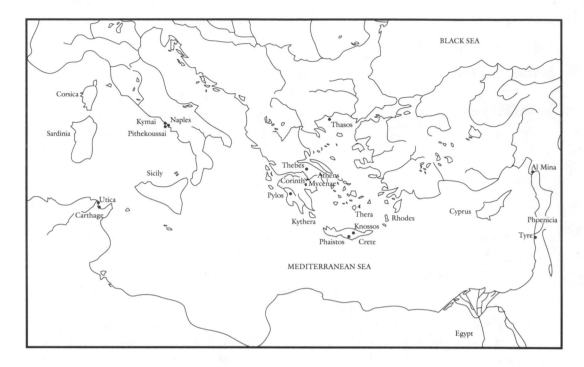

times likened to the hieroglyphics of Egypt, although there is no evidence that the Cretans copied this from their distant southern neighbors. Minoan pictographic writing seems rather to have developed locally from extensive use of engraved sealstones to record on soft clay multiple impressions of familiar objects, such as a man's head in profile, an arrow, or an axe. Thousands of these sealstones survive in a variety of such precious materials as jasper, amethyst, rock crystal, and gold. They preserve an amazing variety of naturalistic designs which illuminate almost all aspects of the physical world of Minoan culture. Originally, the device on a sealstone probably represented its owner's signature. To place one or more such impressions on an object was to make a statement of ownership or to guarantee the quantity or quality of a vessel's contents.

Gradually the method of impressing clay with beautifully carved designs gave way to a linear pictographic script in which the signs were simplified, new signs were added, and the messages recorded became somewhat longer and more complex. This linear script was incised for the most part on unbaked clay tablets or labels. To judge from the frequency of numerals in these texts, it seems to have been employed primarily for inventories or bookkeeping probably connected with the complex life of the palaces. In addition to the old pictographic signs, this script contains many signs which almost certainly represented the sounds of speech. The language they recorded was the same as that found in the Linear A script which developed, as we shall see, out of the linear pictographic. There are still too few surviving tablets bearing this script to permit decipherment and identification of the language they record (fig. 1).[2]

Before leaving Minoan pictographic writing we must pause briefly to examine one of the most puzzling inscribed objects to survive from anywhere in Greece. The clay disk illustrated in figure 2 was recovered intact from excavations in a part of the Minoan palace at Phaistos which dated to the seventeenth century B.C. Its authenticity is, therefore, guaranteed, although it appears to be unique. Measuring about seventeen centimeters in diameter, the disk was stamped on both sides with numerous individual punches which left in the soft clay a series of separate impressed symbols. The disk was later baked hard in a kiln. It has teased and tantalized scholars and visitors to the museum in Heraklion, Crete, ever since it was discovered in 1908.

There are forty-five different symbols in all on the disk, and they are arranged in groups or units consisting of from two to seven signs each. The units are set off by incised lines that also direct the reader to

Figure 1   Clay label with Minoan linear pictographic script from Knossos. Reprinted from *The Cambridge Ancient History*, 3d ed., vol. 2, pt. 1 (Cambridge: Cambridge University Press, 1973), 590. Courtesy of Oxford University Press.

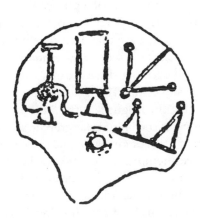

follow a concentric path, probably from the outer circumference spirally inward toward the center. Most of the individual signs represent clearly recognizable objects, such as a running man, a bird, a fish, or an arrow. They differ, however, from the signs employed in Cretan pictographic inscriptions, and many of them recur with enough frequency to suggest that each sign might represent a syllable or have some phonetic value. The language of the Phaistos disk, however, and the content of its text both remain unknown. Since no other examples of this form of writing have been found in Crete, it is an attractive hypothesis that the disk is an import from another culture. If it is a Cretan object, the disk might provide evidence for the contemporary use of a conservative form of pictorial writing while the linear script was also being developed for inventories and accounts. This has led to speculation that the Phaistos disk preserves a religious text, perhaps a ritual hymn in a traditional format. But many other interpretations have been offered, and it is unlikely that this fascinating object will ever exhaust the ingenuity of scholars.[3]

In a manner still imperfectly understood, the linear pictographic script in Crete developed into a much more sophisticated and flexible writing system which Evans labeled Linear A. About one-third of the signs in Linear A were taken over from its pictographic predecessor, the numerical system was refined, and inscriptions in Linear A consistently read from left to right. Most of the surviving Linear A in-

Figure 2 The Phaistos disk. Courtesy of the French School of Archaeology, Athens.

scriptions are on clay tablets which were used primarily to record lists of objects, commodities, and personnel as part of the palace bureaucracy. In a typical Linear A tablet like that in figure 3, a group of incised signs forming a word is followed by an ideogram representing the commodity in question and then by a numerical notation which apparently records totals. In all, about seventy different signs are attested in Linear A, too many for a proper alphabet but too few for a purely pictographic script. Most scholars have therefore concluded that the Linear A script is a syllabary, but efforts to decipher these texts have not yet proved successful. There is general agreement that the language is the same as that recorded in the linear pictographic script and that it is not Greek. While some scholars have attempted to identify the language as Semitic or Luvian, or a Proto-Indo-European tongue, others have maintained that the language of Minoan Crete, like its palaces and its exuberant art, was unlike any other Mediterranean tongue, a unique, unknown, and mysterious language still awaiting decipherment.

Although the total number of surviving Linear A inscriptions is not more than about two hundred, their distribution over more than twenty different sites in Crete and a few places in the islands and the Greek mainland indicates fairly widespread use of Minoan writing. The chronological limits of Linear A extend from about 1650 B.C. to the destruction of many of the palace sites in Crete about two hundred years later.

Figure 3 Linear A tablet from Agia Triada. Reprinted from M. Ventris and J. Chadwick, *Documents in Mycenaean Greek*, 2d ed. (Cambridge: Cambridge University Press, 1973), 35. Courtesy of John Chadwick and Cambridge University Press.

In addition to objects inscribed in the pictographic and Linear A scripts, Evans discovered in the palace of Knossos almost four thousand clay tablets written in a third type of script, which he called Linear B. Originally inscribed with a sharp instrument when the clay was leather hard, such tablets were not fired in a kiln. After being dried in the sun, they seem to have been stored in baskets. It was not expected that they would be kept for a long time. In the intense heat of the great fire that destroyed the huge palace of Knossos about 1380 B.C., however, some four thousand of them were charred and baked hard enough to survive to our day.

Evans and other scholars pointed out that, despite many striking similarities, the texts on the Linear B tablets differed essentially from those written in Linear A. The former are arranged on the tablets within horizontally ruled lines. Words are divided one from the other by short vertical strokes. There is an increased use of ideograms or schematic representations of the object or person named in the text, such as a wheel, a vase, or a man. The overall impression is one of increased efficiency and tidiness over the Linear A inscriptions. Even before Linear B was deciphered, many scholars had concluded that the language it recorded was not that of Minoan Crete.

In 1939, in the last few weeks before the outbreak of World War II, Carl W. Blegen of the University of Cincinnati began excavations at a site in the southwestern Peloponnesos which he identified as Pylos, home of the palace of the Homeric hero

Nestor. Blegen was later able to clear the extensive remains of a rich and important palace of the Bronze Age that reached its heyday in the Mycenaean era. With outstanding good fortune one of Blegen's first trenches went right into the heart of the palace archives. When the dust finally settled at Pylos, more than twelve hundred clay tablets were recovered, most of them from a small office near the main entrance to the palace. It was at once seen that these tablets were strikingly similar to the larger group of Linear B tablets found by Evans at Knossos. Like their Cretan counterparts the Pylos tablets had been baked hard by a conflagration which consumed the palace. This fire, however, did not take place until about 1200 B.C. Blegen's finds of Linear B tablets on the Greek mainland not only widened considerably the range of geographical distribution for this script, but they also extended its life from at least as early as about 1380 B.C. to at least as late as about 1200 B.C. Although no Linear B tablets have been found on Crete outside of Knossos, small but suggestive numbers of them have turned up also in excavations on the Greek mainland at Mycenae, Tiryns, and Thebes.

Blegen's discoveries at Pylos and the presence of large numbers of Linear B tablets in the final phase of the palace at Knossos fueled lively speculation not only about the linguistic identity of the newly attested script but also about the historical implications of the relationship between Knossos and the Greek mainland in the Late Bronze Age. To this day scholars remain in wide disagreement about the latter, but since

1952 there has been general acceptance of Michael Ventris's brilliant decipherment of Linear B as an archaic form of Greek. Although many irksome linguistic difficulties remain in the Greek that Ventris and his followers have reconstructed from the tablets, the decipherment has survived the test of time and many new discoveries remarkably well.

The identification of Linear B as Greek gave new life to the theory that in its final phase the palace of Knossos was presided over by a new dynasty that came from the Greek mainland. Finding a palace bureaucracy using the Linear A script to record transactions in the Minoan tongue, the new masters demanded from the Cretan scribes a new but related script that would enable them to administer the palace in Greek. On this view, then, Linear B was developed in Crete out of Linear A with which it shares a large proportion of its signs. Only the palace at Knossos survived the general destruction of the main centers of Minoan culture about 1450 B.C., when the Greeks are thought to have arrived. Only at Knossos have tablets in Greek been found. Only for about seventy years did the Greek mainlanders or Mycenaeans remain in control of the palace. About 1380 Knossos too suffered final destruction by fire. It must be stressed that this historical reconstruction has not won universal acceptance from archaeologists and linguists. Debate remains vigorous—a healthy sign in a lively field of research.

Like Linear A, the Linear B script is a syllabary. It employs about ninety signs to represent the Greek vowels and combinations of a consonant and a vowel. Ideograms are frequently employed together with a complete numerical system whose highest figure is ten thousand. The texts record for the most part relatively simple, straightforward transactions. Most tablets carry a one-word heading followed by one or more bookkeeping entries each ending in a number. A few longer, more complex tablets appear to present a composite picture of several related transactions. Basically they are all lists of people, animals, commodities, food, implements, and weapons. They record the incomings into the palace of these items and the sending out or distribution of goods into the surrounding countryside. The transactions on the tablets appear exclusively to have taken place in the current year; there is no dating by years, only by months. Aspects of the palace economy and society such as metalworking, sheep raising, wool production, defense, land tenure, agricultural produce, trade in imported luxuries, political institutions, slavery, and religion are only a few of the many facets of Mycenaean culture illuminated by the Linear B tablets (fig. 4).

Linear B was a very conservative and uniform script. For the two centuries of its attested existence few, if any, changes in the shapes of the letters can be discerned. Local variation among Knossos and the four mainland sites is minimal. Nor is there evidence to suggest that this cumbersome syllabary was ever used to record anything but palace inventories; there are no royal letters, no laws, no poems or literature in Linear B Greek. Literacy seems largely to have been confined to the palace scribes of whom some seventy-five have been identi-

Figure 4 Linear B tablet from Pylos. Reprinted from *The Cambridge Ancient History*, 3d ed., vol. 2, pt. 1 (Cambridge: Cambridge University Press, 1973), 623. Courtesy of Cambridge University Press.

fied by their handwriting at Knossos and about thirty at Pylos.[4]

One of the most striking features of Minoan and Mycenaean literacy as exemplified in the scripts of Linear A and B is its abrupt and total extinction. After the destruction of Knossos about 1380 B.C. and the burning of the palace at Pylos about 1200, which accompanied the collapse of other centers of Mycenaean power on the Greek mainland, writing vanishes in Greek lands completely. With the exception of the island of Cyprus, where a local syllabic script survived into classical times, there is a void lasting from about 1200 B.C. to the middle of the eighth century B.C., when the earliest specimens of Greek alphabetic writing begin to appear. As Sterling Dow has aptly remarked, "careful excavation yearly has made the negative more compelling. . . . Literacy ended when the palaces and all that went with them, particularly account-keeping . . . ended. Literacy had only a few and shallow other roots. It probably disappeared almost overnight."[5]

Confirmation of the illiteracy of the Greeks at this time has often been sought in our only available contemporary literature, the Homeric epics. Allowing for the long period of gestation, the requirements of oral composition, and the unknown date at which these poems were first written down, it is nevertheless a striking fact that in over 27,000 verses of the *Iliad* and the *Odyssey* there is only one brief and ambiguous reference to writing.[6] There is no hint that Homer had the slightest knowledge of Linear B, and when the Greeks do begin to write again in the middle of the eighth century B.C., they employ an alphabet that retains no trace whatsoever of the old syllabic signs of Mycenaean days.

Those responsible for the formation of the Greek alphabet have been credited with helping to lead their countrymen out of the dark ages into an exciting new era of expansion and discovery. They have been praised for taking one of the most important steps in the long course of Western civilization. They would have deserved this praise had their invention led to nothing more than

the preservation of the great Homeric epics, but it led, of course, to much more. It is a great pity, then, that we do not know who these men were or where they crafted this new, supple mode of expression. We know no details of how they interacted with their foreign teachers. We have no precise testimony as to when this momentous step was taken. We do not know why the Greeks decided that it would be a good thing to learn how to write their own language again at this time.

Later Greek historians cast little light into these dark caves of ignorance, for the few who do comment on this question attribute the discovery of the alphabet to a god such as Hermes, or to heroes such as Prometheus, Palamedes, or Cadmos. When they specify a date for the formation of the alphabet, it is impossibly early, as in the case of Herodotus (2.145), who states that Kadmos the Phoenician brought letters to Thebes about one thousand years "before my time," that is, in the fifteenth century B.C. Before we set aside this confusing tangle of tales about the origin of the Greek alphabet to look at the inscriptions themselves, however, it is important to note that a strong and persistent tradition in our sources maintains that the Greeks learned their alphabet from the Phoenicians.

It has long been recognized that the earliest examples of Greek alphabetic writing vividly confirm this view. The shapes of the new Greek letters on these earliest objects find their closest parallels in Linear Phoenician inscriptions. The order of the letters is almost identical in the two alphabetic systems. In choosing names for the individual letters in their new alphabet the Greeks turned to Semitic words like *ʾalp, bêt, gaml,* which for the Phoenicians were the names of actual objects, while the Greeks used them exclusively to denote the letters alpha, beta, and gamma. The direction of the writing in some of the earliest Greek inscriptions proceeds, as it does in Linear Phoenician texts, from right to left.[7]

Greek legends and archaeology both provide suitable settings for interaction between Greeks and Phoenicians before the middle of the eighth century B.C. Westward expansion of Phoenician commercial and colonial influence, led perhaps by the city of Tyre, was under way by about the middle of the ninth century B.C. and eventually extended to Malta, Sardinia, Spain, Sicily, and the North African settlements at Carthage and Utica. Greeks in the west had ample opportunities to meet Phoenicians. Herodotus reports Phoenician settlements on the Greek mainland at Thebes and in the islands of Thasos, Thera, and Kythera. There is as yet little archaeological evidence in Greece to support these claims, but excavations have revealed the existence of Phoenician traders and artisans in Cyprus, Rhodes, and Crete, where recently a bronze bowl was discovered bearing a Phoenician inscription of about 950–850 B.C.[8]

In the Phoenician homeland itself extensive evidence of a settlement of Greek traders was revealed by the excavations of Sir Leonard Wooley at Al Mina. Although only one early Greek inscription was found there, the site has seemed to many scholars an appropriate setting for Greeks to have learned the Phoenician alphabet and then adapted it for the purpose of writing their own language.[9] On the Phoenician side there is a complete sequence of Linear Phoenician inscriptions beginning as early as the eleventh century B.C. Enough texts survive to establish a conservative lapidary tradition whose chronology is fairly secure. There were, then, enough texts in stable condition for the Greeks to have seen and copied.

Before turning to the problem of the date of the origin of the Greek alphabet, we shall briefly examine a few of the earliest surviving inscriptions written in this new medium. The patriarch of Greek inscriptions remains the famous Dipylon wine jug from Athens (fig. 5). Nicholas Coldstream, the leading authority on Geometric pottery, has dated the vase to about 740 B.C. on the basis of its shape and painted decoration.[10] Since the inscription was incised after firing, it could be later than the date of the vase, but if, as seems likely, the vessel was awarded full of wine as a prize, then the writing on its shoulder should not be too much later than the date of the pot. A single line of writing running from right to left forms a hexameter which announces a dancing competition: "Whoever now of all dancers performs most nimbly . . ." There follows in another hand a brief tag possibly to the effect that he shall receive this vase as a prize. Although the lettering looks a little awkward and straggling, to have scratched this line of poetry with a sharp instrument through the glaze in an arc around the sloping shoulder of the vase was no mean achievement. In keeping with the early date and possible Phoenician models are the alpha lying on its side, the crooked or three-barred iota, and the hooked pi.[11]

Figure 5 The Dipylon jug from Athens. Courtesy of the National Archaeological Museum, Athens.

Also from the eighth century B.C. are fragments of a late Geometric drinking cup found in a tomb on the island of Ischia, near Capri (fig. 6). Ischia, the ancient Pithekoussai, was the site of a Greek colony founded by the Euboians. Three lines of text are very competently scratched through the glaze. They read from right to left, and at intervals the writer has added marks of punctuation to assist the reader. Again the text is in verse, consisting of a brief heading followed by two dactylic hexameters: "I am the delicious drinking cup of Nestor. Whoever drinks from this cup swiftly will the desire of fair-crowned Aphrodite seize him." Like the verse on the Dipylon jug, this inscription also strikes a lighthearted note. It is conceivable that the name of the owner was indeed Nestor, but much more likely is the suggestion that the author of the verses on this humble clay vessel alludes to the famous gold cup of the Homeric

hero Nestor which is described in detail in the *Iliad* (ll.631–41). Into the old warrior's massive gold cup a serving-girl mixes a soothing, healing potion for Nestor as he comes from battle. In the clay mug from Pithekoussai a drinker will find the sweet delight of Aphrodite.[12]

Unselfconsciously the Greeks wrote messages directly on their offerings to the gods; sometimes these texts speak in the first person. On the side of a marble statue of the seventh century B.C. representing a young girl we read, "Nikandra, daughter of Deinodikes the Naxian, a maid beyond compare, sister of Deinomenes, now wife of Phraxos, dedicated me to the far-darting goddess who delights in arrows" (fig. 7). This dedication to Artemis from the island of Delos is again in verse—three hexameters. It also shows how the Greeks abandoned the uniform right-to-left direction of Phoenician writing. Here the letters read from left to right, but at the end of the first line they turn around and in the second line come back reading from right to left, until they turn again at the beginning of the third line. The Greeks called this arrangement boustrophedon after the path of the plowing ox.[13]

Another variety of boustrophedon writing appears on a little vase from Corinth, where the painted letters wind around the ranks of the young dancers who perform to the accompaniment of a flute player (fig. 8). Next to the latter is the name Polyterpos. The rest of the text not only conveys the message that the leaping youth called Pyrrhias leads the dancers, but the inscription is also an essential part of the decorative scheme of the whole painting.[14]

Despite some affinities between these

Figure 6 Nestor's cup from Pithekoussai. Reprinted from *The Cambridge Ancient History*, 2d ed., vol. 3, pt. 3 (Cambridge: Cambridge University Press, 1982), 100. Courtesy of Cambridge University Press.

earliest specimens of Greek alphabetic writing and Linear Phoenician inscriptions, the differences between the Greek and Semitic alphabets are more striking. With the Semitic alphabet the Greek shares the letters from alpha through tau, but the last four letters, phi, psi, chi, and omega, were added by the Greeks to supplement the range of sounds covered by the Phoenician alphabet. It is, however, in the use of five signs representing consonants in the Semitic alphabet to render vowels in the Greek system that we see the clearest evidence of Greek innovation. This is more than borrowing. The spelling out in the Greek alphabet of vowel sounds, which had remained without individual letters to designate them in Phoenician, was a major step that has had a profound impact on most of the alphabetic systems of the Western

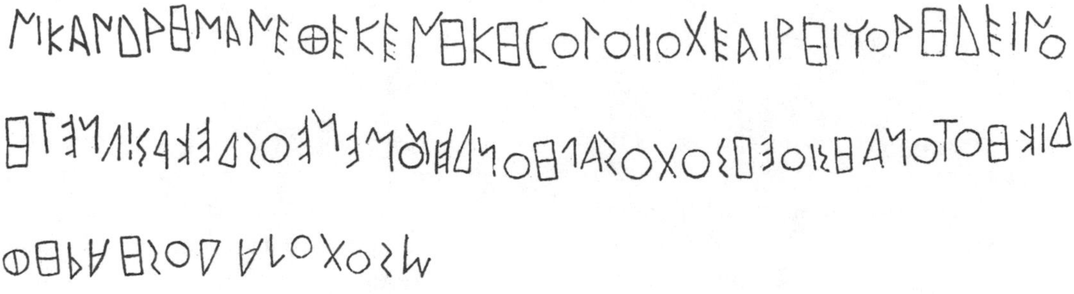

Figure 7 Dedicatory inscription of Nikandra from Delos. Reprinted from H. Roehl, *Inscriptiones Graecae Antiquissimae* (Berlin 1882), 114.

world. That step had already been firmly taken and the details worked out by the time of our earliest surviving Greek inscriptions from widely separated parts of the Mediterranean. Other divergences from the Phoenician model which our earliest Greek inscriptions share have often been cited by scholars to argue against the theory that the Greek alphabet was adopted from the Phoenicians piecemeal on an individual basis by the independent Greek city-states. If the latter had been the case, it is argued, the discrepancies between the Greek and Semitic alphabets would have been much more numerous and varied than they in fact are. At the same time it is immediately obvious from the earliest surviving Greek inscriptions that, although they almost all differ from the Semitic alphabet in the same general ways, there are major divergences among the shapes of the Greek letters in the local scripts of the many different city-states. Such wide diversity in the epichoric scripts is one of the most intriguing features of Greek inscriptions of the Archaic period, and many of these local variations survived in places on into the fourth century B.C.

The shared discrepancies from the Semitic alphabet, which all early Greek inscriptions exhibit, and the wide diversity in letter shapes evident among the local scripts of the Greek states have encouraged the view that our earliest surviving Greek inscriptions had a prehistory. There must have been a formative period in the growth of the Greek alphabet during which it gradually broke free from its Semitic model. The variations in the local scripts will also belong to this prior formative period, and since they too are already present in our earliest inscriptions, a terminus ante quem for the proposed prehistoric period can be set at about 740 B.C. It must be stressed that this formative phase and the Ur-form of the Greek alphabet that was allegedly the result of the first attempts to adapt the Semitic alphabet to Greek are both entirely hypothetical. We do not as yet possess early bilingual inscriptions or experimental pieces that show the process at work.

Scholars are in essential agreement about the logical necessity of postulating a formative period before the appearance of the earliest surviving Greek inscriptions. There is sharp debate, however, about the duration of such a phase. To determine the most likely time before about 740 B.C. when the Greeks transformed their Phoenician model, many efforts have been made to extrapolate from the shapes of the letters on

Figure 8 Painted inscription on a Proto-Corinthian vase from Corinth. Reprinted from *Hesperia* 24 (1955), pl. 64. Courtesy of the American School of Classical Studies at Athens.

our earliest surviving Greek inscriptions a so-called Proto-Greek alphabet. Then, by means of detailed letter-by-letter comparisons with dated Phoenician texts, scholars have sought the era of closest formal resemblance between the two scripts. The lack of bilingual inscriptions has forced this unsatisfactory method on epigraphists, and it is not surprising that a high degree of subjective reasoning has characterized their several conclusions. Even in well-documented periods of Greek history represented by hundreds of dated inscriptions, experienced epigraphists have made major errors when they have sought to date a stone on the basis of letter forms alone. In the proposed formative period the available corpus of Phoenician inscriptions is very small indeed, whereas the Proto-Greek alphabet with which their letter forms are being compared is, after all, only a logical construct. Until more sophisticated methods of dating can be devised or the corpus of comparanda grows significantly we can probably expect scholars to continue to draw the kinds of inferences that character-

ize the debate on the origins of the Greek alphabet.

Hence, it is argued, mostly by Greek epigraphists, that the prehistoric period of the Greek alphabet was quite short indeed, perhaps beginning no earlier than the early eighth century B.C. The adaptation of the Phoenician alphabet was a swift and dynamic invention whose potential was quickly realized. On the other hand some specialists in Semitic inscriptions have urged that the new Greek alphabet must have been independent of the Phoenician script by at least the ninth century B.C., if not earlier. This view has in turn been vigorously extended in recent studies by J. Naveh, who has maintained that the shapes and stance of the letters on our earliest Greek inscriptions, together with the flexibility in the direction of the lines of writing, all point to early Linear Phoenician parallels, which cannot be any later than about 1100 B.C. In pushing back the origins of the Greek alphabet to the end of the Bronze Age, Naveh and his followers also reject the theory of a dark age of Greek illiteracy.

To many students of Greek history and epigraphy, however, the eleventh century B.C. has not seemed a particularly attractive era in which to postulate an innovation of such major significance. Archaeological evidence suggests rather that this was a period of very slow growth in Greece, when close interaction with foreigners was minimal. Long centuries of alphabetic development and adaptation before the appearance of our earliest surviving Greek inscriptions are difficult to accept, particularly when they have yet to produce a single transitional inscription. Greek epigraphists, accordingly, have continued to appeal to the argument from silence, which seems with every new archaeological discovery to point more conclusively to the early eighth century as the period of innovation and adaptation. If the Greeks had learned to write their own language in their own alphabet as early as 1100 B.C., they ask, why do we have to wait over three hundred years for the first tangible evidence of such an achievement in the Dipylon jug?

As Naveh's arguments win more support from students of the Near East, the chronological gap between Semiticists and Hellenists seeking a date for the invention of the Greek alphabet seems to be widening. This is occurring, paradoxically, at a time when the number of newly discovered inscriptions is increasing. We can look forward to a lively new phase of debate in the controversy over the origins of the Greek alphabet.[15]

In the midst of all the debate one aspect of the question that has received less attention than it deserves is the motivation among the Greeks for learning how to write with their new alphabet. There is nothing in the earliest surviving material to suggest that trade and commerce sparked the invention—no contracts or accounts. None of the earliest inscriptions served a public function: no laws, decrees, or royal letters have yet been discovered. Nor is writing the preserve of a professional class of scribes as it had apparently been in the Bronze Age palaces. The earliest texts are all private. Individuals personally record dedications, establish ownership of an object, boast that they made it, or proudly show off their new skills by scratching or painting abecedaria on clay vases. Drinking, dancing, and love are favorite topics. Many of the texts are written in verse. One of them, the Nestor cup, even seems to make a literary allusion. Right at the beginning we see the quick wits, the individuality, and the elegance of expression of the Greeks at work. We have to wonder if poetry, song, and other facets of their cultural life played a more decisive role in the origin of the Greek alphabet than is usually acknowledged.[16]

Whatever the main motivating force might have been, use of the Greek alphabet quickly spread, and the surviving monuments show a wide range of functions. By the second half of the seventh century B.C. the Greek states had officially recognized the value of writing. Law codes and lists of magistrates were inscribed on the walls of temples and displayed in prominent settings in sanctuaries or marketplaces. In late Archaic and classical times official decrees, treaties, and public dedications were chiseled into thousands of stone pillars, engraved into bronze plaques, and put on public view. Nowhere in the Greek world is the obsession with public accountability through stone inscriptions more conspicuous than in the democracy of Athens in the fifth and fourth centuries B.C. High-quality Attic marble was the favored medium. In the Hellenistic Age a monumental style of lettering was developed especially for important monuments set up by prominent people such as King Alexander the Great and his successors. Great masses of Greek writing survive on papyri, thousands of which have been recovered from Greek settlements in Egypt. Many of these are actually parts of ancient books, the direct ancestors of the great medieval and Renaissance manuscripts through which the masterpieces of Greek literature, history, and philosophy have been preserved to our day.

In the West, in Italy, one of the most important by-products of the spread of Greek colonization in the Archaic period was the transmission of the Greek alphabet to the inhabitants of this peninsula. The Greek colony of Kymai, on the west coast near Naples, seems to have played a major role. The exact details of the transmission are still disputed by scholars, but the influence of the Greek alphabet on the earliest preserved inscriptions of the Etruscans and the Latin-speaking people living in the vicinity of Rome is unmistakable.

Whether they learned how to write their own language directly from the Greeks or through Etruscan intermediaries, the debt owed by the Romans to their Hellenic predecessors is obvious in the earliest preserved Latin inscriptions. After rude and somewhat awkward beginning steps, the Latin alphabet by the third century B.C. had reached more or less its classic stage of development. Like the Roman army, it

soon became dominant in Italy, and as the legions gradually extended the borders of the Roman Empire far beyond the shores of the Mediterranean Sea, the Latin alphabet marched with them. One of its most important characteristics—one that would have puzzled Greeks of the Archaic period —is its remarkable uniformity and stability. Without serious modifications it has survived all the fortunes and misfortunes of empire. It has lived on through the Middle Ages and the Renaissance to become the dominant script of modern Europe and the New World.

......

Postscript

New discoveries, only recently reported, may eventually shed additional light on the origins and transmission of the Greek alphabet. They consist of four bronze tablets inscribed on both sides from right to left with an early form of the Greek alphabet from alpha through tau. This alphabetic sequence is repeated continuously on each tablet. One of these objects is in a private collection; two are in the possession of the New York antiquities dealer H. P. Kraus; the fourth went to the Martin-von-Wagner Museum of the University of Würzburg in 1982 as part of the Alexander Kiseleff collection of Egyptian and Greek antiquities. A provenance in the Fayum has been claimed for the two tablets now in New York and a date in the eighth century B.C. or earlier has been suggested.

The tablets remain unpublished, with

the exception of the one in Würzburg on which A. Heubeck has presented a brief preliminary study, "Die Würzburger Alphabettafel," *Würzburger Jahrbücher für die Altertumswissenschaft* 12 (1986): 7–20. On this tablet the alphabetic sequence from alpha through tau is repeated twenty-four times. Heubeck tentatively suggests that these tablets mark the earliest stage of the Greek alphabet, after it had been taken over from the Phoenicians, but before the addition of upsilon and the so-called "extra letters," phi, chi, and psi. He prefers a date of about 800 B.C. and is dubious about an Egyptian provenance for the tablets.

We must await full publication of all four tablets before drawing any conclusions, but it is clear that they will stimulate much scholarly discussion as to their date, contents, and origin.

······

Notes

1. Diodoros, *Historical Library* 12–13, quoted in L. H. Jeffery, *The Local Scripts of Archaic Greece* (Oxford: Oxford University Press, 1961), 12–13.

2. For Minoan pictographic script see S. Dow, "Literacy in Minoan and Mycenean Lands," in *The Cambridge Ancient History*, 3d ed., vol. 2, pt. 1 (Cambridge: Cambridge University Press, 1973), 587–91 (hereafter *CAH*).

3. The bibliography on the Phaistos disk is enormous. See, e.g., Y. Duhoux, *Le disque de Phaestos* (Louvain: Editions Peeters, 1977).

4. On Linear A and Linear B see J. Chadwick, *The Decipherment of Linear B*, 2d ed. (Cambridge: Cambridge University Press, 1967); *Linear B and Related Scripts* (Berkeley: University of California Press, 1986); Dow, "Literacy," 592–608; J. Chadwick, "The Linear B Tab-

lets as Historical Documents," in *CAH*, 3d ed., vol. 2, pt. 1 (Cambridge: Cambridge University Press, 1973), 609–26; M. Ventris and J. Chadwick, *Documents in Mycenaean Greek*, 2d ed. (Cambridge: Cambridge University Press, 1973); D. W. Packard, *Minoan Linear A* (Berkeley: University of California Press, 1974).

5. Dow, *CAH*, 605.

6. In *Iliad* 6.168–177, Proitos writes "grim, deadly signs" on a folded tablet that Bellerophon carries with him to Lykia.

7. For the Linear Phoenician alphabet see chapter 5 above and B. S. J. Isserlin, "The Earliest Alphabetic Writing," in *CAH*, 2d ed., vol. 3, pt. 1 (Cambridge: Cambridge University Press, 1982), 794–818.

8. Published with illustrations by M. Sznycer, "L'inscription phénicienne de Tekke, près de Cnossos," *Kadmos* 18 (1979): 89–93.

9. The inscription, a graffito of five letters on an Attic sherd of the seventh century B.C., is discussed by J. Boardman, "An Inscribed Sherd from Al Mina," *Oxford Journal of Archaeology* 1 (1982): 365–67. The many scholars include, for example, L. H. Jeffery, *The Local Scripts of Archaic Greece* (Oxford: Oxford University Press, 1961), 5–12.

10. Nicholas Coldstream, *Greek Geometric Pottery* (London: Metheun, 1968), 358.

11. The vast bibliography on this important text may best be approached through P. A. Hansen, *Carmina Epigraphica Graeca Saeculorum VIII–V A. Chr. N.* (Berlin: De Gruyter, 1983), 239–40, no. 432 (hereafter *CEG*), and *Supplementum Epigraphicum Graecum* XXX, 46; XXXIII, 59 (hereafter *SEG*); B. B. Powell, "The Dipylon Oinochoe and the spread of Literacy in Eighth-century Athens," *Kadmos* 27 (1988): 65–86.

12. On Nestor's cup see A. J. Graham, *CAH*, 2d ed., vol. 3, pt. 3 (Cambridge: Cambridge University Press, 1982), 99–100; Hansen, *CEG*, 252–53, no. 454; *SEG* XXIX, 975.

13. A bibliography on the Nikandra dedication is collected in Hansen, *CEG*, 221–22, no. 403.

14. A bibliography on the Corinth vase is in Hansen, *CEG*, 251, no. 452, and *SEG* XXX, 346.

15. A helpful bibliography on the work of Naveh and others is collected by F. M. Cross, in chapter 5 above,

n. 12, to which should be added L. H. Jeffery, "Greek Alphabetic Writing," in *CAH*, 2d ed., vol. 3, pt. 1 (Cambridge: Cambridge University Press, 1982), 819–33; Isserlin, "Earliest Alphabetic Writing," 794–818; *Archaeologia Homerica*, ed. F. Matz and H.-G. Buchholz, vol. 3, chap. 10; A. Heubeck, *Schrift* (Göttingen, Vandenhoeck and Ruprecht 1979), 73–184, 196–201; A. Johnston, "The Extent and Use of Literacy: The Archaeological Evidence," *Skrifter Utgivna av Svenska Institutet i Athen* 30 (1983): 63–68.

16. For discussions of this view see K. Robb, "Poetic Sources of the Greek Alphabets," in *Communication Arts in the Ancient World*, ed. E. A. Havelock and J. P. Hershbell (New York: Hastings House, 1978), 23–36; A. Schnapp-Gourbeillon, "Naissance de l'écriture et fonction poétique en grèce archaique: quelques points de repère," *Annales* 37 (1982): 714–23; I. Morris, "The Use and Abuse of Homer," *Classical Antiquity* 5 (1986): 93, 120–27; B. B. Powell, *Homer and the Origin of the Greek Alphabet* (Cambridge: Cambridge University Press, forthcoming).

Cambridge Ancient History. 2d ed. vol. 3, part 1, pp. 819–33. Cambridge: Cambridge University Press, 1982.

———. *The Local Scripts of Archaic Greece*. Oxford: Oxford University Press, 1961.

McCarter, Jr., P. K. *The Antiquity of the Greek Alphabet and the Early Phoenician Script*. Missoula, Mont.: Scholars Press, 1975.

Naveh, J. *The Early History of the Alphabet*. Leiden: E. J. Brill, 1982.

Ventris, M., and Chadwick, J. *Documents in Mycenaean Greek*. 2d ed. Cambridge: Cambridge University Press, 1973.

Excellent bibliographies are provided with each of the chapters in *The Cambridge Ancient History* cited above.

••••••

Further Readings

Chadwick, J. *The Decipherment of Linear B*. 2d ed. Cambridge: Cambridge University Press, 1967.

———. *Linear B and Related Scripts*. Berkeley: University of California Press, 1986.

———. "The Linear B Tablets as Historical Documents." In *The Cambridge Ancient History*. 3d ed. of vol. 2, pt. 1, pp. 609–26. Cambridge: Cambridge University Press, 1973.

———. *The Mycenaean World*. Cambridge: Cambridge University Press, 1976.

Dow, S. "Literacy in Minoan and Mycenaean Lands." In *The Cambridge Ancient History*. 3d ed. of vol. 2, pt. 1, pp. 582–608. Cambridge: Cambridge University Press, 1973.

Isserlin, B. S. J. "The Earliest Alphabetic Writing." In *The Cambridge Ancient History*. 2d ed. vol. 3, pt. 1, pp. 794–818. Cambridge: Cambridge University Press, 1982.

Jeffery, L. H. "Greek Alphabetic Writing." In *The*

8

The Origins and Development
of the Latin Alphabet
· · · · · ·
Rex Wallace

· · · · · ·
The Introduction of the Alphabet
to Italy

Ancient Greek and Roman literary sources
do not agree about who is responsible
for the introduction of the alphabet into
central Italy. According to the tradition
preserved by the Roman historian Tacitus (*Annals* 11.14), the earliest inhabitants
of Latium received the alphabet from the
Arcadian Greek Evander. Pliny the Elder
(*Natural Histories* 7.56.193) attributes the
introduction of the alphabet to the pre-
Etruscan inhabitants of Etruria, the Pelasgi.
The Greek writers Plutarch (*Romulus* 6.1)
and Dionysius of Halicarnassus (*Roman
Antiquities* 1.84.5) offer a third tradition;
they consider the legendary figure Romulus, who was educated by Greeks at Gabii,
the transmitter of the Greek alphabet to the
Latin-speaking world.

These literary sources share the histo-
riographical tendency to attribute important cultural innovations and institutions
to a legendary or mythical past. At the
same time they recognize, and correctly
so, the importance of a Greek element in
the derivation of the Latin alphabet. The
writing system adopted by Latin speakers is derived, though not by way of direct
transmission, from the West Greek system carried by Chalcidian colonists to their
settlements at Pithekoussai (Ischia) and
Cumae in the second and third quarters of
the eighth century B.C.[1]

But the ancient literary sources ignore
the most significant element in the constitution of the Latin alphabet: the Etruscans.
Archaeological and epigraphical evidence
indicates that the Etruscans, who had themselves received the alphabet from the Chalcidian Greeks of Pithekoussai and Cumae,
were responsible for its introduction into
Latium (see map).[2]

The Etruscan influence

At the beginning of the seventh century
Latium enters into the cultural orbit of
Etruria.[3] Evidence for Etruscan presence in
Latium is signaled, initially at least (680–
650 B.C.), by the accumulation of rich materials of Etruscan import (e.g., Greek wine
and oil) and Etruscan craftsmanship (gold
jewelry, ivory ornaments, silver vessels, etc.)
as furnishings in tombs. At Praeneste and
at Tibur the materials in a few tombs are
so splendid that we can only conclude their
owners must have exercised considerable
economic (and presumably political) power
while alive. Although we cannot conclusively determine sociopolitical reality by
considering the quality and quantity of
tomb furnishings, the wealth contained
in these tombs is certainly suggestive of a
powerful Etruscan ruling elite. Tomb furnishings discovered at other sites in Latium,
at Decima and Lavinium in the north and at
Satricum in the south, though not as splendid as the furnishings of the tombs at Tibur

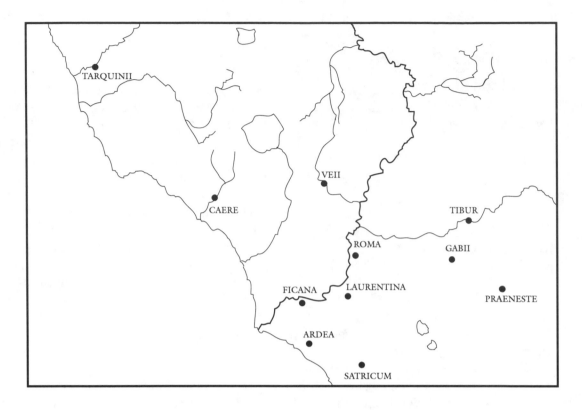

South Etruria and Latium. Map by Bridgette
Stowe.

and Praeneste, confirm a strong Etruscan
economic presence in Latium. By the second half of the century (650–600 B.C.)
Rome joins the increasing number of Latin
settlements which show material evidence
of contact with Etruria. At Rome, however, evidence for Etruscan presence reaches
deeper than that provided by other Latin
settlements. During the last quarter of this
century we find innovations in architecture
(changes in the structure of dwellings and
tombs) and urban organization (rearrang-
ment of the Forum area) which are most
certainly the responsibility of Etruscans.
The Latin literary tradition confirms the
cultural preeminence of Etruscans at Rome

at this time: this is the period of the first
Etruscan king, Lucius Tarquinius.

The literary tradition also provides an
oblique reference to the Greek component
in Latin culture of the seventh century, an
important reference because the archaeological record is tenuous. The Etruscan king
Lucius Tarquinius is the son of a Corin-
thian Greek merchant, Demaratos, who
settled at Tarquinia about 650 B.C. This reference suggests that an important, perhaps
the most important, avenue for transmission of Greek culture to seventh-century
Latium was by means of Etruscan intermediation.

The Etruscans who are responsible for
the introduction of rich material goods and
innovative ideas concerning urban organization are at the same time responsible
for the introduction of writing. Among
the elaborate furnishings of the Bernar-

dini tomb at Praeneste (ca. 650 B.C.) is a silver cup with the name of the owner inscribed just beneath the lip: *vetusia* with archaic possessive morpheme *-ia*, "[I am the property] of Vetus (fig. 1)."[4] Inscribed bucchero cups, of slightly later date (ca. 630–600 B.C.), are found among the remains of votive offerings at Satricum and at Rome: [*mi mulu larisal]e velchainasi*, "[I was given as a gift] for/by Laris Velchaina" (Satricum) and [——]*uqnuś*[——], "of Uqnu" (Rome).[5] Thus, the transmission of the alphabet is certainly one of the results, arguably the most important result, of contact with Etruscans.

The Etruscans responsible for the introduction of writing are without doubt immigrants from the cities of south Etruria. The most prominent candidates are Etruscans from cities which were most active commercially in Latium during the seventh century: the cities of Caere and Veii. And this probability appears to be confirmed by epigraphy. The alphabet used in the Etruscan inscriptions from Latium is the same as the alphabet used at Caere and Veii.

Figure 1 The earliest example of writing in Latium. An Etruscan inscription incised on a silver cup from the Bernardini tomb, Praeneste (ca. 650 B.C.). Drawing by Bridgette Stowe after M. Torelli, "L'iscrizione 'latina' sulla coppa argentea della tomba Bernardini," *Dialoghi di archeologia* 1 (1977): 39, figure a.

The transmission of writing from Etruria to Latium

Precisely how and for what purpose(s) Latins first learned the art of writing remain something of a mystery. There is no evidence, for example, that writing was acquired for economic reasons—to keep accounts on business transactions or the like—although this is a possible motivating factor. Interestingly, the epigraphical evidence in Latium and Etruria suggests a rather different scenario—that writing was acquired by the wealthiest families as a symbol of prestige. Etruscan inscriptions point to the ancient practice of "gift exchange" as a possible source for the transmission of writing. We know that wealthy individuals in Etruria engaged in a ritual exchange of precious objects as a means of confirming friendships, agreements, commercial exchanges, and so forth.[6] Some of the gifts are incised with inscriptions which bear witness to the exchange, generally indicating the name of the owner of the gift (*mi larthia*, "I [am the property] of Larth" [*Testimonia Linguae Etruscae* 54]), the name of the person who dedicated or received the gift (*mini mulvanice mamarce velchanas*, "Mamarce Velchana gave me" [*Testimonia Linguae Etruscae* 57]), or, more rarely, the name of the person responsible for the object's production (*mi qutun lemauśnaś ranazu zinake*, "I [am] the pitcher of Lemausna. Ranazu made [me]" [*Testimonia Linguae Etruscae* 28]). If the practice of gift exchange crossed ethnographic boundaries, and evidence indicates that it did, then we may well imagine members of wealthy Latin families who participated in this exchange learning to write in imitation of this early Etruscan practice.[7] Writing would be an additional mark of the status of the individuals involved in the exchange.

The appearance of writing on precious objects such as the silver bowl from Praeneste and the bucchero cup from Satricum confirms the existence of the practice of gift exchange in early Latium.[8] An analysis of the oldest-known Latin inscriptions appears to support the hypothesis that wealthy Latins were the recipients of the alphabet and that writing was first employed within the context of this ritual exchange of gifts.[9]

The two oldest Latin inscriptions are generally dated to the last decades of the seventh century (ca. 620–600 B.C.). Both inscriptions are incised on wine containers of Latin production. Presumably these containers, when filled with valuable wine, would have been suitable objects for the gift exchange.[10] The first container, found among grave furnishings in a tomb near Gabii, bears an inscription in the form of a salutation: *salvetod tita,* "be in good health, Tita," or "may Tita be in good health," depending on whether the verb is interpreted as second or third person (fig. 2). The second container, whose provenience is unknown (Caere, the *ager Capena*?) but whose source is certainly Latium (perhaps Rome), bears an inscription supplying the name of the recipient and the name of the individual responsible for the container's production: *eco urna tita vendias mamar[cos m]ẹḍ vḥẹ[ced],* "I am the urn of Tita Vendia. Mamar[cos had me made]" (fig. 3). While we cannot determine the context within

which these inscribed objects were given, it is interesting to note that the topic of both inscriptions is a woman, Tita and Tita Vendia, respectively. The container on which the Vendia inscription appears, in all probability attesting to an exchange between a man Mamarcos and a woman Tita Vendia, is perhaps intended as a nuptial gift. Compare the Etruscan model *mi aranth ramuthasi vestiricinala muluvanice,* "Aranth gave me to Ramutha Vestiricina" (*Testimonia Linguae Etruscae* 868).[11]

Although these Latin inscriptions appear to serve the same function as their Etruscan counterparts, inasmuch as they are inscribed on objects which are intended as gifts, they do not parallel the structure of the Etruscan inscriptions in all particulars. The Tita inscription, a salutation, does not, in fact, have parallels among early Etruscan inscriptions. The Latins may have been responsible for adding it to the gift-exchange.[12]

If it is true that wealthy Latin families were responsible for the adaptation of the Etruscan writing system to Latin, writing must very soon have spread beyond the

Figure 2   Latin salutation inscribed on a wine container, Gabii (ca. 620–600 B.C.). Drawing by Bridgette Stowe after G. Colonna, "Graeco more bibere: l'iscrizione della tomba 115 dell'Osteria dell'Osa," in *Archeologia Laziale*, vol. 3 (Rome: Consigilio nazionale della ricerche, 1980), 51, figure a.

ECOYPRATITAYENDIAIMAMAD
ᒼᗪ ᕮᕮᕼ

Figure 3 Latin inscription indicating owner of wine container, origin unknown but possibly Rome (ca. 620–600 B.C.). Drawing by Bridgette Stowe after E. Peruzzi, "L'iscrizione di Vendia," *Maia* 15 (1963): 90.

circles of the wealthy Latins who introduced it. The Forum inscription in Rome, which can be securely dated to about 570–550 B.C., is a "public" inscription prohibiting the desecration of a sacred area.[13] The spread of writing may be tied, as this inscription suggests, to its important public and religious functions. The Roman historian Livy (*Histories* 2.12) provides us with a glimpse of the important role of writing in public life when he describes the function of scribes as secretaries of magistrates at official ceremonies. The role of the priestly caste in the dissemination of writing is amply demonstrated by the scribal schools which existed at important sanctuaries in Etruria. Members of the scribal school at Veii, for example, play a very prominent role in the diffusion of Etruscan writing into Campania. It is not unthinkable that scribal schools appeared also at sanctuaries in Latium and assumed a leading role in the transmission of writing. We know that Roman priests were responsible for recording important events under the names of magistrates in office from the beginning of the republic in about 509 B.C.

Although we are unsure of the manner in which writing spread after its introduction, we know that it spread rapidly. By the end of the sixth century, writing appears, though not in great abundance, at most of the major centers in Latium.

......

Latin Adaptation of the Alphabet

The alphabet introduced into Latium in the seventh century was the alphabet used in the Etruscan cities of Caere and Veii, the so-called "Caeretan" variety of Etruscan alphabet.[14] Formally, the Latin inscriptions of the earliest period show the peculiar characteristics of their ancestor "Caeretan" script. Gamma appears in semilunate form (rather than in the "hooked" form ᒋ characteristic of northern Etruscan scripts; sigma has a three- ⌵ and four- ⌵ stroke variant, the three-stroke variant often written retrograde (the reverse of the direction of writing); and the coda of ypsilon varies in length, giving the variants Y and V.

As a model for the Latin alphabet, the Etruscan writing system possessed, due to differences in the Etruscan and Latin sound systems, both too many and too few signs.[15] As a result, when Latin inscriptions make their appearance at the end of the seventh century, important differences between the two writing systems have already come into

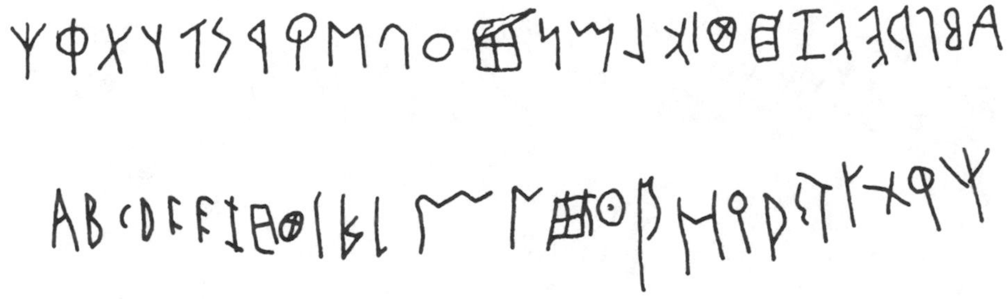

Ƴ⏀ΧƳↃↃϞΡΜΛΟ⊞ϤⅥ⅂ΧↃΘⴹⅠⅎⅎⅅ⅄A

ABᗡⅬⅎⅎⅠⴹⴲↃↃↃ⅂ⅤⅤⅬⅥⴲⴲϸΗↃⴲↃΓↃΧⴲⴲⅤ

Figure 4   Two Etruscan abecedaria: (a), abecedarium on the Ivory tablet of Marsiliana d'Albegna; (b), abecedarium on bucchero amphora from Veii. Figure 4 (a) drawn by Bridgette Stowe after Giuliano Bonfante and Larissa Bonfante, *The Etruscan Language: An Introduction* (Manchester: Manchester University Press, 1986), 101, figure 10a; figure 4 (b) reprinted, by permission, from J. E. Sandys, *Latin Epigraphy* (Chicago: Ares Publishers, 1974), 35.

existence. But these differences fall into place when we consider that the differences in sound systems would have been recognized by those who were responsible for devising the Latin alphabet(s)—namely, Etrusco-Latin bilinguals (that is, Latins who knew how to speak and write Etruscan, and Etruscans who knew how to write Etruscan and speak Latin). Differences in writing systems arise "naturally" when one language's writing system is adapted to another language's sound system.

The authors of the Latin alphabet reject the Etruscan signs ⊕, φ, Ƴ, because they represent sounds (p^h, t^h, and k^h) which do not exist in the Latin sound system. The signs ʃ and ⳋ, which represent two distinct Etruscan sibilant sounds s and ś, are both employed to write the single Latin sibilant s. The function of Etruscan vowel symbols is generalized in Latin to include vowels of both short and long duration as well as the semivowels y and w; for example, Etruscan Ƴ → Latin u, ū, w. Similarly, the function of the three signs used to write the Etruscan velar sound k ΚΑ, ϹⅠ, Ϲⴹ, ϙƳ, are generalized to represent three velar sounds in Latin, k, g, and k^w. But the adaptation of the Etruscan system of writing k must have posed a special problem for the authors of the Latin alphabet; the earliest Latin inscriptions show considerable vacillation in the representation of k (*kalatorem*, Forum inscription [Rome]; *castor*, Castor inscription [Lavinium]) and g (*eco*, Vendia inscription [Rome ?]; *eqo*, Kanaios inscription [Ardea]).

The creation of the Latin alphabetic system involved more than the mere adaptation of an Etruscan writing system. The authors of the first Latin inscriptions make use of signs—for example, omicron with the value o—which are never used to write Etruscan. The existence of these signs in Latin inscriptions indicates that those responsible for the adaptation of the alphabet were familiar with the Greek values for the letters of the alphabet. The existence of abecedaria in Etruria—for example, the tablet of Marsiliana d'Albegna, the Formello vase from Veii—which contain, in addition to the letters used to write Etruscan, letters which are employed for the writing of Greek and Phoenician, indicate that Etruscans preserved and transmitted the alphabet in an unabridged form, presumably that transmitted to them by Greeks (fig. 4).[16] In this context, the appearance of a Greek element, via Etruscan intermediation, in the formation of the Latin alphabet is readily comprehensible.[17]

No archaic Latin abecedaria have as yet been discovered. As a result, we must reconstruct the earliest Latin alphabet by abstracting letterforms from the inscriptions found in the seventh and sixth centuries. Our reconstructed alphabet contains twenty-one letters; their relation to the letterforms of the ancestor script are represented in figure 5.[18]

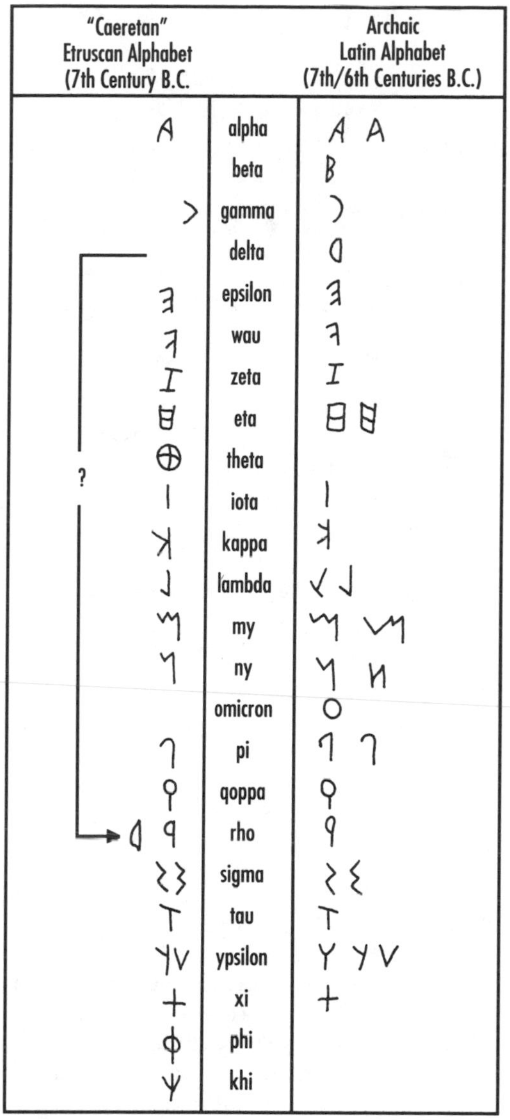

Variations in letter forms on archaic Latin inscriptions

The number of Latin inscriptions attested in the seventh and sixth centuries B.C. is not very large, especially when compared with the abundance of inscriptions from Etruria. Even if we include fragments of writing on ceramics discovered among the remains of votive offerings, the number does not rise much above twenty (see table).[19] Most of the inscriptions from before 550 B.C. are found at Rome; a more democratic distribution appears for those done after the middle of the century. By about 500 B.C. inscriptions are attested at most important settlements in Latium.

The Latin inscriptions produced within Latium before about 500 B.C. are not subject to writing norms. The inscriptions show considerable diversity with respect to letterforms, direction of writing, and, in a few cases, the letters used to represent sounds. The letter ypsilon has variant forms with codas of different lengths: Υ (Tita inscription [Gabii] and Vendia

Figure 5 *Left,* Caeretan Etruscan alphabet from seventh century B.C.; *right,* Latin alphabet abstracted from seventh- and sixth-century inscriptions. Drawing by Bridgette Stowe.

Latin Inscriptions from Seventh and Sixth Centuries B.C.

1. Gabii, Tita inscription	ca. 620–600 B.C.
2. Rome ? Vendia inscription	ca. 620–600 B.C.
3. Rome, Esquiline graffito	ca. 600 B.C.
4. Rome, Duenos vase	ca. 580–570 B.C.
5. Rome, Forum inscription	ca. 570–550 B.C.
6. Ficana	ca. 600–550 B.C.
7. Rome, Palatine graffito	ca. 600–550 B.C.
8. Rome, Sant'Omobono graffito	ca. 560–530 B.C.
9. Rome, Lapis Niger, Vesta graffiti	ca. 550–500 B.C.
10. Lavinium, Castor inscription	ca. 550–525 B.C.
11. Ardea, Kanaios inscription	ca. 550–500 B.C.
12. Laurentina, Karkavios inscription	ca. 525–500 B.C.
13. Tivoli	ca. 525–500 B.C.
14. Satricum, Lapis Satricanus	ca. 500 B.C.

Sources: No. 1: Giovanni Colonna, "Graeco more bibere: L'iscrizione della tomba 115 dell'Osteria dell'Osa," in *Archeologia Laziale III* (Rome: Consiglio Nazionale della Ricerche, 1980), 51–55; no. 2: Emilio Peruzzi, "L'iscrizione di Vendia," *Maia* 15 (1963): 89–92; nos. 3, 6, 7, 8, 9, 11, 12: Giovanni Colonna, "Appendice: Le iscrizioni strumenali latine del VI e V secolo a.C.," in *Lapis Satricanus* (The Hague: Staatsuitgiverig-'s, 1980), 53–69; nos. 4, 5, 10: A. E. Gordon, *Illustrated Introduction to Latin Epigraphy* (Berkeley: University of California Press, 1983), 76–80; no. 13: A. Mancini, "L'iscrizione sulla base di Tivoli CIL 1², 2658: Nuova lettura," *Studi Etruschi* 47 (1979): 370–75; no. 14: G. Colonna, "L'aspetto epigrafico," in *Lapis Satricanus* (The Hague: Staatsuitgiverig-'s, 1980), 41–52.

Note: For a more extensive list and additional references see Cristofani, "Contatti," 32–33.

[?] inscription), Υ , Ṿ , and Ṿ (Forum inscription [Rome]), Ṿ (Duenos vase [Rome]). A five-stroke my appears in several forms (ᴍ , ᴍ, and Ṃ), all of which are attested on the Forum inscription. A four-stroke my (ᴍ) appears (ca. 550–500 B.C.) among the graffiti discovered near the Lapis Niger at Rome and on the Lapis Satricanus [Satricum] (ca. 525–500 B.C.). And the rho sign has two variants, one with straight coda (Ρ), the other with oblique coda (ℓ ; graffito from Regia [Rome]). The Latin inscriptions of the late seventh century are written from left to right, in imitation of the direction of writing which was in vogue at Veii and Caere at this period. But this peculiar southern Etruscan feature is short-lived, and the predominant direction of writing soon becomes right to left once more. Latin inscriptions of the sixth century reflect the southern Etruscan preference for right to left writing (Duenos vase [Rome], graffiti from the Palatine [Rome], Castor inscription [Lavinium]) while also maintaining left-to-right direction of writing as a viable alternative (Ficana inscription, graffiti from the Forum area [Rome], Kanaios inscription [Ardea]). Writing practices peculiar to foreign systems seem to have been adopted in two Latin inscriptions of this period. The Forum inscription [Rome] is written in boustrophedon style ("as the ox plows"), with lines running alternately from right to left and from left to right, perhaps in imitation of Greek writing practice.[20] The inscription from Tivoli is written in serpentine style, a practice probably appropriated from the writing systems of the Sabines and South Picentes.[21] The representations of the velar and sibilant sounds show considerable local and regional variation. The sound *s* is written by a three-stroke sigma in inscriptions produced at Rome, but at Gabii and Ardea sigma is written with four strokes. And the author of the Castor inscription [Lavinium] has apparently devised a system for writing the variant forms of sigma: the three-stroke sigma is used in word-final position, the four-stroke sigma in medial position. The velar sounds are written "phonetically," in the Etruscan manner, in the Forum inscription (Rome), for example, *kapia, recei, quoi,* but in the Castor inscription (Lavinium), the Etruscan system is slightly modified. The letter φ appears before *u* as expected (*qurois*), but (rather than Κ appears before the sound *a* (*castor*).

Interestingly, a variety of sources contributes to the "fluid" state of the Latin alphabet in the seventh and sixth centuries. The variant forms of some letters, for example, ypsilon and five-stroke my, are inherited from the ancestor (Etruscan) script. Variation in direction of writing (left to right, right to left) may be attributed to the continuing influence of southern Etruscan scripts during the sixth century. Contact with other foreign writing systems, in addition to those of southern Etruria, contribute to variation in letterforms (four-stroke my) and direction of writing (serpentine). During this period it is also possible to recognize the first system-internal developments. The appearance of rho with oblique rather than straight coda arises from the need to keep this sign distinct from pi, whose hook in some cases reaches perilously close to the vertical stroke, for example, Ρ.

The somewhat bewildering array of variation which appears in the Latin inscriptions of this period is important because it is a sign that the Latin writing system is alive and well and has taken its place as an autonomous system alongside other writing systems of ancient Italy.

......

The Emergence of Norms for Writing

From the inscriptions which appear at the end of the sixth century, and from the scanty remains of writing which exist for the fifth and fourth centuries, we detect the emergence of norms for writing.[22] The sign (becomes the predominant sign for writing the sounds *k* and *g,* and the sign Κ is accordingly much restricted in its usage. The four-stroke sigma is eliminated in favor of the three-stroke variety, and ypsilon with zero coda replaces Υ. Left to right becomes the preferred direction of writing, in contrast to the right-to-left direction, which becomes the norm in southern Etruria.

The movement to establish norms for writing Latin is attributable in part to the rise of Rome as the preeminent political entity in Latium. The inscriptions produced at the most prestigious center, Rome, could have provided models or standards for writing at other Latin centers. But we should not forget that, although the various settlements in Latium were politically independent at this time, they did share very strong political, commercial, cultural, and linguistic ties. These shared cultural and linguistic bonds must have contributed to the standardization of writing between Latin communities.

An Addition to the Latin Alphabet

At the beginning of the third century, when Rome is clearly the dominant political entity in Latium, inscriptions again become frequent, though by no means plentiful. When the inscriptional record comes into focus, we find that there have been few major changes from the system of the sixth century. There is a stylistic tendency for the oblique strokes on archaic inscriptions to be replaced by horizontal strokes (ꜰ → E). The letter *r* now has an oblique stroke beneath the base of the hook, presumably to enhance the distinction between *p* and *r* (ꝑ → ꝛ). As noted earlier, traces of such a distinction are already in existence by the late sixth century.[23] The function of kappa is clearly marginal; it is restricted to a small number of lexical items, for example, *kalendae,* "the first day of the month." The most important difference between the inscriptions of the Archaic period (seventh to sixth century) and the mid-republican period (third century) is the appearance of a sign for the sound *g*.

Figure 6 Model Latin alphabet from the republican era. Reprinted, by permission, from J. E. Sandys, *Latin Epigraphy* (Chicago: Ares Publishers, 1974), 43.

According to Roman tradition, the introduction of an independent sign for the sound *g* is the responsibility of Spurius Carvilius Ruga, a freedman who, in the mid-third century (ca. 250 B.C.), opened the first school of grammar at Rome. The traditional date for the introduction of the sign is probably not far wrong. It is attested on colonial Latin inscriptions and central Italic dialect inscriptions by the beginning of the second quarter of the third century. The formal origin of the sign *g* is disputed. The view cited most often is that it is an elaboration or remaking of the sign (by extending the lower arc in a vertical direction ((→ ( ). However, the earliest shape of this sign ꜿ suggests that it was derived from zeta by the same principle.[24] When the zeta ceased to be used as an allograph for *s*, it must have survived in the alphabetic series as a "dead" letter. The letter was then revived to represent the sound *g* and subsequently modified in form so as to become more distinct visually from the sign for the sound *k*, (. The appearance of *g* in the position of zeta in abecedaria provides support for this hypothesis. Letters which are created "ex nihilo" or adopted from foreign systems regularly take their place at the end of the abecedarium.

With the addition of the sign ꜿ or, better, with the zeta reutilized to represent the sound *g,* the Latin alphabet assumes the

A B C D E F G H I K L M N O P Q R S T V X

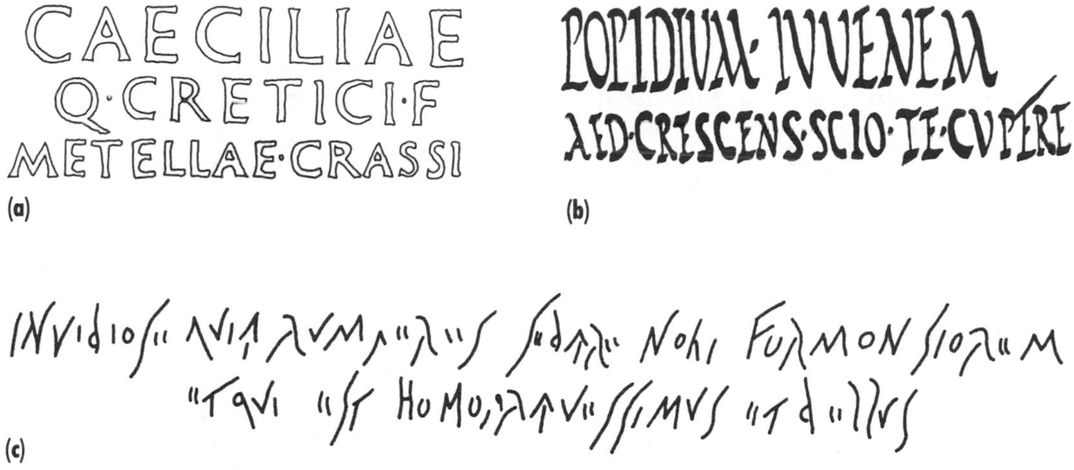

CAECILIAE
Q·CRETICI·F
METELLAE·CRASSI

(a)

POPIDIVM·IVVENEM
AED·CRESCENS·SCIO·TE·CVPERE

(b)

INVidiosi AVIA AVMpnlus fidale Nobi FuRMON siozum
nTavi nft HoMo,zatvnffiMvs nt dnllvs

(c)

Figure 7 Inscriptions illustrating three "styles" of imperial Latin inscriptions. *a*, Monumental style of inscribing; epitaph of Caecilia Metella. *b*, Election advertisement from Pompeii illustrating work of professional calligrapher. *c*, Graffito from Pompeii. Redrawn, by permission, from J. E. Sandys, *Latin Epigraphy* (Chicago: Ares Publishers, 1974), 42, 44, 46, by Bridgette Stowe.

form it was to have throughout the republic and early empire (fig. 6). This is confirmed by the statements of Cicero (*Concerning the Nature of the Gods* 2.93) and Quintilian (*Principles of Oratorical Education* 1.4.9), both of whom note that the alphabet ends in the letter X, and by the numerous abecedaria written on walls at Pompeii and Herculaneum whose final letter is X.

During the imperial period the Greek ypsilon and zeta (with the Greek values *ü* and *z*, respectively) were added to the Latin alphabet. These letters were introduced into the Latin writing system near the end of the republic so that Greek words and names could be written. According to the historian Suetonius (*Augustus* 87/88), who describes the spelling habits of the emperor Augustus, *y* and *z* were all but officially rec-

ognized as part of the alphabet at this time. When these letters are codified as members of the alphabet, they take their place at the end of the alphabetic series following X.

The final attempt to add to the alphabetic series occurred in the early imperial period (ca. 50 A.D.). The emperor Claudius proposed the addition of three signs to the Latin alphabet: ⅃, *ps*; Ⅎ, *ü*; Ⱶ, *w*.[25] Two of these signs actually appear on Latin inscriptions incised during Claudius's reign, but they disappear from inscriptions soon after his death.[26]

The rise of stylistic differences

Diversity in the function of inscriptions (public vs. private) and the acquisition of new and cheaper means for the production of documents (ink and brush) conspired to contribute to the rise of stylistic differences in the forms of letters at the end of the republic. We generally recognize gross, but nonetheless revealing, distinctions in letterforms based on the function of the inscription and on the care and time (that is, expense) taken to have it produced (fig. 7).

The monumental script appears regularly on the most important state-sponsored inscriptions and occasionally on private inscriptions of individuals who were wealthy enough to afford the cost of their production. The letters of the monumental style are generally well defined and incised deeply into the stone, the work of a skilled stone-cutter.[27] The so-called *scripta actuaria* was employed in the production of long state inscriptions, state inscriptions of lesser importance, and inscriptions for the private sector. This script was also used in the painting of election notices and advertisements on the housewalls at Pompeii and Herculaneum. The letters in these documents, owing to the fact they are produced by ink and brush, assume a much more "smooth and flowing" form. This calligraphic style of writing is even imitated by stone masons and subsequently appears in inscriptions cut in stone. The cursive style of writing is attested by the graffiti written on the walls of Pompei and Herculaneum. In this style, the letters, while maintaining the flowing form characteristic of the calligraphic *actuaria* style, show considerable simplification ($S \rightarrow \int$), sometimes to the point of being unrecognizable to the untrained eye.

......

The Spread of the Latin Alphabet

The truly remarkable fact about the Latin alphabet is the rapidity with which it spread from Latium, from the city Rome, over the whole of the Italian peninsula. Between 300 B.C., when Rome emerged as the political master of Latium, and the birth of Christ, the Latin alphabet became the primary writing system on the peninsula, thus replacing the writing systems of Etruscans, Umbrians, Samnites, Picentes, Messapians, and Greeks. Although the spread of the alphabet is obviously a function of the spread of Rome's political and commercial dominion, the adoption of the writing system of Rome by so many diverse peoples so quickly is nonetheless remarkable, since political domination need not entail linguistic and/or cultural domination. This point is clearly illustrated by contact between Romans and Greeks. Rome is the major political force in Greece from the second century B.C., and yet the linguistic habits of the Greeks are not really altered at all. The Greek language continued to be written in the system inherited from the Phoenicians in the ninth century. In fact, it was the Greek system which influenced the Latin. The Greek ypsilon and zeta (re)appear in the Latin of the late republic due to a substantial influx of Greek words, itself an indication that Rome was adopting Greek culture on a rather grand scale.

The rapid diffusion of the Latin alphabet and the Latin language within the Italian peninsula is the result of Rome's successful colonization policy. When Rome conquered cities outside of Latium, the territory controlled by the city was confiscated and the land was distributed to Roman citizens. A substantial number of Roman citizens, somewhere between eight thousand and twenty thousand, were then conscripted and entrusted with the task of colonizing the conquered city. These colonies, with their substantial Latin-speaking (and writing) populace, formed the centers for the spread of Latin culture, the Latin language, and the Latin alphabet.

It is unfortunate that we do not have sufficient evidence to follow in detail the spread of the alphabet throughout the Italian peninsula. In most instances we can only note the dates of the numerous colonies founded by Latins and assume that the establishment of a colony entails the spread of spoken and written Latin.[28] Infrequently, intriguing glimpses of the processes involved in the shift from native writing systems to Latin appear in the inscriptional record. Speakers of several Oscan-Umbrian dialects of central Italy, in territories adjacent to Latium, remain illiterate until contact with Latins. A few inscriptions in these dialects, with substantial Latin superstratum influence, appear in the third and second centuries. But these dialect inscriptions soon disappear because these speakers are among the first to shift to Latin as their primary language. In territories where the shift to the Latin language was a more gradual process, we find that non-Latin speakers often give up their native writing system and adopt the Latin alphabet before giving up their native language. In Campania, for example, Oscan was spoken, and occasionally written, in the first century B.C. We find several examples of Oscan inscriptions written in the Latin alphabet, which suggests that the prestige of the Latin alphabet must have been such that it, even though a foreign system, was preferred over the native writing system. In Etruria and in Umbria, territories north of Latium, the native writing systems have all but disappeared by the second century B.C., giving

way to the Latin alphabet. At this period we find Etruscan funerary inscriptions written in the Latin alphabet. And the lengthy Umbrian religious text, the *Tablets of Iguvium*, switches alphabets, from native Umbrian to Latin, in the middle of the copy of the texts.

Although our knowledge of the spread of the Latin alphabet throughout the Mediterranean basin and beyond, into northern Europe, is even more fragmentary than that for the Italian peninsula, the results of the diffusion of the alphabet are very much in evidence today. The alphabets used to write the languages of Europe, and the colonial languages sprung from them (including American English, of course), are the lineal descendants of the Latin alphabet crafted in Latium in the seventh century B.C.

......

Notes

1. For discussion of the West Greek alphabet used by the Chalcidian colonists of Cumae and Pithekoussai, see M. Guarducci, *Epigrafia Greca I* (Rome: Instituto Poligrafico dello Stato, 1967), 216–28, and L. H. Jeffery, *The Local Scripts of Ancient Greece* (Oxford: Clarendon Press, 1961), 234–39.

2. The transmission of the Greek alphabet to Etruscan-speaking communities is the subject of several important articles by M. Cristofani: "L'alphabeto etrusco," in *Popoli e civiltà dell' Italia antica*, vol. 6, *lingue e dialetti* (Rome: Biblioteca di Storia Patria, 1978), 403–6; "Sull' origine e la diffusione dell' alphabeto etrusco," *Aufstieg und Niedergang der römischen Welt*, no. 2 (1972): 469–71; "Recent Advances in Etruscan Epigraphy and Language," in *Italy before the Romans* (London: Academic Press, 1979), 378–80.

3. The archaeological evidence for Etruscan influence in Latium is admirably evaluated by G. Colonna in

"Preistoria e protostoria di Roma e del Latio, in *Popoli e civiltà dell' Italia antica*, vol. 2 (Rome: Biblioteca di Storia Patria, 1974), 246–73, and "Aspetti culturali della Roma primitiva," *Archeologia Classica* 16 (1964): 1–12. The political influence of Etruscans is discussed by F. Zevi and M. Cristofani, "L'espansione politica," in *Civiltà degli etruschi*, Exhibition catalog (Milan: Regione Toscana Electa, 1985), 121–24.

4. For the Etruscan inscriptions found in Latium, see G. Colonna, "La diffusione della scrittura," in *Civiltà del Lazio primitivo*, Exhibition catalog (Rome: Bretschneider, 1976), 374–75, and C. de Simone, "Gli Etruschi a Roma: evidenza linguistica e problemi metodologici," in *Gli Etruschi e Roma*, Proceedings of the meeting in honor of Massimo Pallotino held in Rome, Dec. 11–13, 1979 (Rome: Bretschneider, 1981), 93–103.

5. Although the Satricum inscription is fragmentary, it can be read in its entirety because of the discovery of an identical inscription incised also on a bucchero cup. The fragmentary Etruscan inscription from Rome may contain a proper name, Uqnu (cf. Ocno, the mythical Etruscan founder of Perugia). For discussion see Zevi and Cristofani, "L'espansione politica," 128–29.

6. M. Cristofani, "Il dono nell'Etruria arcaica," *Parola del Passato* 30 (1975): 145–50.

7. We know that wealthy individuals were "geographically" mobile during the seventh century. We have inscriptional evidence for the appearance of Greeks and Latins at various settlements in Etruria (M. Cristofani, "Contatti fra Lazio ed Etruria in eta arcaica: documentazione archeologica a testimonianze epigrafiche," in *Alle origini del latino*, Proceedings of the conference of the Italian Society of Linguistics held in Pisa, Dec. 7–8, 1980 (Pisa: Giardini, 1982), 33–34.

8. The appearance of the Satricum inscription among votive stipe found at the sanctuary of Mater Matuta does not invalidate this connection. According to Cristofani, "Il 'dono,'" 142–43, the same variety of gift exchange may have occurred between private individuals as between individuals and priestly sanctuaries.

9. Recent investigations of what has generally been considered the earliest Latin inscription, the so-called Praenestine fibula, have cast serious doubts on its

authenticity; see, for example, A. E. Gordon, *The Inscribed Fibula Praenestina: Problems of Authenticity*, University of California Publications, Classical Studies 16. (Berkeley: University of California Press, 1975), and M. Guarducci, "La cosidetta Fibula Prenestina. Antiquari, eruditi e falsari nella Roma dell' ottocento (con un' Appendice di esami e di analisi a cura di Pico Cellino, Guido Devoto et altri)," *Atti della Academia Nazionale dei Lincei, Memorie*, ser. 8, vol. 24, fasc. 4 (1980): 415–574. Until the dispute is decided, either for or against authenticity, the fibula cannot be used as evidence bearing on the origins of the Latin alphabet.

10. G. Colonna, "Graeco more bibere: L'iscrizione della tomba 115 dell'Osteria dell'Osa," in *Archeologia Laziale*, vol. 3 (Rome: Consiglio Nazionale della Ricerche), 51, 53.

11. Colonna, "Graeco more," 51.

12. Interestingly salutations of this type also appear on early Faliscan inscriptions (see G. Giacomelli, *La lingua falisca* [Florence: Leo S. Olschki, 1963], 44–48). The Faliscans, who dwelt in southeast Etruria, spoke a language closely related to Latin.

13. M. Lejeune, "Note sur la stele archaique du Forum," *Collection Latomus* 62 (1961): 1039.

14. See Cristofani, "Recent Advances," 380–83.

15. The characteristics of the Etruscan phonological system are described by M. Cristofani, *Introduzione allo studio dell' etrusco* (Florence: Leo S. Olschki, 1973), 39–54.

16. See G. Colonna, "Il Sistema Alfabetico," in *Proceedings of the Colloquium on the Topic: Archaic Etruscan*, Florence, Oct. 4–5, 1974 (Florence: Leo S. Olschki, 1976), 17–18.

17. Guarducci, *Epigrafia*, 219, and Gianfranco Maddoli, "Contatti antichi del mondo latino col mondo greco," in *Alle origini del latino*, Proceedings of the conference of the Italian Society of Linguistics held in Pisa, Dec. 7–8 1980 (Pisa: Giardini, 1982), 59–60, argue that the appearance of delta and omicron in early inscriptions is evidence for direct Greek interference in the origins of the Latin writing system. But these discussions overlook the Hellenic component in Etruscan culture in the seventh century.

18. The letter beta does not appear on any inscriptions from the seventh or sixth centuries. The first

example of this letter comes from a graffito found on the Palatine hill (Rome) and dated to the second half of the fifth century. This is the form which we use in our reconstructed archaic Latin alphabet. See G. Colonna, "Appendice: Le iscrizioni strumentali latine del VI e V secolo a.C.," in *Lapis Satricanus* (The Hague: Staatsuitgiverig-'s, 1980), 60, 62.

19. Cristofani, "Contatti," 32–33.

20. G. Colonna, "L'aspetto epigrafico," in *Lapis Satricanus*, 49.

21. For Sabine and South Picene alphabets, see A. Marinetti, *Le iscrizioni sudpicene: Testi* (Florence: Leo S. Olschki, 1985), 49–60.

22. Colonna, "Appendice," 68, attributes the lack of inscriptions to the lack of funerary documentation.

23. Colonna, "L'aspetto," 49.

24. R. S. Conway, "Italy in the Etruscan Age," in *The Cambridge Ancient History*, vol. 4 (New York: Macmillan, 1926), 401.

25. Brief discussion of these "reforms" as well as other writing characteristics may be found in M. Leumann, J. B. Hofmann, and D. Szantyr, *Lateinische Grammatik*, vol. 1 (Munich: C. H. Beck, 1977), 12–15.

26. See A. E. Gordon, *Illustrated Introduction to Latin Epigraphy* (Berkeley: University of California Press, 1983), pls. 41 and 43.

27. G. Susini, *The Roman Stonecutter: An Introduction to Latin Epigraphy* (London: Oxford University Press, 1973) contains a concise yet informative discussion on aspects of the production of inscriptions.

28. For discussion of Latin and Roman colonization, see E. T. Salmon, *The Making of Roman Italy* (London: Thames and Hudson, 1982), and J. Pulgram, *The Tongues of Italy* (Cambridge, Mass.: Harvard University Press, 1958), 264–87.

● ● ● ● ● ●

Further Readings

Cristofani, M. "L'Alfabeto etrusco." In *Popoli e Civiltà dell' Italia antica Vol. 6, lingue e dialetti*, 403–28. Rome: Biblioteca di Storia Patria, 1978.

——— . "Contatti fra Lazio ed Etruria in eta arcaica: documentazione archeologica e testimonianze epigrafiche." In *Alle origine del latino*, pp. 27–42. Proceedings of the conference of the Italian Society of Linguistics held in Pisa, Dec. 7–8, 1980. Pisa: Giardini, 1982.

Gordon, A. E. *Illustrated Introduction to Latin Epigraphy*. Berkeley: University of California Press, 1983.

——— . "On the Origins of the Latin Alphabet: Modern Views." *University of California Studies in Classical Antiquity* 2 (1969): 157–70.

Morandi, A. *Epigrafia Italica*. Rome: Bretschneider, 1982.

Sampson, J. *Writing Systems*. Stanford: Stanford University Press, 1985.

9

The Runes: The Earliest Germanic Writing System
······

Elmer H. Antonsen

······

Runes! The very mention of the word evokes a feeling of mystery and conjures up visions of sorcery—so strong has been the influence of medieval and modern enthusiasts of the occult on the study of the earliest Germanic writing system. And yet, a sober review of the materials available to us, that is, of the actual extant inscriptions themselves, reveals that runic writing was no more closely connected to magical practices than was any other of the Mediterranean-based scripts, from some one of which runic writing derives.

At times, it is even maintained that the demise of writing in runes is to be traced to the opposition of the Christian Church to the use of heathen symbols, which because of their supposed inherent magical properties were intimately associated with the Germanic peoples' pagan past.[1] Such a view, however, ignores the abundant examples of pious runic writing found on church-related objects from the time of the introduction of Christianity into the Germanic north until the end of the runic era. Not only do we find stones with inscriptions in runes calling for Christian prayers for the souls of the deceased, but we also find inscriptions in the doorways of churches, on church bells, indeed, even on baptismal fonts. In England, the magnificent Celtic-style stone crosses of Bewcastle and Ruthwell (dating from approximately A.D. 650–750) bear runic inscriptions, and the Ruthwell cross even contains a portion of the *Dream of the Rood (rood* = "cross"), a most Christian Old English poem, inscribed in runes. As R. I. Page points out, nearly all of the thirty-six known Anglo-Saxon runestones come from an ecclesiastical context, as, for example, the Hartlepool namestone I (fig. 1).[2] The coffin of St. Cuthbert was inscribed in runes.[3] On the Continent, the first Christian king of Denmark, Harald Bluetooth, had a stone monument (Jelling stone 2) erected in the last quarter of the tenth century in memory of his pagan parents, King Gorm the Old and Queen Thyra. On side C of this stone can be seen a depiction of Christ, and there is a runic inscription extolling Harald as the one who "made the Danes Christians" (fig. 2).[4] We also have a sizable number of Latin religious texts executed in runes on wooden sticks, most notably those excavated in Bergen, Norway.[5] Although runic finds in present-day Germany are far fewer than those from Scandinavia, there is an inscription on a fibula from Nordendorf (seventh or eighth century), which according to Klaus Düwel represents an abjuration of the old pagan gods and is therefore to be considered a Christian text.[6]

The actual direct evidence available to us strongly contradicts the assumption that the Germanic runes were considered inherently heathen, unsuitable for Christian use, and therefore also contradicts the notion that the runes themselves were thought to be endowed with magical properties. In other words, at the time of the introduction of Christianity, which occurred in the vari-

Figure 1   Hartlepool namestone 1: *upper quadrants,* Alpha, Omega; *lower quadrants,* the woman's name *hildiþryþ*. Photograph copyright R. I. Page, Corpus Christi College, University of Cambridge.

ous regions of the Germanic world over a time-span of some five-hundred years, there was no aversion to using the native writing systems for Christian purposes, whether the text was in the vernacular or in the Latin of the Church. The assumption that the runes themselves had supernatural powers is a secondary development traceable to the period after the decline of runic writing. Already in the Middle Ages, antiquarian interest in the runes flourished and was responsible for the treatises on runic writing and the occasional mentioning of runes in medieval manuscripts.[7] This antiquarian interest quite naturally focused on the unusual, and in the nineteenth century, after the rise of what can be called the scientific investigation of runic inscriptions, there arose a school of investigators who took refuge in the theory of runic magic when-

ever an inscription presented problems of decipherment or interpretation. Even the mere writing of the runic alphabet itself has been interpreted as an attempt to "mobilize all the powers of the runes together" for purposes of magic.[8] And time and again we find inscriptions with no actual reference to any magical or cultic practices interpreted by some scholars as having been written for the express purpose of banning ghosts or warding off evil.[9]

Believers in runic magic base their theory of the supposedly magical powers of the runes on occasional statements referring to runic sorcery found in Old Norse literature dating from a period at least one-thousand years after the development of runic writing and well after the introduction of Christianity into the north. It is significant, however, that not a single inscription from the oldest period, that is, from the first to the fifth century after the birth of Christ, invokes any of the pagan gods, and those inscriptions supposedly intended to ward off ghosts and evil spirits can be interpreted on the basis of sound linguistic analysis as being quite mundane, indeed even arreligious in nature.[10]

One of the mainstays of the magical theory of runic interpretation has been the almost universally accepted view that the very word "rune" had the original meaning "mystery, secret," and that it is related to German *raunen,* "to whisper." It should be noted, first of all, that the word "rune" during the period of the oldest inscriptions never means "runic letter," but rather "inscription, message."[11] Most important, Richard Morris has recently demonstrated in a convincing manner that "rune" has nothing to do with "mystery, secret," but rather is derived from an Indo-European root meaning "to scratch, dig, make grooves" and is therefore simply a designation for writing (cf. English "write," which is cognate with German *ritzen,* "to scratch").[12] As the French scholar Lucien Musset has so cogently remarked, "the obsession with magic of many runologists can be explained more from the psychology of the scholars than from the intrinsic content of the inscriptions . . . for almost all [of these scholars] the aura of mystery which they ascribe to the fuþark was a supplementary attraction in an otherwise austere field of labor."[13] If we are to make the best use of these texts for understanding the culture of the early Germanic peoples and for gaining insights into the early history of the various Germanic languages, or indeed for establishing a plausible history of runic writing itself, we cannot allow ourselves to be led astray by unfounded notions and preconceptions that stand directly in the way of a sober and scientifically verifiable analysis of them. In this regard, I am in complete agreement with the Soviet scholar E. A. Makaev, who took strong exception to the magical bias of most previous runic scholarship and stated unequivocally, "Runology, if it is not to become a heap of unfounded, sterile, fantastic constructions, of which not a few are to be found in its history, can and should become just as exact a discipline as is the comparative grammar of the Germanic languages."[14] We will proceed then from the assumption that runic writing, like all alphabetic writing, was created as a

means of communicating between persons not within hearing and that it could be and was used for any type of communication, whether profane or sacred. Like all other writing systems, the runes could be used for religious purposes and even for purposes of sorcery, but to admit that possibility is a far cry from claiming that such use was the original and primary purpose for the development of runic writing.[15]

As we have seen, the Germanic peoples were already in possession of a system of writing long before the coming of Christianity and of the Latin alphabet used by the Church. We have examples of this writing preserved on objects made of wood, bone, metal, and stone from the first century after Christ down to early modern times. There are also some texts dealing with runes preserved in medieval manuscripts, but these are clearly of an epigonian nature, inspired by a learned interest in things from the past.

The older, or Germanic, runic alphabet consisted of twenty-four letters in an arrangement that differs markedly from the order of letters in all other alphabets (see table 1; the rune þ represents the sound *th* in English "thorn"). Scholars have expended a great deal of effort in trying to determine the reason for this unique sequence in the futhark (so named by modern scholars after the first six letters; cf. "alphabet" = alpha, beta), but it is fair to say that we still have absolutely no idea how this arrangement came about. To my mind, the best guess is that it had to do with the manner in which the runes were taught and learned, the result of some mnemonic device which is no longer retrievable, but

Figure 2   Jelling stone 2 (side C): at the bottom (in younger runes): *auk tani karþi kristnạ* =
'and made the Danes Christians.' Photograph
copyright National Museum, Copenhagen.

Table 1 The Futhark, or Germanic Runic Alphabet

ᚠ	ᚢ	ᚦ	ᚨ	ᚱ	ᚲ	ᚷ	ᚹ
f	u	þ	a	r	k	g	w
ᚺ	ᚾ	ᛁ	ᛃ	ᛇ	ᛈ	ᛉ	ᛊ
h	n	i	j	ǣ	p	z	s
ᛏ	ᛒ	ᛖ	ᛗ	ᛚ	ᛜ	ᛞ	ᛟ
t	b	e	m	l	ng	d	o

which may have left some slight echo in the runic poems preserved in medieval manuscripts.[16] Equally uncertain is the reason for the division of the futhark into three parts (in Old Norse called *ǽttir*, "families," but originally meaning "groups of eight"). It may well be that there was a practical reason which we can no longer reconstruct. In any case, these divisions are used in certain types of cryptic inscriptions, where a particular rune could be designated by citing its position within its own division. Thus, ᚢ = *u* could be cited as the second rune of the first division by means of two branches on one side of a staff (vertical line) and one branch on the other side: ᛇ . In this particular case (on the Körlin ring; see fig. 3), the symbol thus derived can also be interpreted as a bind-rune (ligature) consisting of an inverted ᚨ = *a* attached to ᛚ = *l*, so that the whole can then be read as *al* + *u* = *alu*, a word that appears written out in full just below the cryptic symbol on the ring.[17] Such cryptic use of runes is very rare in the older inscriptions and of itself does not lend support to the magical interpretation of runes, since humans have always delighted in demonstrating their own cleverness and in outwitting others.

While there have been a great number of attempts to provide gematrial explanations of runic inscriptions, it is a fact that we have no indication whatsoever that the runes were ever associated with numbers (although this was true of the Greek and Gothic alphabets).[18] Whenever numbers are mentioned in the older runic inscriptions, they are always written out in words. In this connection, it has also been supposed that the numbers twenty-four (the number of runes in the futhark), eight (the number of runes in each division), and three (the number of divisions in the futhark) had magical significance, but here again we are dealing with pure speculation. Proponents of the

Figure 3 Körlin ring. Photograph reprinted, by permission, from W. Krause, *Die Runeninschriften im älteren Futhark* (Göttingen: Vandenhoeck and Ruprecht, 1966), vol. 2, table 21, no. 46. Copyright 1966 by Vandenhoeck und Ruprecht.

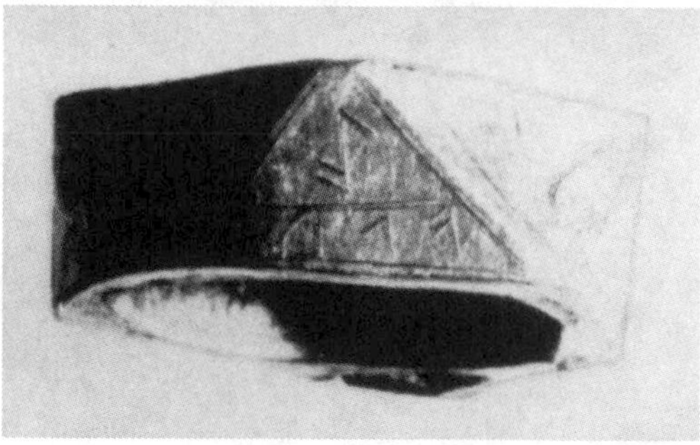

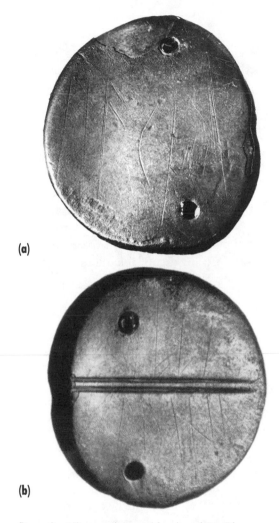

(a)

(b)

Figure 4 Vimose chape (sides A and B). Photographs copyright National Museum, Copenhagen.

magic theory also believe that the reduction of the twenty-four symbols of the older futhark to only sixteen in the younger Scandinavian runic alphabets (to which we will return later) was carried out for magical purposes. We must ask, however, why anyone would have tampered with supposedly sacred numbers if they really had been of any magical significance (in the sixteen-rune futharks, the divisions consisted of six, five, and five runes each).

The shapes of the runes presented above are somewhat standardized. As with all alphabets, variations can be found, so that, for example, *s* is not only ⟨, but also ⟨, ⟨, and ⟨; *d* is usually ⋈ in inscriptions found in Scandinavia but generally has the shape M in those found on the Continent; *e* appears not only as M, but also as Π; *k* has numerous variants, including ⟨, ⟨, and Y.[19] Some runologists attempt to assign dates to inscriptions on the basis of the particular shapes of certain runes. Unfortunately, this assumed dating-aid has proven to be quite illusory, since shapes that once were considered late variants often turn out to be recorded in very early inscriptions. A case in point is the reading of the inscription on the Vimose chape (a metal fitting at the point of a scabbard), which is dated archaeologically to A.D. 250–300 (fig. 4). This inscription, written on both sides of the chape, has been read as:

Side A: *mariha* (left to right)
          iala (right to left
Side B: *makija* (left to right).[20]

On the basis of this reading, two interpretations have been advanced: *Māri hai* [assumed error for *aih] *Alla mākija,* "Alla possesses the Famous One as sword," and *Mārihai Alla mākija,* "To the Famous One, Alla (gives) the sword." Neither of these interpretations is linguistically acceptable for phonological, morphological, and syntactic reasons. Close inspection of this inscription (see fig. 4) reveals that the rune read as *h* = ᚺ actually has an additional branch (nonvertical line) running from the right staff (vertical line) downward to the left staff, intersecting the branch of the "*h*" slightly to the right of its center, so that the rune actually has the shape ᛗ = *d*.[21] With a re-ordering of the sides, the inscription can therefore be read as:

Side A: *makija*   (left to right)
Side B: *marida*   (left to right
        iala   (right to left)

This reading yields *mākija māridē Alla,* "Alla decorated the sword." It requires no assumption of errors on the part of the inscriber (on the spelling *ai* = *ē*, see below) and is phonologically, morphologically, and syntactically irreproachable. It is also runologically incontestable, since it was not unusual to write in a run-on fashion from one line to the next (on our side B) without regard for word divisions. The surface of the Vimose chape has undergone considerable wear, so that the inscription is quite faint in part. The reason the fifth rune of the first line of our side B was read as *h* and the second branch of the rune was ignored, or rather never noticed, can be explained at least partly by the fact that investigators did not expect to find here a *d*-rune with the shape ᛗ , which is rare in

Scandinavia, but is the usual shape in inscriptions from the Continent, which are generally considerably younger. We must admit, however, that we often do not know which shape of a given rune is older than another, nor even whether there were not different "schools" of runic writing that preferred certain shapes over others.

Even a cursory glance at the symbols of the Germanic futhark reveals that this alphabet is closely related to the Greek and Roman alphabets of the Mediterranean world. Clearly identifiable runes include ᚠ = *F*, ᚢ = *U* (inverted), ᚱ = *R*, ᚺ = *H*, ᛁ = *I*, ᛋ = *S* (and ᛝ = Σ), ᛏ = *T*, ᛒ = *B*, ᛚ = *L* (inverted), and ᛉ = Ω. A little explanation suffices to show the relationship of other runes to their Greco-Roman counterparts, for example, ᚨ = *A* reflects archaic ᐱ , ᐱ , while ᛨ = *K* is most likely a development from archaic ᛲ as the result of false separation from bind-runes, as in the combination of ᛗ (*e*) + ᛨ (*k*) = ᛗᛨ (*ek,*) "I," which came to be misconstrued as ᛗ = *e* + ᛨ = *k*. We cannot derive this *k*-rune from Latin C because the rune does not normally occur in full line height.[22] It will be noted that the runic shapes avoid curves and horizontal lines, changing them to angles and oblique lines. This peculiarity of runic writing is the result of its having been developed for carving in wood, where it is difficult to execute curves, and horizontal lines would tend to be obscured by the grain of the wood. Ease of carving in wood also explains the inverted shapes of some runes. Although three or four runes are difficult to account for, it is clear that the runes derive from the Mediterranean writing tradition. The question remaining unresolved, however, is which Mediterranean script was the direct model for the runic alphabet, which in turn is intimately related to the second question: how old is runic writing?

The three main candidates for the honor of being the direct ancestor of the futhark have been the Latin, Greek, and Etruscan alphabets, the latter in the form of the so-called North Italic alphabets of the Alpine region. In 1874 the Dane Ludvig Wimmer undertook the first scientific inquiry into the origin of the runes. Before him, all kinds of wild speculation had prevailed, including the assumption that they were independently developed shortly after the Great Flood.[23] Wimmer came to the conclusion that the runes were derived from the Latin monumental script of the third or fourth century after Christ as the result of the influence of the Romans settled along the Rhine. The Swedish scholar Otto von Friesen, on the other hand, thought the runes had arisen out of a Greek cursive script known to the Goths on the shores of the Black Sea. The Norwegian runologist Carl Marstrander proposed a North Italic origin, not only because of the similarity of shapes, but also because it seemed necessary to posit a point of origin in a southerly region in which Germanic peoples could have come into contact with the Mediterranean writing tradition.[24] Neither Wimmer's nor von Friesen's theories can be maintained today, since they assume a time of origin that is later than the earliest inscriptions now known to us. The supposed North Italic origin leaves unexplained the fact that we have not even one early inscription from middle or southern Germany. In addition, the assumed correspondences

between runes and North Italic letters is exclusively of a formal nature and does not take into account the differences in sound-values. Erik Moltke rightly points out that agreement in the shapes of individual letters is not sufficient evidence to demonstrate a close relationship between two alphabets, but that there must also be a correspondence between the sound-values of the letters.[25] Moltke's objection does not go far enough, however. Writing systems are not normally borrowed as abstract ideas. That is, one does not observe that other people can write and then proceed to invent an alphabet for one's own language, as Moltke assumes happened in the case of the runes vis-à-vis the Latin monumental script in use along the Rhine.

It is indeed striking not only that the shapes of the vast majority of runes correspond to the letter shapes in the Mediterranean tradition, but that sound-correspondences can also be established, provided the comparison is made between linguistic and orthographic *systems* (not just individual letters) of the borrowing and possible donating languages.[26] Most striking of all, however, is the close correspondence between what has often been called the "peripheral" features of the runic writing system and the *Archaic* Mediterranean scripts. These features include the lack of a fixed direction of writing (which may be right to left, left to right, or a combination of both in the so-called boustrophedon style), the lack of designation of nasal consonants before other consonants (e.g., *widuhudaz = Widuhundaz*), the single designation of double consonants (e.g., *hali = halli*), the absence of word divisions, and only occasional use of interpuncts (which, however, agree in both runic and Mediterranean traditions in consisting of a varying number of dots).[27] Most of these features can be found on side A of the Tune stone (fig. 5). This side of the stone contains a typical commemorative inscription, which reads:

I. (left to right)   *ekwiwazafter · woduri*
II. (right to left)   *dewitadahalaiban:*
                      worahto

(*ek Wīwaz after · Wōdurī- / dē witandah^a-laiban : wor^ahtō*), "I, Wīwaz, in memory of Wōdurīdaz the Breadward [i.e., lord, chieftain] wrought [this]."

As indicated, the first line is written from left to right, the second from right to left; individual words are not separated, the *n* of *witanda-* is not written, and there are interpuncts only to set off the name of the person commemorated.

It has been customary in runic scholarship to play down the significance of these so-called peripheral features of runic writing and to ascribe them to the "primitive minds" of the writers. It has even been maintained that writers in runes had no sense of directionality, even though linearity is a sine qua non of all alphabetic writing.[28] It was necessary to explain away these features that runic writing shares with the Archaic tradition as long as it was maintained that runic writing arose after the birth of Christ, since the two traditions did not seem to be chronologically compatible. If, however, we investigate the age of runic writing on the basis of the linguistic and orthographic evidence available in the in-

Figure 5 Tune stone (side A). Photograph copyright University Museum of National Antiquities, Oslo.

scriptions themselves and in the light of the known historical development of the Germanic languages, rather than on the basis of an ad-hoc assumption that this writing cannot be much older than the oldest inscription known to us, then the question of the relationship between the runes and Mediterranean scripts becomes much clearer. It is then possible to view the development of runic writing in a normal frame of reference, in which the person or persons responsible must have been bilingual and must have learned to read and write in the model language before adapting its writing system for a Germanic language. In learning to write the model language, the adaptor(s) would, of course, also have learned the *entire system, including the so-called peripheral features,* which are part-and-parcel of that system.

The dating of runic inscriptions in the older period is a matter that can be carried out only with the help of archaeology. When an object with an inscription is discovered in an archaeological context that lends itself to relative dating, then we have a definite point of reference. It happens, however, that runic objects are sometimes found in isolation and archaeologists are unable to suggest a relative date of origin. Inscriptions on stone are not amenable to archaeological dating in most cases. Even when archaeologists provide us with a dating, however, runologists have not always been eager to accept their help. A classic example is the dating of the Vimose woodplane, which archaeologists ascribe to the period A.D. 100–300. Wolfgang Krause has difficulty accepting this finding: "The . . . usual dating of the finds from Vimose

(100–300) cannot be easily applied to the inscriptions of the woodplane. . . . A dating to the 3rd century would be possible only on the assumption that the *k*-rune B 2, which is actually perfectly clear, is merely a writing error.[29] On the basis of the shape of this one rune, Krause ascribes the inscription to the sixth century, that is, between 200 and 400 years later than the archaeologists suggest. As I have pointed out above, however, we do not know the full history of variant shapes for the runes, and it is highly speculative to date inscriptions on the basis of such shapes. The archaeological evidence remains, therefore, our best guide in this instance.

Also largely on the basis of the shape of the *k*-rune, Krause dates the inscription on the whetstone from Strøm (fig. 6) to about A.D. 600.[30] This interesting little object has an inscription of two lines, one on each of the narrower sides (those not used for sharpening a tool). It is clearly a type of worksong:

watehalihinohorna / *hahaskaþihaþuligi*
(wātē halli hinō, horna! haha, skaþi! haþu,
ligi!)

"Wet this stone, horn! Scythe, scathe! Hay, lie!" Since this whetstone was found alone, archaeologists cannot date it. From a linguistic and runological point of view, there is nothing that would justify our dating it later than about A.D. 450, and it may be even older.[31] We choose the year 450 as the terminus ante quem for the relative dating of this and other inscriptions because it is the midpoint in the so-called bracteate period. Bracteates are thin gold medallions

Figure 6 Strøm whetstone (sides A and B). Photographs copyright Universitetet i Trondheim, Vitenskapsmuseet.

impressed from one side with decorative motifs, intended to be worn on a thong or other support around the neck. Hundreds of them have been found in the north, and some bear runic or pseudorunic inscriptions (fig. 7).

Bracteates are imitations of Roman coins and medallions, and archaeologists have dated the period in which they were in use from approximately A.D. 350–550.[32] These bracteates are significant for the relative dating of runic inscriptions in general because some of their inscriptions reveal linguistic and runological-orthographic developments that mark a transition from the language of the oldest inscriptions (before the bracteate period) toward the language and writing system of the younger Scandinavian inscriptions. In other words, the period of the bracteates marks a watershed in the linguistic history of Scandinavia. From this period on, we have definite indications that the language of Scandinavia has developed certain characteristics that

are peculiarly Scandinavian, whereas the language before this period showed no special Nordic traits.[33] It is therefore often possible on the basis of linguistic criteria and of spelling peculiarities to determine whether a given inscription should be assigned chronologically to the period before or the period after the bracteates. For those inscriptions that display none of the linguistic and runological changes that begin in the period of the bracteates (roughly before A.D. 500), we have no guideposts whatsoever in the inscriptions themselves that could indicate their relative age. This means that in the absence of archaeological datings, all of the oldest runic inscriptions must be lumped together in a chronologically amorphous mass. We have, in other words, no way of knowing whether the inscription on the Tune stone is older, younger, or contemporaneous with any given archaeologically datable inscription from the period before the bracteates. These considerations make it obvious that any attempt to determine the age of runic writing on the basis of the age of extant inscriptions is simply doomed to failure. Fortunately, there are other, more reliable indicators of this age.

It is a curious fact that the Germanic futhark displays six vowel symbols, even though only five would suffice to designate all ten vowels in the language of the oldest known runic inscriptions, since each symbol can represent both a long and a short vowel (table 2). The sixth vowel rune, ⌡ , is not found in any meaningful inscriptions from the oldest period, although it is present in the futhark itself. In Old English inscriptions from a much later period, this rune is occasionally used in place of both the *i*-rune and the *h*-rune, a clear indication that its original function has been lost. In seeking to explain the presence of this sixth vowel rune in the futhark, some scholars

Table 2   Vowel Phonemes and Symbols in the Oldest Inscriptions

/i/ I	/u/ ∧	/ī/ I	/ū/ ∧
/e/ M	/o/ ⋈	/ē/ M	/ō/ ⋈
	/a/ ⊦		/ā/ ⊦

have proposed that it represented a kind of *i*-sound different from that represented by the rune I .[34] The Russian scholar M. I. Steblin-Kamenskij emphatically rejected this interpretation because there never existed a vowel corresponding to this "different *i*" at any time in the history of the Germanic languages.[35] The only reason for positing such a sound is the ad-hoc assumption that the rune ⌡ represented some kind of *i*-sound, which in turn is based on the very late and sporadic use of the rune in place of the rune I (as well as in place of the *h*-rune). Steblin-Kamenskij came to the conclusion that the rune ⌡ was superfluous from the very inception of runic writing, but this assumption leaves unexplained the very presence of the rune in the futhark.

If wc look into the prehistory of the Germanic languages, we find that at a stage older than our oldest known inscriptions, the stage we refer to as Proto-Germanic, the vowel system consisted of only eight vowel-phonemes, which can be arranged as in table 3 to indicate their interrelationships. The vowels /ǣ/ and /ō/ had approximately the sound-values found in English "*had*" and "*laud,*" respectively. I need not go into the details of the reconstruction

Figure 7   Fyn bracteate 1. Under the horse's head, *right to left: horaz;* around the outer edge, beginning over the horse's head; *left to right: laþu aadraaaliiu alu.* Photograph copyright National Museum, Copenhagen.

Table 3	Proto-Germanic Vowel System		
/i/	/u/	/ī/	/ū/
/e/			
	/a/	/æ/	/ɔ/

Table 4	Original Fit of Vowel Phonemes and Runes (Proto-Germanic)		
/i/ ᛁ	/u/ ᚢ	/ī/ ᛁ	/ū/ ᚢ
/e/ ᛖ			
	/a/ ᚨ	/æ/ ᛇ	/ɔ/ ᛟ

of this vowel system. Suffice it to say that internal Germanic evidence, comparative Indo-European evidence, and the evidence of loanwords both from and into non-Germanic languages all require the positing of such a system.[36]

It will be seen that this vowel system has only two pairs of vowels that correspond to each other as short/long counterparts, /i/ : /ī/, and /u/ : /ū/. As was the practice in the Mediterranean scripts, these pairs (but only these pairs) could each be designated by a single symbol: ᛁ = /i, ī/, and ᚢ = /u, ū/. All of the other vowels required a separate symbol each, since none of them corresponded to any other in a short/long correlation. Since /e/ and /a/ were always short, the runes ᛖ and ᚨ could have represented originally only these short vowels, respectively. Since there was no short */o/, the rune ᛟ must have represented originally only the long vowel /ɔ/ (corresponding to Greek Ω). This means that there is only one vowel left undesignated and one rune left to be accounted for. Clearly, ᛇ must have been originally the designation for the long vowel /æ/, and the relationship between sound and symbol was originally as shown in table 4. We can therefore ex-

plain the presence of the sixth vowel rune, ᛇ, in the futhark on the basis of linguistic evidence and need not assume in an ad-hoc fashion that it never had a function, or that it represented a vowel for which there is no other evidence to be found. The absence of the rune ᛇ from meaningful inscriptions known to us is readily comprehensible from the history of the Germanic languages, since /æ/ later became /ā/ in accented (root) syllables but became /ē/ in unaccented (nonroot) syllables. These new long vowels could then be designated by the runes for the corresponding short vowels, whereby ᚨ = /a, ā/ and ᛖ = /e, ē/, and the rune ᛇ became superfluous for the language we find in our oldest inscriptions.

There is also runological evidence that the state of affairs I have outlined actually obtained in the earliest stage of runic writing. Each rune had a name beginning with the sound represented by that rune (so-called acrophonic principle), for example, ᚠ /f/ = *fehun, "cattle, movable property" (cf. Ger. *Vieh,* Eng. *fee*); ᚺ /h/ = *haglaz, "hail" (cf. Ger. *Hagel*), and so on. These names are known to us only from relatively late medieval sources, but in most cases (though not all), the correspondence between the Old English and Old Norse evidence ensures that these names are ancient.[37] As far as the vowel runes are concerned, we can consider as certain the following names in table 5. We do not know the original name for ᛃ. From this list, however, it is apparent that the runes ᛗ and ᚨ originally represented only short vowels, since their names begin with short vowels. Had they also been the designations for long vowels, their names would have begun with a long vowel, as is true of the runes ᛁ and ᚢ, and is still true of the names for letters of the alphabet in the West European tradition (cf. Eng. *e* as in "feed," not "fed"; Ger. *e* as in *Beet*, not *Bett*, etc.). There is therefore an exact fit between the vowel system of Proto-Germanic and the orthographic system provided by the futhark. This must mean that runic writing arose during the Proto-Germanic period, that is, well before our earliest runic records.

There is yet further evidence pointing to the origin of runic writing in the Proto-Germanic period. In Proto-Germanic, it was possible to have diphthongs in unaccented (nonroot) syllables, for example, Proto-Germanic */dágai/ (masc. dat. sing.),

Table 5 Rune Names and the Acrophonic Principle

ᛁ	/i, ī/	=	**īsaz / īsan*, "ice"
ᚢ	/u, ū/	=	**ūruz*, "aurochs"
ᚨ	/ō/	=	**ōþalan / ōþilan*, "inherited [real] property"
ᛗ	/e/	=	**ehwaz*, "horse"
ᚨ	/a/	=	**ansuz*, "[a kind of] god"

"day." In all the later Germanic languages, including our oldest runic inscriptions, these diphthongs have undergone monophthongization in nonroot syllables, for example, Gothic *daga*, OE *dæge*, OS *dage*, OHG *tage*, OIc. *dege*. This monophthongization has already occurred by the time of our oldest runic records, as can be seen from the masculine dative singular ending *-e* of *woduride* = *Wōdurīdē* "(to, for), Wōdurīdaz" on the Tune stone. On the Möjbro stone (fig. 8), however, this same ending is written *-ai*. The inscription appears in two lines, both written right to left, with the last rune of the first line, *z*, written above the line for lack of room: *anahahaislaginaz / frawaradaz (ana hanhē slaginaz, Frawarādaz)*, "Slain on [his] steed, Frawarādaz." In itself, the spelling *-ai* for /-ē/ in *hahai* = *hanhē*, "steed," can only be explained as an archaic (conservative, inherited) spelling from a time when the diphthong was still pronounced as a diphthong (our form is therefore comparable to modern English spellings like "knight," which corresponded to the pronunciation in Chaucer's day, but from the point of view of present-day English are conservative, etymological spellings). Perhaps even more telling, however, is the testimony of inverse spellings, that is, spellings which are historically incorrect and arose because sound-changes made it impossible for the writer to distinguish between two spellings that had come to represent the same sound (cf. Eng. "whole," related to "hale" and "health," with its ahistorical *w*). Such inverse spellings are among the best clues we have to phonological changes in older stages of written

Figure 8 Möjbro stone. Photograph copyright
Riksantikvarieämbetet, Stockholm.

Figure 9 Stenmagle wooden box (with detail). Photographs copyright National Museum, Copenhagen.

languages. On the wooden box from Stenmagle (similar to an old-fashioned pencil box with sliding cover; fig. 9), we find the inscription:

hagiradaz ⋮ *tawide* ⋮ *(Hagirādaz : tawidē)*

"Hagirādaz made [it].[38] The verb *tawidē,* "made," appears in the third-person singular, preterit indicative, and has the expected, historically correct ending -*e*. On the Nøvling clasp, however, the inscription reads:

bidawarijaz.talgidai (Bīdawarijaz talgidē),

"Bīdawarijaz carved."[39] Here, the ending of the verb *talgidē,* "carved," is not spelled -*e,* but rather -*ai,* and the same is true of

the verb *māridē* (= *maridai*) on the Vimose chape already discussed. These spellings with -*ai* for expected -*e* are explicable only on the basis that there was a writing tradition already established at a time when the actual diphthong */-ai/* was still pronounced in unaccented syllables and that its correct spelling with -*ai* continued in use even after the diphthong had undergone monophthongization. The continued use of -*ai* to represent the new /-ē/ from older */-ai/* created an unstable orthographic situation, since now /-ē/ was sometimes spelled -*e* and sometimes -*ai*. Such a situation inevitably results in spelling errors (cf. the difficulties some semiliterate speak-

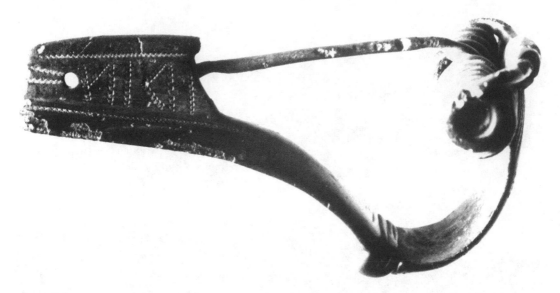

Figure 10 Meldorf fibula. On the catch-plate, *right to left: irih*. Photograph copyright Archäologisches Landesmuseum der Christian-Albrechts-Universität, Schleswig, Federal Republic of Germany.

ers of English have with "their," "they're," "there"), and this is precisely the case with the verbs ending in *-ai*. They are inverse spellings that, along with the historically justifiable *-ai* in the noun *hahai,* indicate beyond doubt that the runic writing tradition had already evolved during the Proto-Germanic period, the only period in which diphthongs were still present in unaccented syllables.

If we take into consideration all of the evidence available to us, including the shapes and sound-values of the runes themselves, the rune names, inverse spellings, the known historical development of the Germanic languages, and the peripheral features that runic writing shared only with the Mediterranean writing practices of the Archaic period, then the conclusion is inescapable that runic writing must have arisen during the Proto-Germanic period, at a time when the standardizations characteristic of the classical periods of Greek and Latin had not yet been fully carried out. We most certainly have not yet discovered the earliest runic text ever executed, but new discoveries continue to be made, such as the spectacular finds from Meldorf in Holstein, Germany, and in the Illerup River Valley of Jutland, Denmark.

In 1979, Michael Gebühr discovered in the storeroom of the Schleswig-Holsteinisches Landesmuseum für Vor- und Frühgeschichte a bronze fibula with characters resembling writing (fig. 10). Archaeologists were able to date this fibula to the first quarter of the first century after Christ.[40] The German runologist Klaus Düwel inspected the characters and came to the conclusion that they could not be Latin letters, but because of the early date of the fibula, he was reluctant to pronounce them runes, thinking they might be "proto-runes."[41] As we

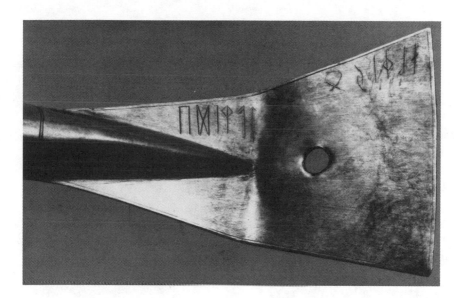

Figure 11 Illerup shieldgrip-fitting 2. Starting at top, *right to left, niþijo tawide,* "Niþijō made (this)," in which the runes for þ and *w* have double (mirrored) pockets. Photograph copyright National Museum, Copenhagen.

have seen, we must assume that runic writing antedates our known inscriptions by a considerable period of time, and the dating of the Meldorf fibula is a pseudoproblem with regard to establishing the runic character of its inscription. It is without doubt the oldest archaeologically datable runic inscription yet found, but we have no reason to conclude that even this (as yet uninterpreted) inscription is close to the beginnings of runic writing.[42]

From the archaeological digs in the valley of the Illerup River in central Jutland, significant runic finds have come to light in the course of cleaning the various objects found there. The first inscription, on a bronze fitting for a shieldgrip, was found in 1977, while two lanceheads were found in 1980 to bear identical inscriptions, one stamped into the metal, the other incised. Further, a woodplane (for making spearshafts) was found to carry an inscription in 1981, and perhaps most spectacular, in 1983, inscriptions with hitherto unknown runic shapes were found on two silver shieldgrip fittings (fig. 11). All of these objects have been dated by archaeologists to the last decade of the second century after Christ.[43] These finds are significant for a number of reasons: they are the oldest datable inscriptions yet found in present-day Denmark; two of the shieldgrip fittings and the two lanceheads display hitherto unknown runic shapes; and the lanceheads, with identical inscriptions executed in different manners, present us with the first clear evidence of a "master's signature" in runes.[44] All of the recently found inscriptions present runologists with new challenges in the never-ending search for the origin of runic writing, but they also give us hope of finding still more, even older inscriptions in the future.

The Germanic futhark underwent profound changes in the period after the bracteates. In England, it developed into an alphabet with thirty-one (and more) runes.[45] The increase in the number of symbols can be accounted for to a large extent by the phonological changes which Old English underwent in its development from the older stages of Germanic, but they are too complex to be discussed here.[46] Similarly, in Scandinavia significant changes occurred in the language, but instead of increasing the number of runes, the Scandinavians reduced the twenty-four-letter futhark to several variants of sixteen runes each.[47] Here, too, the changes in the futhark can be traced largely to phonological developments too complex for treatment here, but it should perhaps be noted that in Scandinavia, phonological changes in the names of the runes played a significant role in the reduction.[48] The Old English futhorc was well suited to represent the phonological system of the language. Nevertheless, in the long run it could not compete with the Latin alphabet, and the runic tradition did not survive the Norman conquest, except as the object of antiquarian interest. In Scandinavia, where the new futharks represented numerous sounds with the same rune and the runes had taken on simplified shapes, the system was a boon to the carver, but the bane of the reader. It was nevertheless manageable enough to remain in use for approximately four hundred years (until ca. 1050), when it was replaced by the medieval system of dotted runes with more adequate representation of the sounds of the language.[49] After approximately 1400, even this improved system yielded to the Latin alphabet, and runic writing no longer represented a living tradition, although in certain quarters, knowledge of the runes persisted into early modern times.

......

Notes

1. Cf. the discussion by M. Halsall, *The Old English Rune Poem: A Critical Edition* (Toronto: University of Toronto Press, 1981), 15.

2. R. I. Page, *An Introduction to English Runes* (London: Methuen, 1973), 134.

3. Page, *Introduction*, 173.

4. E. Moltke, *Runes and Their Origin, Denmark and Elsewhere*, trans. Peter Foote (Copenhagen: National Museum of Denmark, 1985), 207–20.

5. A. Liestøl, *Norges innskrifter med de yngre runer 6.1: Bryggen i Bergen* (Oslo: Norsk historisk Kjeldeskrift-institutt, 1980), presents all the Latin materials found in the excavations under the burned-out Hanseatic wharf in Bergen.

6. K. Düwel, *Runenkunde*, 2d ed. (Stuttgart: J. B. Metzler, 1983), 128.

7. R. Derolez, *Runica Manuscripta: The English Tradition* (Brugge: De Tempel, 1954).

8. W. Krause, *Die Runeninschriften im älteren Futhark* (Göttingen: Vandenhoeck und Ruprecht, 1966), 13.

9. The pioneering work in refuting the magical theory is A. Bæksted, *Målruner og troldruner* (Copenhagen: Gyldendal, 1952).

10. E. H. Antonsen, "Den ældre fuþark: en gudernes gave eller et hverdags-alfabet?" *Maal og Minne* 1980: 129–43, and E. H. Antonsen, "On the Typology of the Older Runic Inscriptions," *Scandinavian Studies* 52 (1980): 1–15.

11. Antonsen, "Den ældre fuþark," 139.

12. R. Morris, "The Etymology of NwG *rūnō-*." *Beiträge zur Geschichte der deutschen Sprache und Literatur* 107 (1985): 344–58.

13. L. Musset, *Introduction à la runologie* (Paris: Aubier-Montaigne, 1965), 142–43.

14. E. A. Makaev, *Jazyk drevnejšix runičeskix nadpisej* (Moscow: "Nauka," 1965), 98.

15. A cultic-religious origin of runic writing is proposed by G. Høst, *Runer: Våre eldste norske runeinnskrifter* (Oslo: Aschehoug, 1976); but cf. Moltke, *Runes and Their Origin* 69.

16. Page, *Introduction*, 69–89.

17. On the meaning of *alu*, see G. Høst Heyerdahl, "'Trylleordet' *alu*," in *Det Norske Videnskaps-Akademis Årbok* 1980: 35–49, and E. H. Antonsen, "On the Mythological Interpretation of the Oldest Runic Inscriptions," in *Languages and Cultures: Studies in Honor of Edgar C. Polomé*, ed. M. A. Jazayery and W. Winter (Berlin: Mouton de Gruyter, 1988), 43–54.

18. The most recent such attempt is H. Klingenberg, *Runenschrift—Schriftdenken—Runeninschriften* (Heidelberg: Carl Winter, 1973).

19. On runic variants, see E. H. Antonsen, "The Graphemic System of the Germanic Futhark," in *Linguistic Method: Essays in Honor of Herbert Penzl*, ed. I. Rauch and G. Carr (The Hague: Mouton, 1978), 287–97, and R. L. Morris, *Runic and Mediterranean Epigraphy NOWELE* Supplement vol. 4 (Odense: Odense University Press, 1988), 109–21.

20. C. J. S. Marstrander, *De nordiske runeinnskrifter i eldre alfabet* (Oslo: *Viking: Tidsskrift for norrøn arkeologi* 16, 1953), 37–44, and Krause, *Die Runeninschriften*, 57–58.

21. Antonsen, "The Graphemic System," 291–92.

22. E. H. Antonsen, "Zum Ursprung und Alter des germanischen Fuþarks," in *Festschrift für Karl Schneider*, ed. K. Jankowsky and E. Dick (Amsterdam: John Benjamins B.V., 1982), 3–25, esp. 6–7.

23. See the résumé in Moltke, *Runes and Their Origin*, 70 n. 1.

24. For a concise review of these theories, see Düwel, *Runenkunde*, 90–95.

25. Moltke, *Runes and Their Origin*, 38–39.

26. Antonsen, "Zum Ursprung und Alter des germanischen Fuþarks," 7–12.

27. The most thorough treatment to date of the peripheral features is found in Morris, *Runic and Mediterranean Epigraphy*, esp. 125–39.

28. See, for example, E. Moltke, "Järsbergstenen, en mærkelig värmlandsk runesten," *Fornvännen* 76 (1981): 81–90, in which the attempt is made to equate runic writing with the erratic arrangement of motifs on Gotlandic picture stones; E. H. Antonsen, "On Reading Runic Inscriptions," *NOWELE (North-West European Language Evolution)* 2 (1983): 23–40, demonstrates that there was no lack of a sense of directionality on the part of writers in runes.

29. Krause, *Die Runeninschriften*, 63.

30. Ibid., 113.

31. E. H. Antonsen, "The Inscription on the Whetstone from Strøm," *Visible Language* 9 (1975): 123–32.

32. Cf. Moltke, *Runes and Their Origin*, 108–13.

33. E. H. Antonsen, *A Concise Grammar of the Older Runic Inscriptions* (Tübingen: Max Niemeyer, 1975), 26–28.

34. This view is propounded, for example, by Krause, *Die Runeninschriften*, 5, and Düwel, *Runenkunde*, 5–6.

35. M. I. Steblin-Kamenskij, "Kakuju sistemu glasnyx vyrožal pervonačal'no runičeskij alfavit?" *Skandinavskij Shornik* 4 (1959): 153–58, and M. I. Steblin-Kamenskij, "Noen fonologiske betraktninger over de eldre runer," *Arkiv för Nordisk Filologi* 77 (1962): 1–6.

36. For a detailed discussion of the reconstruction of the Proto-Germanic vowel system, see E. H. Antonsen, "The Proto-Germanic Syllabics (Vowels)," in *Toward a Grammar of Proto-Germanic*, ed. F. van Coetsem and H. Kufner (Tübingen: Max Niemeyer, 1972), 117–40.

37. Convenient reviews of the material can be found in Page, *Introduction*, 69–89, and Düwel, *Runenkunde*, 106–10.

38. Moltke, *Runes and Their Origin*, 87–88.

39. Moltke, *Runes and Their Origin*, 124 and 129–30. Moltke insists on interpreting the spelling with *-ai* as a copying error by an illiterate metalsmith. We have no basis for assuming that the writer was either a metal-

smith or an illiterate; see E. H. Antonsen, "The Oldest Runic Inscriptions in the Light of New Finds and Interpretations," in *Runor och runinskrifter: Föredrag vid Riksantikvarieämbetets och Vitterhetsakademiens symposium 8–11 september 1985* (Stockholm: Almqvist and Wiksell International, 1988), 17–28.

40. K. Düwel and M. Gebühr, "Die Fibel von Meldorf und die Anfänge der Runenschrift," *Zeitschrift für deutsches Altertum und deutsche Literatur* 110 (1981): 159–75, esp. 161; and K. Düwel, "The Meldorf Fibula and the Origin of Runic Writing," *Michigan Germanic Studies* 7 (1981): 8–14, esp. 9.

41. Düwel, "The Meldorf Fibula," 12.

42. Düwel proposes a reading *hiwi* for this inscription. However, the middle rune can only be an *r* of the type also found on the Fyn bracteate 1 and on the clasp from Aquincum, i.e., ᚺ ; see Antonsen, "The Graphemic System," 294–95.

43. On the archaeological data, see J. Ilkjær and J. Lønstrup, "Der Moorfund im Tal der Illerup-Å bei Skanderup in Ostjütland (Dänemark)," *Germania* 61 (1983): 95–116.

44. The most recent treatment of these inscriptions is M. Stoklund, "Neue Runenfunde in Illerup und Vimose," *Germania* 64 (1986): 75–89.

45. See Page, *Introduction*, 39–51.

46. In addition to Page, ibid., see E. H. Antonsen, "On the Origin of Old English Digraph Spellings," *Studies in Linguistics* 19 (1967): 5–17, esp. 11-16.

47. See Moltke, *Runes and Their Origin*, 28–30 and 173–83.

48. The best treatment to date is A. Liestøl, "The Viking Runes: The Transition from the Older to the Younger Futhark," *Saga-Book* 20 (1981): 247–66.

49. See Moltke, *Runes and Their Origin*, 30–32.

• • • • • •

Further Readings

Antonsen, Elmer H. *A Concise Grammar of the Older Runic Inscriptions*. Tübingen: Max Niemeyer, 1975.

Düwel, Klaus. *Runenkunde*. 2d ed. Stuttgart: J. B. Metzler, 1983.

Krause, Wolfgang. *Die Runeninschriften im älteren Futhark*. Göttingen: Vandenhoeck und Ruprecht, 1966.

Moltke, Erik. *Runes and Their Origin, Denmark and Elsewhere*. Translated by Peter Foote. Copenhagen: National Museum of Denmark, 1985.

Page, R. I. *Introduction to the English Runes*. London: Methuen, 1973.

10

Ogham: The Ancient Script of the Celts

· · · · · ·

Ruth P. M. Lehmann

· · · · · ·

The Celts make up an important branch of the Indo-Europeans and can culturally and linguistically be distinguished from others of this language group by the first millennium B.C. Some scholars place the Celts in Central Europe at the beginning of the second millennium.[1] Through discoveries of characteristic archaeological artifacts, a distinct Celtic culture has been traced as early as the Bronze Age, most notably around Hallstatt, in what is now Austria. From about 800 B.C. to 450 B.C. the Celts remained in the region of present-day Salzburg but gradually moved west and north along the river valleys. They left vestiges of their culture in the names of many of the rivers of Germany, notably the Rhine and its tributaries and the Inn, and also in many place names along these routes. Here, they constructed the hill forts and hill towns ringed by earthworks so characteristic in their later migration to the British Isles. Another group went southward to Switzerland and southern France and built on lower ground, often in lakes for protection. While parts of this group continued to move onward through Spain to the most northwesterly province of Galicia, others turned back east, inhabited the Po valley in northern Italy or proceeded east into Asia Minor, settling in Galatia about modern Ankara during the second and first centuries B.C.

On the basis of a typological bifurcation in which Proto-Indo-European *k^w developed either as a velar or as a labial, it is customary to divide the Celtic languages into the so-called Q-Celtic, or Goidelic, and the P-Celtic, or Brythonic, groups. For example, Latin *quis,* "who," appears in Old Irish as *cia* but in Welch as *pwy.* Also, the German hill town Dünenberg has the front vowel like the Welsh *dinas,* "fort," compared with the Irish *dun,* "fort" or "enclosure", like English "town." It is generally believed that both dialects existed in Gaul, but we have no way of knowing by what routes the Celtic peoples made their way to Britain nor any hope of constructing isoglosses to determine the regions where the dialects were spoken, for while the Celts were a vocal people with great memories, a love of story and song, they had no writing system borrowed or invented before coming to Britain, except for a very few inscriptions in Gaul and Spain written in Greek or Latin letters.

Important to the prehistory of the writing system of the pagan Celts was a caste of priests known as the druids. The druids were jealous of their important functions as the source of divine law and ritual and, as Julius Caesar informs us, were prohibited by religion from committing their teachings to writing.[2] Only a few pupils were chosen for the rigorous training to carry on the pagan rites that were kept a mystery to the uninitiated. The *brehons* guarded the laws, and aided the kings and chiefs in giving judgment. Druids and poets (*filid*) were

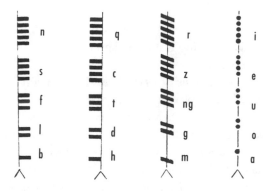

Figure 1 Ogham characters. From *Introduction to Old Irish* by R. P. M. Lehmann and W. P. Lehmann (New York: The Modern Language Association, 1975).

prophets and along with the brehons kept alive an oral tradition of history, myth, and story, as well as the genealogies and great deeds of the leaders and their ancestors.

With Christianization in the third century A.D. the laws and the verse and tales of the Celtic people began to be recorded. The laws were probably the earliest writings to be codified, and are the oldest written form of Celtic text. For the druid lore our best information comes from early Greek and Roman travelers and historians—men who did not understand the foreign culture and made the best sense of it they could in terms of their own religion.

But what of ogham? In truth, we know very little and can make only uneducated guesses. The accuracy of our knowledge is further complicated by the fact that the ogham alphabet employed strokes and notches in a way that defies clear-cut derivation from a parent alphabet (fig. 1). The Celtic scholar J. Vendryès has ventured the theory, however, that the unusual shapes

of ogham characters are linked to their origin in wooden tally sticks used for counting sheep.[3] This is only one of many theories of the origin of ogham which will be discussed in this chapter.

Although ogham may have developed on the Continent, the only records we have of it are in the British Isles, either in Ireland or in territory settled by the Irish or strongly influenced by them. Ogham stones were either grave markers, as we hear in the ancient tales, or they were boundary markers. Possibly they were used for both, for though graves have not been found below them, the stones have not infrequently been moved or used in later constructions so that the archaeological evidence cannot be relied on in all its detail.

Besides these relatively stable evidences for the use of the writing system, manuscripts written well after the time when the country was Christianized inform us of the alphabetical equivalents of the symbols and tell their names. Occasionally marginal notes in ogham are added to manuscripts of the seventeenth and eighteenth centuries. The old stories tell not only of raising a stone and marking it in ogham above the grave of important figures but also of using it for magic purposes to halt opponents.

First, what is the origin of the name "ogham"? What are the ogham characters? What are their Roman equivalents, their names, and precisely where are they to be found? The name for the script may come from Oghma, a Celtic deity of culture, but L. J. D. Richardson derives it from *agma,* an old Greek letter for *ng*.[4] Many scholars, such as Kenneth Jackson, would date all written Celtic from the time of Christian-

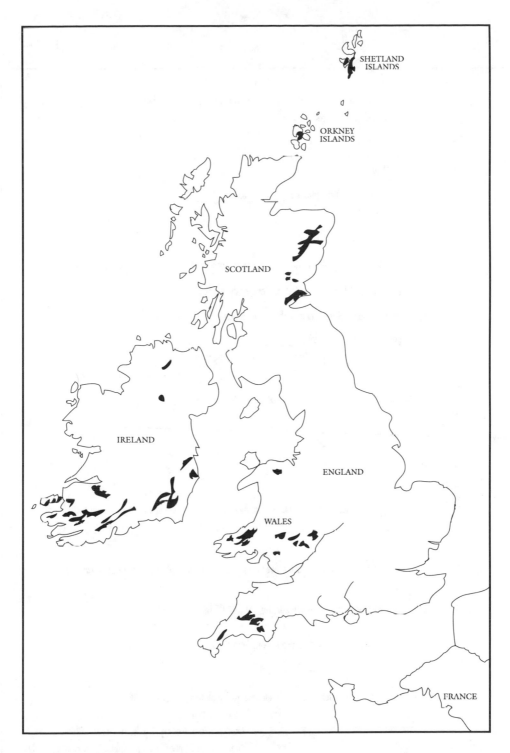

Outline map of the British Isles showing by
shaded areas where carved ogham markers have
been found. Guide for shading: Kenneth Jackson, 1950.

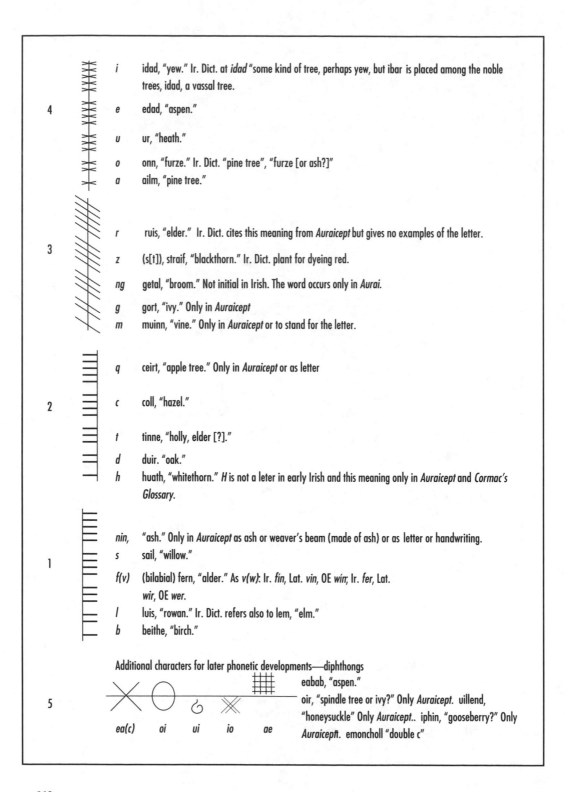

4

i — idad, "yew." Ir. Dict. at *idad* "some kind of tree, perhaps yew, but ibar is placed among the noble trees, idad, a vassal tree.

e — edad, "aspen."

u — ur, "heath."

o — onn, "furze." Ir. Dict. "pine tree", "furze [or ash?]"

a — ailm, "pine tree."

3

r — ruis, "elder." Ir. Dict. cites this meaning from *Auraicept* but gives no examples of the letter.

z — (s[t]), straif, "blackthorn." Ir. Dict. plant for dyeing red.

ng — getal, "broom." Not initial in Irish. The word occurs only in *Aurai.*

g — gort, "ivy." Only in *Auraicept*

m — muinn, "vine." Only in *Auraicept* or to stand for the letter.

2

q — ceirt, "apple tree." Only in *Auraicept* or as letter

c — coll, "hazel."

t — tinne, "holly, elder [?]."

d — duir. "oak."

h — huath, "whitethorn." *H* is not a leter in early Irish and this meaning only in *Auraicept* and *Cormac's Glossary.*

1

nin, — "ash." Only in *Auraicept* as ash or weaver's beam (made of ash) or as letter or handwriting.

s — sail, "willow."

f(v) — (bilabial) fern, "alder." As *v(w)*: Ir. *fín,* Lat. *vin,* OE *wín;* Ir. *fer,* Lat. *wir,* OE *wer.*

l — luis, "rowan." Ir. Dict. refers also to lem, "elm."

b — beithe, "birch."

5

Additional characters for later phonetic developments—diphthongs

eabab, "aspen."

oir, "spindle tree or ivy?" Only *Auraicept*. uillend, "honeysuckle" Only *Auraicept*.. iphin, "gooseberry?" Only *Auraicept*. emoncholl "double c"

ea(c)   *oi*   *ui*   *io*   *ae*

ization, that is, the fourth century A.D.[5] In 1942, however, H. O'Neill Hencken reported the excavation of a crannog (an ancient wooden lake dwelling preserved by the acidity of the bogs) at Ballinderry II.[6] Among the findings, he described dice of bone or wood in a crannog that may date from the second century A.D.[7] None of the dice is the familiar cube of modern gaming; two are the tarsal bone of a sheep and a third is a squared rod about the length of the bone dice. On both bone dice the numbers one and two are represented by the two ends unmarked. The narrower edges have three and four dots, the odd number in a cluster, the even with two dots drilled toward each end. But on one bone die, number five is indicated by the ogham for *V* as in Latin; on the other, five is indicated by two dots at each end and one in the center; on both, six has three dots at each end. The use of *V* for five makes clear that Roman numerals were known. The wooden die is marked, not with dots but with verti-

Figure 2 (Left) The Beithe-Luis-Nin with the names of the characters. Inscriptions should be read from the ground up.

Figure 3 (Below) Ogham characters in alphabetical order and written as in late manuscripts and on Pictish stones from eastern Scotland.

cal lines. Side three has one at each end and one in the center; side five has three vertical lines in the center—like the ogham *V* on one of the bone dice. The ogham letters are given in the traditional order in figure 2 in the form found on standing stones. But in manuscripts the arrangement is horizontal, and the vowels, mere notches on the edges of the stones, are drawn as vertical lines (fig. 3). The ogham letters in the beithe-luis-nin (the first, second, and fifth letters of ogham) are rearranged in alphabetical order (fig. 2). This form of ogham appears both in later manuscripts and on late monuments, as in eastern Scotland (Pictish).

As for the earliest form of ogham, many think it was derived from the Roman alphabet, although it is not in alphabetic order. Runes have a similarly unorthodox order, but the shapes of the characters reflect the classical alphabets, except for the avoidance of curves to facilitate carving. But ogham also abandoned the *abc* order and traditional character shapes and arranged its alphabet in groupings of five characters (fig. 2).

The arrangement in groups of five (runes are grouped in eight) led R. A. S. Macalister to suggest that originally the signs had been a finger language for transmitting the secret lore of the druids. But Vendryès's connection of ogham with tally rods

A B C D E F G H I L M N O Q R S T U Z NG

would account for it. Clearly nothing can be proved when speculating about origins that may well precede the introduction of writing. Ogham was never used for texts and only for very conventional records. Indeed it is an uneconomical form of writing, therefore the finger-language theory is attractive, for five fingers can be signed and read as rapidly as one. The lack of early evidence for the finger-language theory notwithstanding, the "Book of Ballymote," a folio vellum manuscript of the early fifteenth century, seems to offer a modicum of possible corroboration:

Cossogham = Leg Ogham: the fingers of the hand about the shinbone for the letters and to put them on the right of the shinbone for group B. To the left for group H. Athwart the shinbone for group M. Straight across for group A, viz. one finger for the first letter of the groups, two for the second letter, till it would reach five for the fifth letter of whichever group it be.[8]

Also listed are Nose ogham ("the fingers of the hand about the nose") and Palm ogham, where one hand strikes the other for the letters. Although this manuscript is much too late to prove that ogham began as a finger alphabet, it furnishes more indirect evidence than we have for any of the other theories about the origins of the script.

Ogham inscriptions are merely names in the genitive case, even the head word, "stone," "boundary," "grave," is omitted and we read: "of X the son [or grandson or descendant] of Y." Rudolf Thurneysen and Daniel Binchy, who had worked with the oldest Irish texts, the law tracts, thought these grammatical forms older than the fourth century. However, the Irish were frequent and clever archaizers and gave their writings a more august and ancient authority, just as they wrote of chariot fighting and scythed chariots in the late medieval and early modern retellings of their ancient battles. Richard Brash gives the following reading of a Gaedhil stone tomb: "of Toictheach son of Sagi Rettos" (fig. 4 is Brash's drawing of the stone and its reading).[9] The Gaedhil stone was found in Kerry, but many of these inscribed stones have been removed to museums for preservation; some have become lintels (thresholds above openings) and even the altars of churches. In his book, Brash shows not only ogham monuments but also small artifacts in metal or bone with ogham.

Carl Marstrander suggested that runes and ogham—the two sets of signs independent of alphabetical order—arose at the same time, perhaps while the peoples were close together in northern Italy.[10] But German scholars, notably Hermann Arntz, thought runes the older by a couple of centuries. Certainly the order of letters in these sets of signs is entirely unrelated, but since the discovery of the dice in Ballinderry Crannog II, Marstander's suggestion that the two writing systems might be contemporaneous cannot easily be discounted. I will return to this intriguing theory in more detail later.

Since the earliest work of John MacNeill, further stones have been discovered. Many had been used in souterrains and Christian churches. Françoise Henry describes the moving and misplacing of a stone with

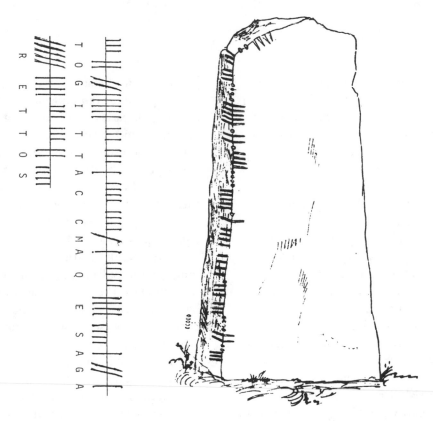

Figure 4 A drawing of an ogham inscription from Kerry, specifically from Cahernagat. Reprinted from Richard Rolf Brash, *The Ogam Inscribed Monuments of the Gaedhil in the British Islands* . . . (London: George Bell, 1879), pl. 25, discussion p. 220.

an ogham inscription at Killogrone.[11] In his later work John MacNeill considers the problem of archaizing by writing ogham markers in a language older than the current speech.[12]

In spite of such efforts, however, the scribes made errors, and from such occurrences as well as from whether the inscriptions run up one side and down the other of a stone or consistently from the bottom up, or even along a line (as in the later manuscripts and on the Pictish stones of Scotland), scholars have dated these inscriptions. Those running up and down or

up, across, and down are the oldest, determined by the absence of errors in archaization. Kenneth Jackson dates the Irish inscriptions from the fourth to sixth centuries in Ireland; the Welsh, which occur where Irish had settled, especially in the south and west, from the sixth perhaps to the eighth, and those in eastern Scotland still later, perhaps seventh to ninth.[13] Many of these are undecipherable and have been explained as composed in the Pictish language.[14] But because of the utter unintelligibility of many examples, Macalister also suggests that some of the stones may have been carved by imperfectly trained workers who were simply imitating the stones they had seen, and therefore the inscriptions were merely illiterate scribbles, or even that the inscribers were paid by the stroke and profited by doubling letters, even if they produced gibberish.[15] Some of the Welsh ogham and a few of the Pictish stones are accompanied by Latin, which made confirmation of readings easier.

In Irish studies we are fortunate that the Irish were so well trained and articulate. They have left detailed descriptions of verse forms with examples, chiefly for the later verse forms, and the information we have acquired about ogham is likewise from the later period as the old way of teaching by rote memory gave way to the special Irish modification of the Latin letters that we call Insular script. The table of ogham characters with their names and the interpretation of the names is chiefly from the "Book of Ballymote," which contains some much older material than its dating to the early fifteenth century would suggest.[16] The treatise on ogham is the *Auraicept na n-Eces* (the Scholars' primer). In the manuscript, a horizontal line is drawn and the fifth *aicme* (or fifth grouping of characters; fig. 2) contains additional letters necessary for making distinctions that developed when endings were lost and changes in the quality of consonants, phonetic or allophonic, became phonemic. The Irish call them *forfeda*.

There is another question about the ogham Beithe-Luis-Nin in figure 2: why is the order of characters different from other alphabets that we know? Vendryés gives a brief list of proposals.[17] Macalister—proceeding from a secret alphabet based on Chalcidic Greek—believes that the Germanic runic futhark was a source; Thurneysen and a number of later scholars hold

that the Latin alphabet was the origin. John Rhys derived it from Phoenician.[18] Considering the early date of contacts with the Continent and the possibility that ogham was, as Macalister has suggested, a finger language used by the druids to communicate religious rites to the novices, any of these might be the source. Some scholars have attempted to explain it as a system of ciphers, perhaps intended to confuse or to convey occult doctrine. James Carney frankly terms ogham a cipher and demonstrates how the Latin alphabet might have been written out to give the ogham order.[19] Thurneysen called attention to Donatus's arrangement of that alphabet for easier teaching in the schools.[20] Carney and Arntz mention this, but add that Quintilian had suggested such an arrangement about A.D. 95.[21] These early teachers had recognized classes of sounds: vowels, semivowels, mutes, and *y* and *z*, necessary only in Greek words. But within these categories (which were not just what we would include under these names) the letters were listed in alphabetical order. The Beithe-Luis-Nin has no such order in its four aicme, nor in the later fifth aicme, and by convention ogham is normally transcribed in capitals.

First, the vowels are represented in the fourth group, which begins with *A*. The *B* group is, however, first, and *B* is the first consonant. But *B* is not phonetically related to the rest of its group, which is made up of continuants. Nor is any group but the *A* group and perhaps the *M* aicme headed by a letter that has any clear reason for being in its group. Moreover, though rough breathing probably was used in early times as it is now, *H* was not used in writing any ogham inscriptions, nor was the Roman letter in the manuscripts until long after ogham had fallen into disuse. Yet *H* heads the second aicme. All the rest of that group are stops: *D/T C/Q*.

The third group is headed by *M* and followed by *G/NG*. These two are clearly related. Though hardly similar to these, *Z* and *R* are related to each other after a fashion, yet *Z* seems to have been pronounced *st-* as in spellings like Zefanus and Stefirus in the manuscripts. The association with *r* may have seemed natural because the cluster *s(t)-* is regularly followed by *r* in the names for the ogham in the manuscripts.

The additional letters, the forfeda, which form the fifth group are sometimes called the diphthongs, but clearly they are based chiefly on some of the Greek letters. *X* is chi, *O* is omicron and the double *X* to the right or below the line probably was originally called emoncholl, that is, double *C*. John MacNeill speculates that the Greek abbreviations chi-ro for Christos and ΙΗΣ for Iesu led to using the ogham sign for both *C* and *Ea*, that is, for *e* followed by a nonpalatal consonant.[22] These additions to the Beithe-Luis-Nin show that the distinction between palatal and nonpalatal consonants (phonemic when the endings were lost) were now recognized. In the original *A* group, vowel quality had been recognized in the order of vowels: *a/o/u* the back vowels, then the front vowels *e/i*.

Even more inventive were the Picts, who apparently tried to adapt ogham (learned from the Celts) to their own language.[23] They varied the ogham strokes by linking the tops and bottoms and sometimes bending such boxes, or the strokes at the line.

They carved inscriptions in the manuscript manner along a line. Macalister believes these new signs were vowels of Pictish, but they may have been added magic. Since we cannot read the signs and know nothing of the Pictish language, this interpretation remains, again, only a guess. Also, the forfeda and Pictish inscriptions are younger than the rest and are found only as late inscriptions.

Carl Marstrander suggests a plausible explanation that although the Celts knew both the Greek and Roman alphabets and their uses, runes and ogham came into use at about the same time in central Europe and mutually influenced each other.[24] He points to the similarity of the word "rune" in Germanic and Celtic. In Irish, *run* is "mystery" or "secret," later "secret love" = "darling," and in Germanic similar meanings have been offered (see Antonsen's interpretation in chapter 9 above). Moreover, the futhark (runic alphabet) is, as mentioned earlier, also in an unusual order, and its name is simply the letters in the order of runes. But neither is it in anything like the phonetic order of ogham. Yet ogham may have been influenced by it to the extent of heading the second aicme with *H*, as does the second *ætt*, the name for the division or groupings of the runes, of the futhark. The letter is not used in early inscriptions nor written in early Irish. Marstrander also points out that aicme and Old Norse *ætt* both mean "family" as well as "group." The Old Norse is thought to derive from "eight," for there are eight runes in an *ætt*. Marstrander points to the *Book of Ballymote*, which lists "vassal trees," of which there are eight, "noble trees," and shrubs, though these are more often seven. Furthermore a rune for *ng* parallels the third letter of the third aicme in ogham. Naming ogham characters for plants is probably a later development. Both Charles Graves and Howard Meroney have questioned the authority of these supposed plant names.[25] Thurneysen also had misgivings, but decides from the evidence that the names of the characters are late.[26]

The evidence of suspicious plant names is indicated on the table of the Beithe-Luis-Nin (see fig. 2). Doubts about the precise tree or plant are suggested in some of the names given (chiefly from glosses in the Royal Irish Academy's *Dictionary of the Irish Language*) and are strengthened by the fact that the only source for the name is the *Auraicept*. Meroney lists the only undeniable common plant names as *beithe, fern, sail, duir,* and *coll* (see fig. 2). One name that has been especially troublesome is that for *Q*. In the Salzburg text of the Gothic runes occurs the rune *gertra* as well as *pertra*, which might easily be doublets in Goidelic (Q-Celtic) and Brythonic (P-Celtic). Marstrander has suggested that the names are from just such a source, borrowed from the ogham name for *Q, ceirt*. Not all runic futharks have both *p* and *q*, but the names are regularly *peorth* and *cwearth,* the first probably is the modern Welsh *perth,* preserved in English in the Scottish (Pictish) name of a city, and meaning "bush," "brake," "hedge." In the Old English *Rune Poem,* the rune for *P* seems to have something to do with the joy in the hall and is

thought to have been the name of a board-game or of a chessman, or perhaps the specific material from which the men were carved. At any rate, it would seem that the Germanic names for *P* and *Q* came from the Celtic names for ogham characters.

René Derolez discusses the matter of runes and ogham. He especially points to St. Gall, where several Irish monks had had residence, as a center for the development of cryptographic ogham that he considers especially like the *isrunar* and *hahalrunar,* secret runes in Scandinavia.[27] There are, to be sure, very imperfect correspondences between ogham and any other alphabet. But with the discovery of the Ballinderry dice, the objection that ogham is too late to influence runes can be dismissed.

Although scholars have done much speculation about the sources, the age, the place of origin, and the ciphers that may account for the order of the characters, the only real facts we have are the inscriptions themselves. As is the case in the next chapter on the origins of ancient Chinese, the archaeologists have provided the surest and least questionable evidence for interpretation. It seems unlikely that the phonemic classes of the ogham characters could have been arrived at haphazardly through a fortuitous cipher. Only the Irish, imperfectly, and the Hindus, perfectly in the devanagari, have ordered their letters on a rational principle. The forms of ogham are the most easily inscribed of any alphabet, though the least challenge to the calligrapher. The script surely was developed long before we have any examples of ogham. It may have been a finger language and almost surely had been carved on wood before it was chiseled on stone. That is not much to know of a script, but beyond that we can only speculate.

••••••

Notes

1. Myles Dillon and Nora Chadwick, *The Celtic Realms* (London: Weidenfeldt and Nicolson, 1967), 3.

2. Julius Caesar, *The Conquest of Gaul*, trans. S. A. Handford (Harmondsworth, Engl.: Penguin Books, 1960), 32.

3. J. Vendryés, "L'écriture ogamique et ses origines," *Etudes Celtiques* 4 (1948): 83–116.

4. See L. J. D. Richardson, "Agma, a Forgotten Greek Letter," *Hermathena* 58 (1941): 57–69.

5. See Kenneth H. Jackson, "The Pictish Language," in *The Problem of the Picts*, ed. F. T. Wainwright (Westport, Conn.: Greenwood Press, 1956), 129–66.

6. See H. O'Neill Henken, *Ballinderry Crannog No. 2*, Proceedings of the Royal Irish Academy (*PRIA*) 47C no. 1 (1942).

7. Cited by Eoin Mac White, "Contributions to a Study of Ogam Memorial Stones," *Zeitschrift für Celtische Philologie* 28 (1961): 301.

8. George Calder, ed. and trans., *Auraicept na n-Eces*, chiefly from the "Book of Ballymote" (Edinburgh: John Grant, 1917), 297, BB 311, a 24.

9. Richard Rolf Brash, *The Ogam Inscribed Monuments of the Gaedhil in the British Islands. . . .* (London: George Bell, 1879), 220.

10. See Carl S. J. Marstrander, "Om Runene og Runenavnenes Oprindelse," *Norsk Tidskrift for Sprogvidenskap* 1 (1928): 88–188.

11. Françoise Henry, "Early Monasteries, Beehive Huts, and Dry-Stone Houses in the Neighbourhood of Caheraveen and Waterville (Co. Kerry)," *PRIA* 58C (1957): 45–166.

12. John MacNeill, "Archaisms in the Ogham Inscriptions," *PRIA* 39C (1929–31): 35–53.

13. Kenneth Jackson, "Notes on the Ogam Inscriptions of Southern Britain," in *Chadwick Memorial Studies:* *Early Cultures of Northwest Europe*, ed. Sir Cyril Fox and Bruce Dickins (Cambridge: Cambridge University Press, 1950), 197–214.

14. K. Jackson, "Pictish Language"; R. A. S. Macalister, "The Inscriptions and Language of the Picts," in *Essays and Studies Presented to Eoin MacNeill*, ed. Rev. John Ryan (Dublin, 1940), 184–226.

15. Jackson, *Pictish Language*, 129–66.

16. R. I. Best, *Bibliography of Irish Philology and of Printed Irish Literature*, 2 vols. (Dublin: Browne and Nolan, 1913; repr., Dublin: Dublin Institute for Advanced Studies, 1942), 64.

17. Vendryès, "L'écriture ogamique," 83–116.

18. John Rhys, *Lectures on Welsh Phonology* (London, 1877), 272–432.

19. James Carney, "The Invention of the Ogom Cipher," *Eriu* 26 (1975): 53–65.

20. Rudolf Thurneysen, "Zur Ogam," *Beiträge zur Geschichte der deutschen Sprache und Literatur* 61 (1937): 188–208.

21. Carney, "Invention of the Ogom Cipher," 53–65; Hermann Arntz, "Das Ogom," *Beiträge zur Geschichte der deutschen Sprache und Literatur* 59 (1935): 321–413.

22. See John MacNeill, "Notes on the Distribution, History, Grammar and Import of the Irish Ogham Inscriptions," *PRIA* 27C (1908–1909): 35–53.

23. R. A. S. Macalister, *The Secret Languages of Ireland* (Cambridge: Cambridge University Press, 1936), 106.

24. Marstrander, "Om Runene," 85–188.

25. Charles Graves, "The Ogham Alphabet," *Hermathena* 2 (1875–1876): 443–72; Howard Meroney, "Early Irish Letter-Names," *Speculum* 24 (1949): 19–43.

26. See Thurneysen, "Zur Ogam" 188–208.

27. René Derolez, *Runica Manuscripta: The English Tradition* (Brugge: "De Tempel," 1954), 154–61.

······

Further Readings

Arntz, Hermann, *Handbuch der Runenkunde: Sammlung kurzer Grammatiken germanischer Dialekte.* Halle:Niemeyer, 1935.

———. "Das Ogom." *Beiträge zur Geschichte der deutschen Sprache und Literatur* 59 (1935): 321–413.

Binchy, Daniel A. "The Background of Early Irish Literature." *Studia Hibernica* 1 (1961): 7–18.

Brash, Richard Rolf. *The Ogam Inscribed Monuments of the Gaedhil in the British Islands.* . . . London: George Bell, 1879.

Calder, George, ed. and trans. *Auraicept na n-Eces.* Chiefly from the *Book of Ballymote*. Edinburgh: John Grant, 1917.

Carney, James. "The Invention of the Ogom Cipher." *Eriu* 26 (1975): 53–65.

Derolez, René. *Runica Manuscripta: The English Tradition.* Brugge: "De Tempel," 1954.

Diack, F. C. "Origin of the Ogam Alphabet." *Scottish Gaelic Studies* 3 (1929): 86–91.

Gelb, I. J. *A Study of Writing: The Foundations of Grammatology.* Chicago: University of Chicago Press, 1952.

Graves, Charles, Lord Bishop of Limerick. "The Ogham Alphabet." *Hermathena* 2 (1875–76): 443–72.

Jackson, Kenneth H. *Language and History in Early Britain.* Edinburgh: Edinburgh University Press, 1953.

———. "Notes on the Ogam Inscriptions of Southern Britain." In *Chadwick Memorial Studies: Early Cultures of Northwest Europe*, ed. Sir Cyril Fox and Bruce Dickins, 197–214. Cambridge: Cambridge University Press, 1950.

———. "The Pictish Language" In *The Problem of the Picts*, ed. F. T. Wainwright, 129–66. Westport, Conn.: Greenwood Press, 1956.

Jensen, Hans. *Sign, Symbol, and Script.* 3d rev. and enl. ed. Trans. from the German by George Unwin, 579–82. London: Allen and Unwin. 1970.

Macalister, R. A. S. "The Inscriptions and Language of the Picts." In *Essays and Studies Presented to Eoin MacNeill*, ed. Rev. John Ryan, 184–226. Dublin: The Sign of the Three Candles, 1940.

———. "A New Ogham Inscription." *Journal of the Royal Society of Antiquaries* 72 (1942): 76.

———. *The Secret Languages of Ireland.* Cambridge: Cambridge University Press, 1936.

———. *The Archæology of Ireland.* London: Methuen, 1949.

———. *Corpus Inscriptionum Insularum Celticarum.* Vol. 1. Dublin: Stationery Office, 1945.

MacNeill, John. "Archaisms in the Ogham Inscriptions." *PRIA* 39C (1929–31): 35–53.

———. "Notes on the Distribution, History, Grammar and Import of the Irish Ogham Inscriptions." *PRIA* 27C (1908–09): 329–70.

MacWhite, Eoin. "Contributions to a Study of Ogam Memorial Stones." *ZCP* 28 (1961): 294–308.

Marstrander, Carl S. J. "Om Runene og Runenavnenes Oprindelse." *Norsk Tidskrift for Sprogvidenskap* 1 (1928): 85–188.

Meroney, Howard. "Early Irish Letter-Names." *Speculum* 24 (1949): 19–43.

Plummer, C. "On the Meaning of Ogam Stones." *R.C.* 40 (1923): 387–90.

Raftery, Joseph. "A Suggested Chronology of the Irish Iron Age." *Essays and Studies Presented to Professor Eoin MacNeill.* Dublin: The Sign of the Three Candles, 1940.

Rhys, John. *Lectures on Welsh Phonology: Lectures vi and vii*, 272–432. London, 1877.

Thurneysen, Rudolf. *A Grammar of Old Irish.* Translated from the German by D. A. Binchy and Osborn Bergin. Dublin: The Dublin Institute for Advanced Studies, 1961.

———. "Zur Ogom" *Beiträge zur der deutschen Sprache und Literatur* 61 (1937): 188–208.

Vendryès, J. 1948. "L'ecriture ogamique et ses origines." *Etudes celtiques* 4 (1948): 83–116.

11

The Origins of Writing in China: Scripts and Cultural Contexts

......

David N. Keightley

......

The Significance of the Topic

The origins of writing are closely associated with the great shift from Neolithic culture to Bronze Age civilization. This shift is of particular interest in China, where it occurred roughly in the second millennium B.C., because it lies at the genesis of one of the world's great civilizations and because it largely occurred in isolation. The writing system that emerged was, like most of the features of China's Bronze Age civilization, indigenous.[1]

The origins of writing in China are also of particular interest because there have been few cultures where high literacy, high civilization, and aesthetic prowess have been so intimately combined. Literacy in China involved not only a profound knowledge of the written classics but also the ability to wield a brush effectively, either to paint a landscape, usually with a poem inscribed at its side, or to write Chinese characters in a way that conveyed not just their meaning but also their aesthetic vitality and the taste of their composer. As Michael Sullivan has put it:

> From the merchant who hoists up his newly written shop-sign with ceremony and incense to the poet whose soul takes flight in the brilliant sword-dance of the

brush, calligraphy is revered above all other arts. Not only is a man's writing a clue to his temperament, his moral worth and his learning, but the uniquely ideographic nature of the Chinese script has charged each individual character with a richness of content and association the full range of which even the most scholarly can scarcely fathom.[2]

A man absorbed with writing was absorbed not just with words but with symbols and, through the act of writing with the brush, with a form of painting and thus with the world itself. To the lover of high culture, the way in which something was written could be as important as its content.

There is still a third reason why the origins of Chinese writing are of interest: namely, the seminal and overriding importance of Chinese script in the general history of East Asia. It is hard for us today to conceive of the cultural dominance that imperial China exerted over Korea, Japan, and much of Southeast Asia. China was to this area what the Near East, Greece, and Rome were to Europe. China was the source of all high culture, and its influence, including that of its writing system, was accordingly great during the early periods when civilization was developing in the neighboring countries.

This influence derived in part from China's early start. China was developing an advanced Bronze Age civilization by about the middle of the second millennium B.C., well before the surrounding areas reached such a stage. The influence also derived from the remarkable attractive-

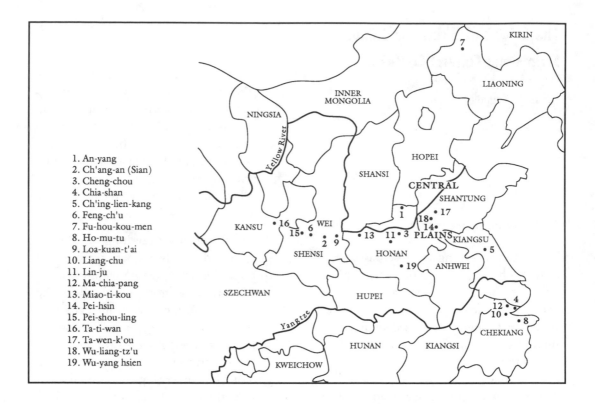

Map of Sites Referred to in This Chapter

ness of Chinese civilization, including its writing system. The majestic words with which Edward Gibbon opened his *Decline and Fall of the Roman Empire*—"In the second century of the Christian era, the Empire of Rome comprehended the fairest part of the earth and the most civilized portion of mankind"—might equally well have been applied to the empire of China in the middle of the second century before Christ, and certainly to several high points of the dynastic cycle since. China's impact on Japan from the Nara period of the seventh century onward, to cite but one example, was immense. Nara was modeled on the T'ang

capital of Ch'ang-an (see map), and its administration, law codes, court rituals and ceremonies, and even Buddhist religion, were all based on Chinese prototypes. The Chinese writing system, with its multistroke characters and its emphasis on elegant calligraphy, was a key element in this wave of sinification.

......

The Evolution of Chinese Writing

In tracing the evolution of Chinese writing I shall move from the known to the lesser known, proceeding backward from two Han-dynasty scripts, the *li shu* and *hsiao chuan,* whose graphs were quite similar in appearance to those of modern times, to the Shang-dynasty script, which was truly archaic; my account, for which the graphic

Table 1 Principles and Graphic Evolution of Chinese Writing: Pictographs

Modern pronunciation / meaning	Oracle-bone form (Shang dynasty)	Greater seal (W. Chou)	Lesser seal (E. Chou-Han)	Modern form (3d cent. A.D. on)
Objects				
1. *jen* / man				
2. *nü* / woman				
3. *erh* / ear				
4. *yü* / fish				
5. *jih* / sun				
6. *yueh* / moon				
7. *yü* / rain				
8. *ting* / cauldron				
9. *ching* / well				
Relationships				
10. *shang* / above				
11. *hsia* / below				

Table 2 Principles and Graphic Evolution of Chinese Writing: Phonetic Loans and Homophones

Archaic / modern pronunciation; meaning	Oracle-bone form (Shang dynasty)	Greater seal (W. Chou)	Lesser seal (E. Chou-Han)	Modern form (3d cent. A.D. on)
12. *ləg / lai (a) weed, plant	朩		茉	萊
(b) to come			來	來
13.1. *tiěng / cheng to divine	貞	鼎	貞	貞
13.2. *ȶiěng / cheng to regulate	正	正	正	正

Note: Archaic pronunciations are indicated by an asterisk.

Table 3 Principles and Graphic Evolution of Chinese Writing: Phonetic + Semantic Compounds—*hsieh sheng,* "corresponding in sound"

Archaic / modern pronunciation	Modern meaning	Modern graph
14. *təng / teng	lamp	燈
15. *d'iəng / ch'eng	strain, filter	澄
16. *dz'iěng / ching	quiet, chaste	姘
17. *dz'iěng / ching	hole, pitfall, snare	穽
18. *tâ / to	many	多
19. *t'â / t'o	tired, sick	痑
20. *t'ia / ch'ih	take away	拸
21. *dia / yi	move	迻

Note: Archaic pronunciations are indicated by an asterisk.

Table 4 Principles and Graphic Evolution of Chinese Writing: Phonetic + Semantic Compounds—*hui yi,* "combining the meaning"

Archaic / modern pronunciation	Modern meaning / semantic elements	Oracle-bone graph	Modern graph
22. **miǎng / ming*	bright (moon + sun or window)		明
23. **χôg / hao*	good (woman + child)		好
24. **·ân / an*	peace (woman + roof)		安
25. **t̞iông / chung*	multitude (three men + sun)		衆

Note: Archaic pronunciations are indicated by an asterisk.

evidence is adumbrated in tables 1–4, is inevitably simplified. In the second half of this chapter I will consider one possible scenario for the earliest development of the Chinese writing system.

Li shu 隸書

The so-called *li shu,* "clerkly script" or script of people of low status, was characterized by its rapid, flowing strokes that were suited to the needs of the clerks who staffed the growing imperial bureaucracy of the Han dynasty (206 B.C.–A.D. 220). The marked differences in the width of those strokes gave the graphs a varied and aesthetically pleasing appearance and promised future calligraphers considerable freedom of expression (fig. 1). The *li shu* was not invented all at once; it probably existed in rudimentary form as far back as the time of Confucius in the sixth century B.C., if not earlier.

Hsiao chuan 小篆

The clerkly script is traditionally thought to have evolved from an earlier script known as *hsiao chuan,* "lesser seal"—"seal" referring to the fact that its graphs were engraved or cast on the seals or "chops" of wood, ceramic, or bronze by which administrators, in particular, would sign their documents and letters. The characters look carved, the strokes being unmodulated, of uniform width, and rather mechanical and geometric in appearance (fig. 2). The austerity, dignity, balance, and symmetry of the graphs is well captured in the traditional appellations for the script: *t'ieh hsien,* "iron wires," or *yü chin,* "jade muscles." The lesser-seal calligraphy reproduced in figure 2 is a late copy, supposedly of the inscription on a stele erected by Ch'in Shih Huang Ti, the First Emperor, two years after he unified China in 221 B.C.; the stele was one of six "propaganda posters" he erected in various parts of China, praising his benevolent rule.[3] Political unity was reinforced by the unification of many aspects of culture, involving the various regional writing systems that had flourished during the Eastern Chou. Ch'in Shih Huang Ti's prime minister, Li Ssu, is, in fact, credited with inventing the lesser-seal script and standardizing both the size and the shape of its characters. The Ch'in state in general and Li Ssu in particular relied heavily on totalitarian methods of social control, and one can understand how critics of the Ch'in have seen these totalitarian qualities reflected in the rigidity of its graph forms. Such retrospective prejudices aside, *hsiao chuan* remained the script for formal official writing during the Han dynasty. It continues in use to this day in certain consciously archaicizing contexts, such as posters and greeting cards, and even in advertisements with cultural pretensions.

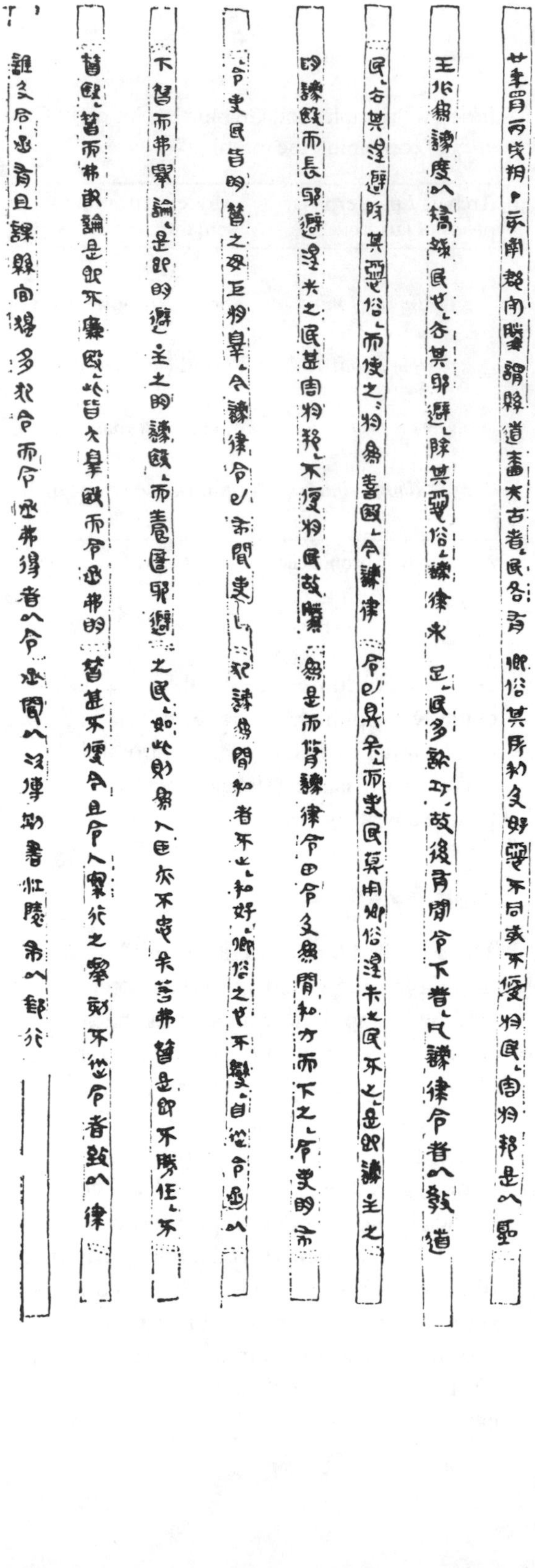

Figure 1 The rapid, modulated strokes of the *li shu,* or "clerkly script" (presented here in a modern hand copy, for clarity of reproduction). The text is a letter, consisting of 327 characters on eight bamboo strips, from the Ch'in Governor of the Southern Commandery to his subordinates. The document starts (right strip, reading from the top): "In the twentieth year [227 B.C.], the beginning of the fourth month, the days ping-hsu (day 23) and ting-hai (day 24)." The days were numbered according to the sixty-day calendrical cycle that had been in operation since at least Shang times (see the dating formulas given in the captions to figs. 4, 6, and 7 below). "'Nan-chün shou T'eng wen-shu' ho Ch'in ti fan fu-pi tou-cheng." Reprinted from *K'ao-ku* 1976.5: 307, fig. 1.

Ta chuan 大篆

Moving back into the Western Chou and Late Shang dynasties (twelfth to eighth centuries B.C.), it is evident that the lesser-seal script evolved from what has been called the *ta chuan*, "greater seal," script (also known as *chou wen* 籀文). This was the style of writing used in the numerous inscriptions cast into the bronze vessels, both secular and sacred, of the Late Shang and, in far greater numbers, the Chou dynasties (figs. 3, 4). Since the inscriptions are generally intaglio in the body of the vessels, one can see that skillful carving of clay was required to produce these results. Various methods were employed, but in general, designs were first written with brush and ink

Figure 2 A tenth-century rubbing of what may have been a recarving of the *hsiao chuan* script on the stone stele erected by Ch'in Shih Huang Ti on Mount Yi in southern Shantung in 219 B.C. Reprinted from Jung Keng, "Ch'in Shih Huang k'e-shih k'ao," pl. 1.

on a clay surface; the graphs were then cut into the clay to produce an intaglio mold; from that mold, a negative clay cast of the inscription, in relief, was made, and that clay, bearing the "negative" of the inscription, was inserted into the outside of the clay model which was to form the central core about which the outer piece molds were then placed (fig. 5).[4] The calligraphy of these greater-seal inscriptions, accordingly, as we see it in the bronze vessels, betrays its carved, seal-like, ceramic origins, again manifesting, as the lesser seal was to do, rather stiff and mechanical qualities. The form was a product of the technology.

Figure 3   A Late Shang *ta-chuan* inscription cast on the inside of the so-called Rhinoceros *tsun*, a wine vessel in the shape of a rhinoceros, which is now in the Avery Brundage Collection, Asian Art Museum, San Francisco. Reading down the columns, and reading the columns from right to left, the twenty-six-character inscription, which has been dated to the first part of the eleventh century B.C., may be translated as follows: *col. 1:* "On the day ting-ssu [day 54 of the 60-day cycle], the king inspected the ancestral temple of K'uei"; *col. 2:* "The king bestowed upon the Junior Servitor, Yü, cowrie shells from K'uei"; *col. 3:* "It was the time when the king came from attacking the Jen-fang. It was [*col. 4:*] the king's 15th sacrificial cycle, a Yung-ritual day." Reprinted with permission from Noel Barnard and Cheung Kwong-yue, *Rubbings and Hand Copies of Bronze Inscriptions in Chinese, Japanese, European, American, and Australian Collections* (Taipei: Yee Wen, 1978), 318.

Figure 4 A *ta-chuan* inscription on the *Li kuei,* an early Western Chou bronze vessel excavated in 1976. My tentative translation reads: *col. 1, on the right:* "It was when King Wu was campaigning against the Shang, the morning of that chia-tzu (day 1) when Jupiter [*col. 2:*] was regulating (the year). I (Li) was able to report: 'By dusk, we have the Shang.' On hsin-wei (day 8), [*col. 3:*] the king being in the Chien encampment, awarded bronze to (me) the Manager of Affairs, Li. [*col. 4:*] I thereupon made this treasured and honored vessel for Sire T'an." "Shanhsi Lin-t'ung fa-hsien Wu Wang cheng Shang kuei," *Wen-wu* 1977.8:2.

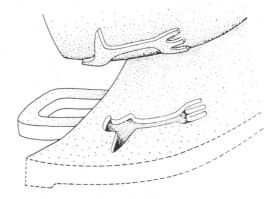

Figure 5 Relievo character on the outer surface of the clay core (*top*), cast as an intaglio normal character into the inner wall of the bronze vessel (*bottom*). Reprinted with permission from Noel Barnard, from *Bronze Casting and Bronze Alloys in Ancient China,* Monumenta Serica Monograph 14 (Tokyo: Monumenta Serica, 1961), 158, fig. 50.

Chia-ku wen 甲骨文

The bronze inscriptions represented the earliest Chinese writing known until the turn of the century, when the discovery and gradual decipherment of what has come to be called oracle-bone inscriptions (literally, *chia-ku wen,* "writings on [turtle] shell and [animal] bone") revolutionized our understanding of the origins of the Chinese script. These inscriptions (figs. 6, 7) were written by scribes of the Shang (also known as Yin) dynasty, which dominated significant areas of the Central Plains from about the middle of the sixteenth to the middle of the eleventh century B.C.[5]

The true worth of these precious objects was not appreciated until 1899, but the political and military upheavals of the war-lord era, the Sino-Japanese War, and

Figure 6 Rubbing of an inscribed Shang oracle bone (*Ping-pien* 247) from the reign of Wu Ting (ca. 1200–1180 B.C.). Numbered cracks may be seen at the bottom of the half plastron, running "1," "2," "3," from the central spine outward to left and right in the top row, with "4," "5," and (on the right side) "6" on the bottom row. The inscription on the right, starting on the right edge and reading the columns from top to bottom, may be translated as follows: (Preface:) "Crack-making on chia-shen (day 21), Ch'ueh divined:" (Charge:) "Fu Hao's childbearing will be good." (Prognostication:) "The king, reading the cracks, said: 'If it be a ting day childbearing, it will be good. If it be keng day childbearing, it will be extremely auspicious.'" (Verification:) "On the thirty-first day, chia-yin (day 51), she gave birth. It was not good. It was a girl." The inscription on the left side is virtually identical, except that the charge is in the negative mode ("Fu Hao's childbearing may not be good") and the inscription starts on the left edge and runs toward the center.

Figure 7 Photograph of an inscribed scapula (*Ching-hua* 4, reduced 58 percent), also from the reign of Wu Ting. Starting from the right and reading downward, the three right columns record the following divinatory results: [col. 1] (Prognostication:) "The king, reading the cracks, said: 'There will be harm.'" (Verification:) "On the eighth day, keng-hsu (day 47), there was . . . [col. 2] arriving clouds from the east and [two graphs of uncertain meaning]; in the afternoon, there was also . . . [col. 3] the coming out of a rainbow (the third graph, depicting a two-headed snake) from the north which drank in the (Yellow) River."

the subsequent civil war considerably delayed the scientific excavation and decipherment of the Shang oracle-bone inscriptions, which came primarily from An-yang in the northern Honan panhandle. Thanks, however, to the labors of dedicated scholars in China and Japan and, to a lesser extent, in other parts of the world, we are now in a position to start using the oracle bones as historical documents for the reigns of the last nine Shang kings (ca. 1200 to 1045 B.C.). The historical value of these inscriptions is all the greater because they

lay in the ground for some three thousand years, unknown to the authors of the Chinese Classics, to scholars, and to Confucian editors; the result is that they have come down to us unmediated by revisionist interpretations or errors in transmission. They are the actual bones themselves that the Shang king or his officers had handled and, given their inscribed flat surfaces, they are ideal for the making of mechanically accurate rubbings. More than 150,000 pieces of oracle bone have now been recovered, a figure that may represent about 10 percent of the number originally engraved. Inscribed turtle plastrons and cattle scapulas, some of considerable historical importance, continue to be excavated.[6]

The oracle-bone inscriptions, the earliest body of writing we yet possess for East Asia and written in a script that was ancestral to all subsequent forms of Chinese writing, merit our particular attention. An oracle bone was either a turtle plastron (fig. 6) —turtle carapaces were used occasionally —or a cattle scapula (fig. 7) that had been used in a form of divination known as plastromancy or scapulimancy, depending on the material used.[7] The diviner took the bone and applied heat to it so as to produce stress cracks; the cracks were then "read" in some way to foretell the future. This form of pyromancy was widespread in human history, being found throughout much of Asia and as far east as Labrador in North America. It was only the Chinese, however, who carved the subject matter of their divinations into the bone itself.

The practice is possibly far older, but the earliest pyromancy that has left archaeological traces in China may be dated to about the middle of the fourth millennium B.C. (at Fu-ho-kou-men in Liaoning), with the cracks being formed in a random manner. By the time of the Shang dynasty, however, the diviners were drilling and boring a series of regular hollows in the backs of the bones (fig. 8); they applied the heat at these weakened points to produce a series of highly regular cracks on the bone front. These cracks, generally numbered from one to five (as in fig. 6), provided the framework, as it were, around which the diviners or their scribes incised the divination record.

Although most of the oracle-bone records were carved into the bone, a few have been found in which the writing was actually done by a brush in red or black ink (fig. 9). As the illustration reveals, however, the aesthetic influence of the brush appears to have been minimal; the brush-written script looks stiff and angular, resembling the carved script. That the Shang scribes could have written all their inscriptions with a brush but chose not to do so raises the interesting question of why they expended considerable time and labor to carve the characters into the bones. One cannot be sure of the answer, but two facts are suggestive. First, the diviners also carved out some of the cracks as well, rendering them deeper and more visible, and second, the diviners frequently filled the incised graphs and the cracks with red- or black-colored pigments. These practices suggest that the carving itself served some

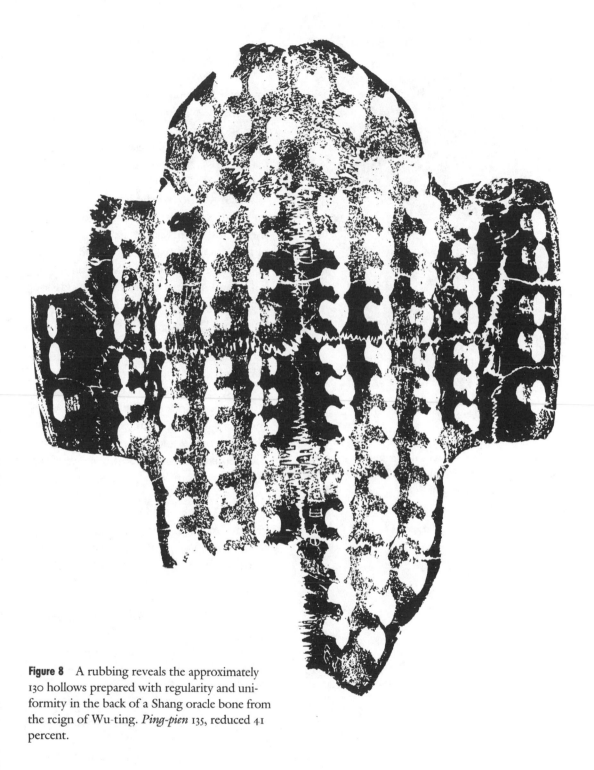

Figure 8 A rubbing reveals the approximately 130 hollows prepared with regularity and uniformity in the back of a Shang oracle bone from the reign of Wu-ting. *Ping-pien* 135, reduced 41 percent.

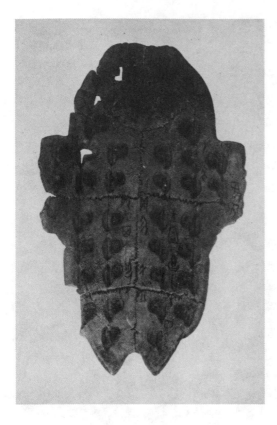

Figure 9 Oracle-bone writing written by a brush in red ink on the back of a turtle plastron, *Yi-pien* 3380; Tung Tso-pin, *Chia-ku-hsueh liu-shih nien* (Taipei: Yi-wen, 1965), pl. 40.

aesthetic function—permitting the coloration of the writing—and that it may also have served some magical function in which the actual carving, by establishing a sympathy between the crack and the record, helped to "fix" or induce the desired event.

When we turn to the graphs recorded on the oracle bones, we can see that there was considerable continuity between many of the Shang forms and the graphs subsequently used to write *ta chuan, hsiao chuan, li shu,* and modern Chinese; the kinds of graphic filiations involved may be seen in tables 1, 2, and 4. Literate Chinese of today, untutored in oracle-bone script, would probably find much of it incomprehensible at first glance—and it is true that many Shang graphs have no modern descendants, just as many modern graphs have no Shang ancestors—but after only a few moments of study they would begin to see the connections and begin to identify some of the early graph forms that preceded those of the modern script.

A particularly striking instance of both graphic and semantic continuity may be seen in the inscription recorded in figure 7. The prognostication recorded the appearance of a rainbow—depicted as a snake or dragon with heads at both ends—which the Shang, unlike the authors of the Book of Genesis, regarded as ominous. More than thirteen hundred years later, in the second century A.D., Han-dynasty shrine reliefs at Wu-liang-tz'u in southwest Shantung portray the same arched, two-headed dragon in a struggle with the spirits of wind and rain (fig. 10). The dragon-cum-rainbow apparently symbolized the forces of drought.[8] In this instance, early graph form and later iconography belong to the same tradition of representation.

The content of another Shang divination, which, like the previous example, may be dated to the reign of the powerful king, Wu Ting (ca. 1200 to 1180 B.C.), is translated in the caption to figure 6. The verification tells us much about the dominant role of the male in dynastic and religious matters, but several other observations may also be made. First, one should note that there was a remarkable symmetry in placement of the positive charge ("Fu Hao's childbearing will be good") on the right side and of the negative charge ("Fu Hao's childbearing may not be good") on the left side of the plastron; both charges start at the outer edge and are written downward in columns which move toward the central spine. The same symmetry may be observed in the T-shaped cracks whose horizontal arms also run from right and left toward the center. Second, this inscription bears on the important legitimating role of these records. It clearly would not have been to the Shang king's advantage to employ scribes who would carve into bone a record of his divinatory mistakes. The king's reputation, much like that of modern leaders, depended in part upon his ability to present himself as a successful forecaster. It seems to have been a general rule, accordingly, that when a verification was recorded—not all divination charges were provided with verifications—the Shang king was virtually never shown to have been wrong.[9] In the case of the inscription reproduced in figure 6, the king made auspicious forecasts for ting- and keng-day childbearings (rather like saying "if the child is born on Tuesday or Friday, that will be good"—except that the Shang used a ten-day week); the baby in fact was born on a chia day and the birth was "not good." The king's reputation as diviner was protected, because he had made no prognostication about a chia day.

Finally, one may note the bureaucratic nature of Shang pyromancy. Not only were the hollows drilled in the back of the bone with great regularity (fig. 8), not only were the cracks themselves numbered (fig. 6), not only were the divinations frequently paired in positive and negative mode (fig. 6), but there was evidently some kind of filing system that enabled sets of bones and shells to be reused over a certain period of time. By the reigns of the last Shang kings, not only were many hunting inscriptions divined in the field and then returned to the cult center at An-yang for storage, but certain scapulas were being reserved exclusively for particular topics, such as the royal hunt or the luck of the coming ten-day week, and were used over a period of several weeks, if not several months. The longest span between one divination charge and its verification, in fact, appears to have covered some 170-odd days in the reign of king Wu Ting, during which time, presumably, the divining staff had kept track of the bone in question.[10] The inscription format itself, of course, with its prefatory record of the date and the name of the diviner (fig. 6), may also be seen as bureaucratic in nature.

The Origins of Writing in China

There is little doubt that Chinese writing was entirely indigenous. Its system of graphs developed without any genetic connection to Sumerian, Egyptian, or Hittite written forms.[11] The argument, however, that certain scratches (fig. 11) found on Neolithic pots at Yang-shao culture sites such as Pan-p'o village, just east of Sian in the Wei River valley, represented numerals and were thus the earliest attempt to create a script anywhere in the world is unconvincing for a number of reasons. In the first place, it is not likely that the peoples of Neolithic China in the fifth millennium B.C. needed a writing system; their culture, so far as we can recover it from the archaeological record, was not yet sufficiently complex. Second, it is almost inconceivable that, had the inhabitants of China invented writing at this time, they

Figure 10 Portion of a second-century A.D. tomb relief from Wu-liang-tz'u in Shantung. The second register is thought to depict the legendary struggle between "a water-concentrating reptilian rainbow" (on the right) sent by the Yellow Lord, and the Wind Baron and the Rain Master (on the left), summoned by Ch'ih Yu to resist the drought that the Yellow Lord had sent (Berger, "Rites and Festivities," 38–42). Edouard Chavannes, *Mission archéologique dans la Chine septentrionale: Planches*, Publications de l'école française d'extrême orient (Paris: Leroux, 1909), pl. 68, no. 132; *Mission archéologique . . . : La Sculpture à l'époque des Han*, Publications de l'école française d'extrême orient, vol. 13 (Paris: Leroux, 1913), 240–41.

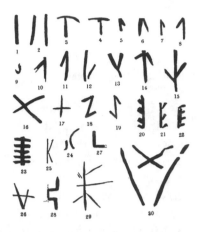

Figure 11 Scratches found on Neolithic pots from Pan-p'o village, Sian, Shensi. Reprinted from *Hsi-an Pan-p'o* (Peking: Wen-wu, 1963), 197, fig. 141.

would have taken more than three thousand years to develop it to the stage represented by the oracle-bone inscriptions of the Shang. Finally, to the extent that one would expect the earliest writing to be pictographic in nature, these scratches do not qualify.[12] It is conceivable that the marks represented signs or symbols, but there was certainly no attempt to record a sequence of *words*. The scratches may have been part of a human marking system; they were not yet part of a *Chinese* writing system.

The principles of the early writing system

In turning to the origins of Chinese writing, which, once the basic idea had been invented, may have evolved quite rapidly, it is important to comment briefly on the various principles of graph formation we can discern in the Shang script. These principles continue in use to this day and they also bear on the nature of the invention itself. As entries 1–9 in table 1 reveal, the

simplest—and presumably, the earliest—graphs were pictures: of men, body parts, animals, the sun and the moon, falling rain, vessels, and so on. Such a use of pictures is, of course, found at the origin of writing systems throughout the world; in the absence of precise and consistent graphic and phonetic similarities between early writing systems, the use of pictographs must be understood as representing only an analogous developmental stage, not a homologous genetic connection. The writers of early Chinese also developed pictorial symbols to express relationships like "above" or "below" (table 1, entries 10–11). Since, however, we cannot always be sure if a graph was written for its pictographic accuracy or its phonetic value, "pictograph" can be an ambiguous analytical category.

The question of pictography is of some importance because even early Chinese writing, *as writing*, was logographic and not, as is frequently claimed, ideographic. That is to say, the Chinese, once they were writing true writing, were using graphs to record *words*; they were not using them to draw pictures or ideas even though pictographic elements may originally have been used to construct the logographs and record the sounds of the words.[13] The Chinese, in other words, were using their writing system then, as they do now, to record their spoken language. Thus, the word *lai*, "to come," was actually written with a picture of a weed or plant; this was because the word for growing grain had the same pronunciation and could thus be "loaned" to write the nongrain word (table 2, entry 12). The principle was essentially that of the rebus in which we might draw a picture of a pear, for example, to write the word "pair." As in the case of the early pictographs discussed above, use of the rebus principle, which is found in many early writing systems, provides no evidence, by itself, of any genetic connection between such systems.

The early Chinese used this principle of borrowing the sound of one word to help write another word extensively, but in many cases they did not signal what they were doing. Thus, when we see a graph drawn like a *ting*-cauldron (table 1, entry 8) —a graph that was a standard part of the divination preface in the oracle-bone inscriptions—we cannot assume that it meant "cauldron" (though it may have).[14] What we can tell is that this was the way the Shang chose to write, that is, to "spell," one of a number of homophones that all had the archaic sound of **tieng,* one of which meant "cauldron" (modern pronunciation, *ting*) but another of which meant "to divine," another "to regulate," and so on (these two words, entries 13.1 and 13.2 in table 2, are now generally pronounced *cheng*).[15]

One of the major difficulties in deciphering early inscriptions derives precisely from this "looseness" of the spelling system and the irregularity with which early scribes equipped, as it were, their naked phonetic symbols with semantic clothing. Just as Shakespeare spelled his own name in a variety of ways, Shang and particularly Western Chou scribes might spell the same word with a variety of different phonetic graphs, a variety of different "rebuses," recording the sounds inconsistently and ambiguously. The difficulties are well illustrated by the start of the inscription on the *Li kuei,* a

vessel found in 1976 in a cache of Western Chou bronze items some thirty kilometers east of Sian.[16] The thirty-two-character inscription (fig. 4), written in elegant *ta chuan* calligraphy, records a royal gift made only eight days after the Chou conquered the Shang on January 15, 1045 B.C.; it is, accordingly, a document of major historical importance.[17] While there is little disagreement about the meaning of the first seven characters in the right-hand column, there is, as yet, no agreement about the meaning of the next five characters or even their punctuation. Several, though not all, scholars agree that the last graph in the right-hand column, for example, should be read as *sui,* but whether the word meant "the year" or "Jupiter (the planet)" is unclear. There is no doubt that the next graph, at the top of the next column, is a picture of a ting cauldron, but whether the word being written meant "cauldron," "regulate," "divine," or even "then," is much contested. As a result, a number of conflicting translations for just these two graphs alone (italicized in the passages below) are possible: *"Jupiter being in the (proper) position. . . ."*; *"performed the sui-sacrifice and divined"*; *"'Sacrifice to Jupiter, then* victory'"; ". . . performed the dawn *sui-sacrifice by means of a cauldron,"* and so on.[18]

The confusion inherent in such a system was resolved in two ways: first, by the standardization of the phonetic forms chosen to write particular words, and second, by the development, at an early stage, of another principle of graph formation—the writing of compound graphs (traditionally classified as *hsieh-sheng* 諧聲 , literally, "corresponding in sound," or *hsing-sheng* 形聲 , literally, "shape [i.e., the meaning] and sound," compounds) which were constructed by combining semantic classifiers with phonetic elements. In these cases we have, as it were, rebuses with signals attached, as if one drew a pear with a "2" beside it to indicate "pair." The graph for *lai,* a growing grain, for example, was distinguished from the homophonic *lai,* "to come," by the addition of a semantic classifier meaning "grass" or "vegetation" (table 2, entry 12). Similarly, the graph for *ching* (table 1, entry 9), which depicted a view from above of the "Lincoln log"-style frame used to line a well, served as a phonetic symbol in other words that had the same or similar pronunciation (table 3, entries 16, 17). The most important point is that, in the early stages of the script, many of the meanings of *ching*—"well," "quiet, chaste," "hole, pitfall, snare"—could have been written with the "unclothed" phonetic; the *hsieh-sheng* graphs provide the semantic clothes. The semantic classifier served as the ideograph, for it indicated the idea, not the word. In China, as in Egypt and Mesopotamia, these semantic classifiers, somewhat misleadingly referred to in Western textbooks about Chinese as "radicals," were secondary, "nonradical" accretions, added to avoid homophonic confusion.[19]

Graphs constructed with these semantic classifiers were already in use by the time of the Shang dynasty, as figure 12 reveals. We cannot tell, without detailed study, if all the 190-plus Shang graphs in this section of the concordance index necessarily had a "wooden" meaning. In many cases, no modern descendant exists, or we are dealing with a proper name whose "woodenness" cannot be ascertained, or both. Nevertheless, it may be crudely estimated that over 50 percent of all oracle-bone graphs were of this compound form.[20] The eventual adoption and standardization of these *hsieh-sheng* spellings naturally involved larger cultural and political questions; it was only in reforms after the unification of China in 221 B.C., accordingly, that a national system of spelling and writing, alluded to in the discussions of *hsiao chuan* and *li shu* above, was eventually established.

What at first glance appears to be another principle of graph formation has been called *hui yi* 會意 , "combining the meaning," by Chinese scholars. Graphs traditionally assigned to this category (table 4) were, like the *hsieh-sheng* graphs that combined semantic and phonetic elements, also constructed according to what might be called the componential principle, the ability to combine semantic and graphic elements to create new graphs to record different words. For example, as entry 22 in table 4 reveals, "moon" (table 1, entry 6; now pronounced *yueh*) and "sun" (table 1, entry 5; *jih*), or moon and window (*ch'uang*) appear to have been written together to form the word "bright" (now pronounced *ming*); a woman element (*nü*; table 1, entry 2) was combined with a child element (*tzu*) to form the word "good" (*hao*; table 4, entry 23); a woman element (*nü*; table 1, entry 2) was also placed under a roof to form the word "safety, peace" (*an*; table 4, entry 24), and so on. It has traditionally been thought that these combinatory graphs were entirely semantic in their inspiration, so that the sun and moon conceived in combination,

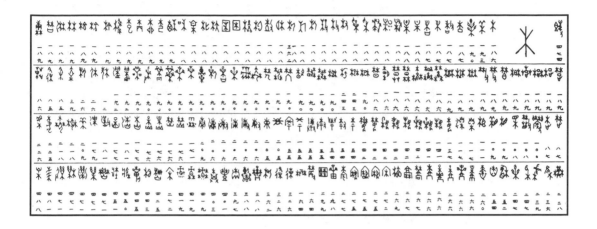

Figure 12 Oracle-bone graphs composed with the "wood" or "tree" classifier. Reprinted with permission from Shima Kunio, *Inkyo bokuji sōrui*, 2d rev. ed. (Tokyo: Kyūko, 1971), 595.

or the moon shining on a window, had suggested the use of the two elements to write the word for "bright," that a woman with a child was "good," and so on. While such explanations cannot yet be universally rejected, recent research suggests that in such cases one of the graphic elements was chosen for its phonetic, as well as its semantic, role, even though that phonetic reading may have been a secondary one that, as the above examples demonstrate, is not now easily discernible; if further study proves this to be true, then *hui yi* graphs would, in origin, have been nothing more than *hsieh-sheng* graphs, combining elements of sound and meaning, rather than combining elements of meaning and meaning.[21]

One final comment on the composition of early Chinese graphs is in order. Although the *hsieh-sheng* principle of combining semantic and phonetic elements to write homophonic words in distinctive ways offers a potentially systematic way of spelling Chinese characters, so that, for example, every graph containing the element 多 (table 3, entry 18), modern pronunciation *to*, ought to be pronounced *to* today, the purity of the principle either never existed in fact or was corrupted at an early date. Unlike Sumerian signs, Chinese graphs seem to have been rarely endowed with multiple semantic and radically different phonetic values; in a large number of cases, however, the same phonetic element was used to write words whose sounds were close but not identical. Subsequent sound changes, resulting from these originally minor dissimilarities, have led to the existence of graphs containing the same phonetic element whose modern pronunciations are, nevertheless, extremely dissimilar; an archaic **ta* has become modern *to*, a **t'a* has become *t'o*, a **t'ia* has become *ch'ih*, a *dia* has become *yi* (table 3, entries 18–21). This "breakdown" in the spelling system is one reason why it may be harder today than it was two thousand years ago to learn to write Chinese; many graphs contain no unambiguous or precise graphic clues as to their correct pronunciation.

The principle of componential construction, in any event, which combined graphic elements in this way had certainly become well established by the time the Late Shang oracle-bone inscriptions were recorded (ca. 1200–1045 B.C.). It was so firmly established and, evidently, so well liked, that the written language in China never advanced to what was, in other cultures, the next and seemingly natural step, the development of a syllabary in which graphs were used purely for writing sounds rather than for writing words. The potential was clearly there: most, if not all, graphic forms had definite phonetic values associated with them (e.g., entries 9, 14–17 in tables 1 and 3). The Japanese, indeed, were to use the Chinese logographs to invent their own *kana* syllabary in the ninth and tenth centuries A.D.—although even they were unable to turn the kana script into the preferred system of writing. It was the inflected nature of their language that encouraged the Japanese, it may be noted, to develop a spelling system for the word endings that they appended to the Chinese characters. The Chinese lacked such a stimulus, just as they lacked the stimulus that had been present in ancient Mesopotamia, of having to write two such entirely dissimilar languages as Sumerian and Akkadian.

Twentieth-century modernizers have tended to think in terms of China's "failure" to syllabize or alphabetize. Not only is this judgment anachronistic, but it fails to consider the relatively high literacy rates in traditional China; the prestige attached to mastering a script of such difficulty and

beauty helps account for these high rates.[22] The genesis and maintenance of the logographic Chinese script, in fact, can only be explained in terms of the whole mental set of the Late Neolithic and early Bronze Age in China. I should like to consider in closing, accordingly, the social and intellectual context in which Chinese writing developed.

The Neolithic background

Speaking in terms both general and incomplete, the Neolithic cultures of China in the sixth to fourth millennia B.C. can be divided into: (1) those of the East Coast, which embraced both the Lower Yangtze and the eastern part of North China and gave rise to such cultures as Ho-mu-tu, Ch'ing-lien-kang, Ma-chia-pang, Liang-chu, Pei-hsin, Ta-wen-k'ou, Hou-kang, Hung-shan, and late Miao-ti-kou; and (2) those of the Northwest, which also includes the western half of the North China plain, where such cultures as Lao-kuan-t'ai, Ta-ti-wan, Pei-shou-ling, Pan-p'o, and early Miao-ti-kou flourished. These two cultural systems have sometimes been referred to as that of the black pottery, or Lung-shan, culture in the East, and that of the painted pottery, or Yang-shao, culture in the Northwest.[23] Whatever terms one uses, and they are in need of considerable refinement, one of the main differences was not the paint or lack of paint on the pot surface but the way the peoples of the two major regions actually made the pots themselves.

The pots of the Northwest tradition (fig. 13) were on the whole made quite simply with natural, globular, smooth-

Figure 13 Pots of the northwest tradition. *Above,* Yang-shao painted ware; *below,* Yang-shao unpainted ware. Reprinted from Feng Hsien-ming et al., *Chung-kuo t'ao-tz'u shih* (Peking: Wen-wu, 1982), 10, 11.

contoured shapes; they may be referred to as "holistic" in both conception and execution, being either built up by coiling or, in the later stages, turned on a slow wheel. The shapes were efficient, in terms of most volume for least clay used. Indeed, they represent the kinds of shapes that most of us, as amateur potters, might first devise. One may notice, too, that the bottoms of these pots were generally unpainted; presumably they were set down into the ground to give them stability.

The potters of the East Coast were motivated by a different set of aesthetic concerns that was, in many ways, alien to the more natural tradition of the Northwest. The eastern potmakers created vessels with arbitrary, carinated profiles in which shape took priority over efficiency (fig. 14). Their pots were almost invariably unpainted; the aesthetic impulse focused on pot form rather than on surface design. Their repertoire of pot shapes was far larger and more varied than that of the Northwest potters. Not only did they produce vessels like the *kuei*-tripod pitcher (see fig. 14) and *ho*-kettle with hollow, bulbous legs, but they also frequently equipped them with appendages like spouts and handles. Above all, it is evident that many of their pots with sharp profiles or with appendages were made componentially. That is, the body sections or component elements—such as handles, legs (whether bulbous or solid), and spouts —were first made separately and were then assembled in accordance with some prescribed plan.[24]

Since the eventual rise of Shang culture in the North China plain in the first

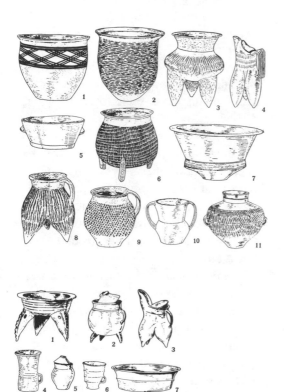

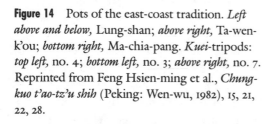

Figure 14 Pots of the east-coast tradition. *Left above and below,* Lung-shan; *above right,* Ta-wen-k'ou; *bottom right,* Ma-chia-pang. *Kuei*-tripods: *top left,* no. 4; *bottom left,* no. 3; *above right,* no. 7. Reprinted from Feng Hsien-ming et al., *Chung-kuo t'ao-tz'u shih* (Peking: Wen-wu, 1982), 15, 21, 22, 28.

half of the second millennium B.C. was intimately associated with the increasing dominance of vessel shapes and other cultural traits, such as burial customs, jade working and bone carving, and certain artistic motifs, associated with the cultures of the East, one may speculate that some analogous connection existed between the componential nature of the eastern pots, which displayed a genius for combination,

for putting things together in a prescribed way, and the componential character of the Shang written script which emerges, fully formed, in the oracle-bone inscriptions of northern Honan by about 1200 B.C.[25]

The demand for writing

Presumably writing was needed in Shang China by the time of the great public works like the monumental rammed-earth enceinte which surrounded the Middle Shang capital at Cheng-chou (ca. 1500 B.C.), a city wall some eight kilometers in length that, it may be estimated, would have taken the labor of some ten thousand laborers twelve years to construct. Enterprises such as this imply some form of labor recruitment and record keeping. The Late Shang royal tombs at Hsi-pei-kang (approximately ten kilometers northwest of An-yang), massive cruciform pits dug into the ground like inverted pyramids, up to forty-two feet deep, would have required similar mobilization of labor. And, to offer a third example, the piece-mold process of bronze casting itself, with its assemblage of ceramic cores and outer segmented molds (as in fig. 5), was a quintessential componential activity, conducted on an industrial scale, that coordinated the labor of hundreds of miners, woodsmen, haulers, ceramicists, and foundrymen.[26] All of these large-scale activities would have required the centralized, bureaucratic control that written instructions and records greatly facilitate. The oracle-bone inscriptions, so bureaucratic themselves in form, indeed reveal that the Shang king divined about mobilizing conscripts by the thousands for both military and economic purposes.

But would writing have been needed earlier? Can we identify a social or technological activity in the late Neolithic, particularly in the East, where many of the Shang roots lay, which would have stimulated the development of a written script? Writing in the ancient Aegean seems to have arisen partly to assist in problems of mensuration and calculation.[27] The archaeological evidence suggests that it was indeed the cultures of the Neolithic East that were primarily concerned with such problems. For componential pot construction implies attention to scale and measurement, particularly when three-footed vessels are involved, which must be made with legs of equal size. The parts—legs, handles, spouts, lids—have to be measured so that they will fit the vessel body. The whole approach to pottery making would have been quite different from that of the holistic potter of the Northwest and Central Plains who could, as it were, let the clay take its natural course, not simply with regard to the globular shape of the final product, but also with regard to its size.

Turning from clay to wood, the concern with mensuration in the cultures of the East is also seen in the exactitude of the mortise-and-tenon construction used in the pile dwellings at Ho-mu-tu (ca. 4000 B.C.), in the regularity of the planks used in house construction at Ma-chia-pang in the fourth millennium, and in the exact measurements used to construct wooden well shafts in the late Liang-chu site, about 2000 B.C., at Chia-shan; these sites are all in northern Chekiang.

The most striking precision craftsmanship, however, is seen in the highly worked, perforated jade *pi*-disks and *ts'ung*-tubes (fig. 15) which served as grave goods in eastern burials in the Yangtze delta area from at least the third millennium B.C. onward. The disks show little variation in diameter (frequently no more than one millimeter in any direction); the walls of the tubes bored from either end into the center of the *ts'ung* frequently met exactly; the *ts'ung* registers are of virtually identical size, again with differences of less than one millimeter. Because of its hardness, jade has been referred to as a "sublimely impractical" material; it is extremely difficult to work. And yet

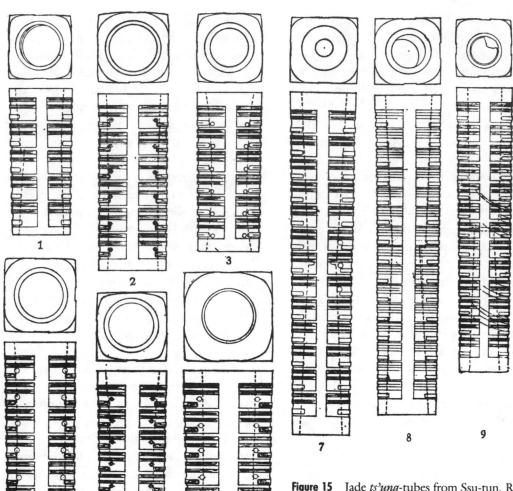

Figure 15 Jade *ts'ung*-tubes from Ssu-tun. Reprinted from "1982 nien Chiang-su Ch'ang-chou Wu-ching Ssu-tun yi-chih ti fa-chueh," *K'ao-ku* 1984.2:119, 120.

the peoples of the East had the tenacity to shape it with this remarkable precision.[28]

I would suggest, in short, that it is in the lithic, woodworking, and ceramic technologies of the East Coast Neolithic that precise mensuration would have been most widely practiced, and that the need for recording measurements would first have been most urgently felt.[29] And when we consider that fine ceramics and jades played a crucial role as grave goods, used in venerating the dead and in validating the status of their living descendants, we can see that religious and lineage concerns might have provided important encouragement for the invention of a written script. It is a mere accident of archaeological preservation and discovery that the earliest corpus of Chinese writing, the Shang oracle-bone inscriptions, was religious in nature; one cannot, on this basis, argue that early Chinese writing was developed to communicate with dead ancestors.[30] The strength of the lineage and the concern shown for the care of the dead in early Chinese culture, however, does suggest that lineage-related activities—such as the manufacture of mortuary jades in the Neolithic, and of ritual bronzes in the Shang, as well as the creation of some system of lineage identification—might have stimulated the development of writing.[31]

There is, even now, some support for the hypothesis that Chinese writing originated in the East Coast. The textual evidence for the existence of ancient bird totemism in the Shantung region appears to be supported by a series of pictorial designs on Eastern pots and jades that combine bird and solar motifs (fig. 16). It has been plau-sibly proposed that some of the Liang-chu designs carved on jade should be read as the words *yang niao*, "sun birds," the name of a local eastern Yi group which, according to early texts, had settled in the Lower Yangtze.[32]

Whatever the precise meaning of the schematic, emblematic designs reproduced in figure 16, one can regard them as componential, involving the putting together of two or more independent graphic elements, sun and bird, to form a composite sign. I doubt that we will ever be able to recover their precise meaning. Indeed, they probably served as emblems of ownership or identity on these pots and jades, rather than as words in a writing system which were recording true speech (see n.31 above). Nevertheless, few if any componential signs have been found in the Neolithic traditions of the Northwest.[33] And it is surely significant that similar emblems, thought to mark the lineages of the men who ordered their casting, have been found on Shang and Chou bronzes (fig. 16f). There is no certainty that these signs recorded spoken words rather than certain ideas, such as identity and ownership, but it seems likely that they lay on the border between ideographic notation and logographic writing. Their preservation on the Chou dynasty bronzes suggests the cultural importance that the early Chinese attached to them, long after the writing system was fully developed.

I would suggest, therefore, as a hypothesis to be tested against future archaeological discoveries, that, on the basis of craft prac-

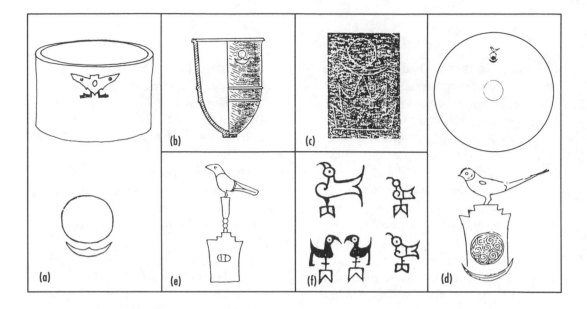

Figure 16 Bird and sun motifs on eastern pots and jades: (a) bird and sun-moon motifs carved on a Liang-chu culture jade ring; (b) sun-moon motif incised on a *tsun*-vase from Ling-yang-ho, Shantung; (c) sun-moon-mountain (or fire?) motif incised on a *tsun*-vase from Ling-yang-ho; (d) jade *pi*-disk of Liang-chu culture; bird on a cartouche with sun and moon motifs; (e) bird, cartouche, and sun motif incised on a Liang-chu culture *pi*-disk; (f) bird emblems cast on Shang and Chou bronzes. Reprinted with permission from Wu Hung, "Bird Motifs in Eastern Yi Art," *Orientations* 16.10 (Oct. 1985), 34–36, figs. 9, 10, 11, 13, 15, 17.

tice, social need, and actual graphic finds, the origins of Chinese writing, in the form of composite emblems (fig. 16) rather than linear scratches (fig. 11), are probably to be found in late-third-millennium (B.C.) sites of the Eastern Neolithic in China. The argument is not that only those who made componential pots were likely to invent a componential writing system. The argument is rather that, given the increasing social and craft complexity evident in the Late Neolithic, writing was more likely to develop first in the region where such habits of organization, in various aspects of life, were more pronounced and valued.[34]

Given the relative newness of scientific archaeology in China and the large number of revolutionary discoveries that are made almost every year, such hypotheses must naturally be treated with caution.[35] Whatever the truth about the geographic and functional origins of Chinese writing, the deep-rooted cultural dispositions, which encouraged and then maintained a system that combined phonetic and signific elements, were so strong and so congenial to the Shang and subsequent descendant cultures that, to this day, one of the aesthetic and cultural glories of Chinese civilization has been its characteristic logographic and componential writing. That writing, as we have seen, was indigenous, being deeply rooted in the cultural practices of the late Neolithic and the early Bronze Age within China itself. We will better understand the earliest origins, subsequent nature, and remarkable longevity of this writing system as more detailed knowledge about the way it was first used becomes available.

······

Notes

1. The first Westerners who made contact with China tended to presume that its culture was derivative. In the realm of language, consider, for example, John Webb's essay, "An Historical Essay Endeavoring a Probability that the Language of the Empire of China Is the Primitive Language," published in 1669. This work is cited by T. Watters, *Essays on the Chinese Language* (Shanghai: Presbyterian Mission Press, 1889), 6 n.1; Watters's first chapter, "Some Western Opinions," is instructive and entertaining on such matters.

2. Michael Sullivan, *The Arts of China* (Berkeley: University of California Press, 1973), 183. For a discussion of the term "ideographic," see below.

3. The fact that no reference is made to the text of this particular inscription before the Sung, together with various anomalies in the inscription itself, carved in A.D. 993, raises serious questions about its authenticity. See Jung Keng, "Ch'in Shih Huang k'e-shih k'ao" (A study of the stone inscriptions of Ch'in Shih Huang), *Yen-ching hsueh pao* (Yenching Journal of Chinese Studies) 17 (June 1935); 130–32; Derk Bodde, *China's First Unifier: A Study of the Ch'in Dynasty as Seen in the Life of Li Ssu, 280? 208 B.C.* (Leiden, 1938; repr., Hong Kong: Hong Kong University Press, 1967), 175–78, "The Unification of Writing." Regardless of its authenticity, it is a superb example of *hsiao chuan* graph forms.

4. Noel Barnard, *Bronze Casting and Bronze Alloys in Ancient China*, Monumenta Serica Monograph 14 (Tokyo: Monumenta Serica, 1961), pp. 158–59.

5. For an introduction to these inscriptions, see David N. Keightley, *Sources of Shang History: The Oracle-Bone Inscriptions of Bronze Age China* (Berkeley: University of California Press, 1978).

6. Significant discoveries were made at Anyang in 1973 and at Feng-ch'u, some 350 miles to the west in the Wei River valley, in 1977; this last find was particularly important because the inscriptions appear to be associated with the Chou dynasty, which conquered the Shang, rather than with the Shang themselves. For the latest total of oracle-bone inscriptions, see Hu Hou-hsuan, "Pa-shih-wu nien lai chia-ku-wen ts'ai-liao chih tsai t'ung-chi" (Recount of the oracle-bone materials of the last eighty-five years), *Shih-hsueh yueh-kan* (History monthly) 1984. 5:15–22.

7. "Plastromancy" refers to the pyromantic cracking of turtle plastrons; "scapulimancy," to the pyromantic cracking of animal scapulas. For these terms and the nature of the bones involved, see Keightley, *Sources of Shang History*, 3–12, and "Appendix I: Identification of the Inscribed Turtle Shells of Shang," by James F. Berry, 157–64.

8. I assume that a rainbow meant harm to the Shang diviners and drought to the Han iconographers because it is seen only when sun and rain appear together, thus suggesting an inadequate rainfall. The ominous significance, for the Shang, of a rainbow in the north (as in fig. 7) was still felt by modern peasants. David Arkush notes the popularity in "virtually every province" of the saying, "East rainbow sudden thunder, west rainbow rain; south rainbow torrential showers; north rainbow—sell your children!" ("Economic Calculation and Social Morality as Seen in Chinese Peasant Proverbs" [Paper presented at the Conference on Orthodoxy and Heterodoxy in Late Imperial China: Cultural Beliefs and Social Divisions, Montecito, Calif., August 20–26, 1981], 21.) A letter (May 12, 1981) from Yang Hsi-chang, one of the archaeologists at the site of Hsiao-t'un, An-yang, where the oracle-bone inscriptions were excavated, reveals that a similar proverb is still current among the peasantry of northern Honan: "When a rainbow is in the east, thunder will strike; when a rainbow is in the west, rain will fall; when a rainbow appears in the south, sell sons and daughters; when a rainbow

appears in the north, resort to arms (because times will be bad in both cases)." This is striking evidence of the endurance of folk belief over a period of some three thousand years. The relative popularity of the two-headed dragon motif in the regions of Shantung and Kiangsu during the Han dynasty (Patricia Berger, "Rites and Festivities in the Arts of Eastern Han China," [Ph.D. diss., History of Art, University of California, Berkeley, 1980], 41) provides further grounds for linking Shang iconography and writing to the Late Neolithic cultures of the East.

9. I know of only one possible exception to this generalization, *Ping-pien* 368–369, and even in that case it seems clear that the diviners and record-keepers were attempting to save the king from his mistaken forecast that it would rain on a ping day. (For the full record of the abbreviated references to published collections of oracle-bone inscriptions used here and elsewhere in this article, see Keightley, *Sources of Shang History*, 229–31.)

10. The inscription is *T'ieh-yun* 5.3; see the discussion at Keightley, *Sources of Shang History*, 45 n.84.

11. See, e.g., I. J. Gelb, *A Study of Writing*, rev. ed. (Chicago: University of Chicago Press, 1963), 98, fig. 54, who provides a comparative table of graphs from Sumerian, Egyptian, Hittite, and oracle-bone Chinese; Ping-ti Ho, *The Cradle of the East: An Inquiry into the Indigenous Origins of Techniques and Ideas of Neolithic and Early Historic China, 5000–1000 B.C.* (Hong Kong: Chinese University of Hong Kong, and Chicago: University of Chicago, 1975), 246–52, who provides a similar comparison of Sumerian and Chinese graphs.

12. David N. Keightley, "Ping-ti Ho and the Origins of Chinese Civilization," *Harvard Journal of Asiatic Studies* 37 (Dec. 1977); 389–91; William G. Boltz, "Early Chinese Writing," *World Archaeology* 17, no. 3 (1986); 429–32.

13. These phonetic considerations apply even in the case of the rainbow (figs. 7 and 10), discussed above. It seems likely that there was both a semantic and phonetic similarity between **g'ung/hung,* "rainbow," and **l'iung/lung,* "dragon"—archaic pronunciations are indicated by an asterisk (i.e., an ideograph!)—and that

both words derived from a still earlier word, which may be reconstructed as close to **kliung,* which had the basic meaning of "arched," "vaulted." See Marty Gerald Backstrom, "The *Dong Ming Ji*: Marvellous Episodes from the Court of Emperor Wu" (M.A. diss., Department of Oriental Languages, University of California, Berkeley, 1985), 61 n.83; Edward Schafer, *The Divine Woman: Dragon Ladies and Rain Maidens in T'ang Literature* (Berkeley: University of California Press, 1973), 13–14.

14. E.g., fig. 6, fifth graph from the top in the columns on both the far right and the far left. It also appears as the first graph in column 2 in fig. 4 and as the fifth graph in the lefthand column in fig. 7.

15. Archaic pronunciations (indicated by an asterisk) for these and other graphs may be found in Bernhard Karlgren, *Grammata Serica Recensa* (Stockholm: Museum of Far Eastern Antiquities, 1957).

16. Wen Fong, ed., *The Great Bronze Age of China: An Exhibition from the People's Republic of China* (New York: Metropolitan Museum and Knopf, 1980), 203.

17. For the date of the conquest, see David S. Nivison, "The Dates of Western Chou," *Harvard Journal of Asiatic Studies* 43 (Dec. 1983): 481–580.

18. In addition to the studies by Chao Ch'eng, Hsu Chung-shu, and Huang Sheng-chang in *Wen-wu* 1978.6 see Chang Cheng-lang in *Kao-ku* 1978.1:58–59 and Huang Jan-wei in *Kōkotsugaku* 12 (1980): 67–75. My own highly tentative translation, which has drawn upon their discussions, is given in the caption to fig. 4.

19. Boltz, "Early Chinese Writing," 428.

20. Li Hsiao-ting, "Ts'ung liu-shu ti kuan-nien k'an chia-ku wen-tzu" (Oracle-bone graphs from the viewpoint of the six ways of writing), *Nan-yang ta-hsueh hsueh-pao* 2 (1968): 91–95. For reasons explained below, I combine his figures for "compound ideographs" (*hui-yi* [see below]; 32 percent) and classifier-plus-phonetics (*hsieh-sheng*; 27 percent). Such percentages are approximations, since they depend in many cases on the fallible understanding of the modern interpreter. The fact, however, that Shima, in compiling his invaluable concordance of oracle-bone graphs (see Keightley, *Sources of Shang History*, 61–62), was able to classify nearly all oracle-bone graphs under 164 "radicals" of his own devising indicates the degree to which

most of the four thousand or more Shang graphs were composed componentially, i.e., with more than one graphic unit, whatever the components' precise functions may have been. (For the total number of Shang graphs, see Keightley, *Sources of Shang History*, 59 n.8, and 61 n.20.)

21. "Characters were not invented by just putting together two or more elements based on their semantic values alone. At least one of the components must have had a phonetic function" (Boltz, "Early Chinese Writing," 428).

22. It has been suggested that literacy rates in nineteenth-century China, for example, were probably higher than those in much of preindustrial Europe. See Evelyn Sakakida Rawski, *Education and Popular Literacy in Ch'ing China* (Ann Arbor: University of Michigan Press, 1979), esp. chap. 7, "Popular Literacy in Perspective."

23. For an introduction to these major Neolithic traditions, see Louisa G. Fitzgerald Huber, "The Relationship of the Painted Pottery and Lung-shan Cultures," in David N. Keightley, ed., *The Origins of Chinese Civilization* (Berkeley: University of California Press, 1983), 177–216. The distinctions between the two major cultural systems are discussed in Keightley, "Archaeology and Mentality: The Making of China," *Representations* 18 (Spring 1987): 94.

24. See Keightley, "Archaeology and Mentality," 94–102, for a fuller exposition of the argument.

25. Kwang-chih Chang, *Shang Civilization* (New Haven: Yale University Press, 1980), 345; Keightley, "Archaeology and Mentality," 116–17.

26. Barnard, *Bronze Casting*, 48–59, 65, 87; Ursula Martius Franklin, "The Beginnings of Metallurgy in China: A Comparative Approach," in George Kuwayama, ed., *The Great Bronze Age of China: A Symposium* (Los Angeles: County Museum of Art, 1983), 94–99.

27. Colin Renfrew, *The Emergence of Civilisation: The Cyclades and the Aegean in the Third Millennium B.C.* (London: Methuen, 1972), 407.

28. Keightley, "Archaeology and Mentality," 111–12, provides more information on mensuration and jade-working in the Chinese Neolithic.

29. Some memory of this East Coast concern with mensuration may be found in the *Tso chuan* account of the bird ministers who were supposed to have administered part of Shantung at the time of the legendary ruler, Shao Hao Chih. These included "the five Pheasant (officers) who presided over the five classes of artisans; they saw to the provision of implements and utensils, and to the correctness of the measures of length and capacity, keeping things equal among the people" (trans. based on that by James Legge, trans., *The Chinese Classics*, vol. 5, *The Ch'un Ts'ew with the Tso Chuen* [Oxford: Oxford University Press, 1872], 667, Chao 17.) This legend, recorded in Chou texts, supports the conclusions suggested by the Neolithic artifacts.

30. This, for example, was the claim made by Jacques Gernet, "Ecrit et histoire en Chine," *Journal de Psychologie Normale et Pathologique* 56 (1959): 36–38.

31. K. C. Chang has proposed that "the overwhelming majority of these ceramic marks, both Shang and prehistoric, were markers and emblems of families, lineages, clans, or divisions of these" (*Art, Myth, and Ritual: The Path to Political Authority in Ancient China* [Cambridge, Mass.: Harvard University Press, 1983], 85).

32. Wu Hung, "Bird Motifs in Eastern Yi Art," *Orientations* 16, no. 10 (Oct. 1985): 34–36. For the increasingly common view that the symbols on the eastern pots and jades, like those in fig. 16, were indeed early Chinese characters, see Li Hsueh-ch'in, "Lun hsin-ch'u Ta-wen-k'ou wen-hua t'ao-ch'i fu-hao" (The symbols on newly discovered Ta-wen-k'ou pots), *Wen-wu* 1987.12:75–80, 85.

33. One possible exception is the picture of a stone axe and a stork holding a fish (a silver carp?) in its beak painted on a *kang* crock found in Yen ts'un, Lin-ju county, in central Honan in 1978; the site is possibly late fourth millennium in date. This design, remarkable for its singularity, has been interpreted by one scholar as a totemic representation, on the urn used for the burial of the victorious chief, to commemorate the domination of the stork over the carp tribe (Yen Wen-ming, " 'Kuan yü shih-fu t'u' pa" [Postscript on the "Stork, Fish, Stone-Axe Painting"], *Wen-wu* 1981. 12:79–82). No later texts or myths are cited to support this speculation; nor is any claim made that the symbols can be read as words.

34. For increasing social differentiation in the cultures of the East Coast, see Richard Pearson, "Social Complexity in Chinese Coastal Neolithic Sites," *Science* 213 (Sept. 4, 1981): 1078–86. Increasing distinctions of social and economic status may well have led to developing notions of property and ownership that might also help explain the markings found on the Late Neolithic jades and pots of the East.

35. One recent discovery, if correctly dated, would certainly challenge some of the observations offered above. Conversations I had with archaeologists in China in September 1987 indicated that the single skeletons in two P'ei-li-kang burials, from Chia-hu, in Wu-yang hsien, northern Honan, had each been buried with a turtle-shell "box," composed of the carapace and plastron together, at the waist, the box containing small white stones. Carved on one shell was the graph for "eye," carved on the other was the graph for "day" or "sun" (see table 1, entry 5). These graphs are said not to have been representational drawings, but graphs such as we might find on the oracle-bone inscriptions of ca. 1200 B.C. Since carbon-14 dating puts the P'ei-li-kang culture at about 6,000 B.C., these graphs appear to be some 4,500 years earlier than the fully formed writing system that appears in the oracle-bone inscriptions of Shang. Even if the date of these forms is confirmed, it would not follow that these symbols of 6,000 B.C. were writing, for they do not appear in a social context where writing is likely to have been useful, nor do they appear in sentences. But it is remarkable to find that Chinese symbol makers of the Central Plains were abstracting pictographic designs for sun and eye and turning them into stylized, standardized, nonnaturalistic depictions at such an early date. They did so with such success, apparently, that the forms they chose endured for the next 4,500 years. For a brief account of these finds, see "Yü ch'u-t'u chia-ku ch'i-k'e fu-hao ho ku ti" (Symbols carved on shell and bone and bone flutes excavated in Honan), *Jen-min jih-pao* (overseas edition), Dec. 13, 1987, p. 1.

· · · · · ·

Further Readings

Boltz, William G. "Early Chinese Writing." *World Archaeology* 17, no. 3 (1986): 420–36.

Ch'en Chih-mai. *Chinese Calligraphers and Their Art*, esp. "The Oracle Bone Inscriptions," 10–20, "The Ancient Scripts," 21–34, and "Han Innovations," 35–51. Melbourne: Melbourne University Press, 1966.

Chiang Yee. *Chinese Calligraphy: An Introduction to Its Aesthetic and Technique*, esp. "The Origin and Construction of Chinese Characters," 18–40. Cambridge, Mass.: Harvard University Press, 1963.

Chu, Yu-kuang. "The Chinese Language." In *An Introduction to Chinese Civilization*, ed. John T. Meskill, 587–615. Lexington, Mass.: Heath, 1973.

Crump, James and Irving Crump. *Dragon Bones in the Yellow Earth*. New York: Dodd Mead, 1963.

DeFrancis, John. *The Chinese Language: Fact and Fantasy*, esp. "Rethinking Chinese Characters," 69–130. Honolulu: University of Hawaii Press, 1984.

Karlgren, Bernhard. *The Chinese Language: An Essay on Its Nature and History*. New York: Ronald Press, 1949.

Tsien, Tsuen-hsuin. *Written on Bamboo and Silk: The Beginnings of Chinese Books and Inscriptions*. Chicago: University of Chicago Press, 1962.

12

The Ancient Writing
of Middle America

······

Floyd G. Lounsbury

······

It is not generally known that true "writing" existed in the Middle American region of the New World before the coming of the Europeans and that it had here a considerable antiquity. Nor has it been appreciated, even by scholars until fairly recently, that its nature and the history of its development parallel in important respects those of the early systems of writing in the Old World —this in spite of the rather striking differences in its visual impact, graphic conventions, and artistry. Any antiquity claimed for a tradition of writing is of course dependent on the definition that we have in mind for that cultural invention. I use the term here in a sense broad enough to encompass the employment of word-signs of nonphonetic derivation (as well as of phonetic), but narrow enough to exclude the employment of such signs, or signs of any variety, when not generally disposed in such a manner as to represent the constituent elements of compound expressions in the user's language. Even the latter restriction allows of some scaling. I speak of "writing" in its fullest sense in those instances where we find graphic representation of complete sentences and the concatenation of sentences into texts; but I also accept as "writing," though in a more attenuated sense, those instances in which compound words and phrases are the maximum attested units (as in representations of place names, personal names, composite numerals, numerals with signs for things tallied, etc.) but where the representation of fully formed sentences is not general.

As many as thirteen different systems or traditions of writing have been distinguished for the Middle American area.[1] Of these, the hieroglyphic system of the Classic Lowland Maya qualifies as writing in the fullest sense described here. Its earliest surviving specimens date from A.D. 292 and 320; but they, and other monuments, give evidence of a lengthy history of earlier developments leading up to them. Certain others of these systems, some earlier and some later, qualify only in the weaker sense of the term. The Mixtec and the Central Mexican codices, for example, abound in compound personal and place-name designations and in calendrical specifications, but their method of narration is fundamentally pictorial. In these, writing is employed to identify the "who," the "where," and the "when" of their story, but the primary medium for the "what" is serial pictorial representation, with the written annotations superimposed as identifying labels.[2]

The Middle American culture area— "Mesoamerica" as it is commonly called— extends from Central Mexico southward and eastward through southern Mexico, Guatemala, Belize, western Honduras, and El Salvador (see map). It was an area of complex civilizations and political developments prior to the Spanish intrusion. Its populations spoke (and still do) languages of more than a dozen different linguistic families, and they represented numerous

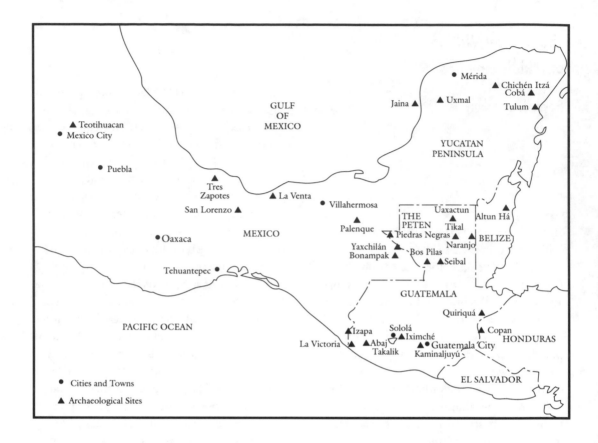

The Middle American culture area.

distinguishable ethnic groups. It was an area, however, of many shared cultural features. One of these, diagnostic of the area, was the common possession of a 260-day almanac and a 365-day annual calendar, which, running simultaneously, resulted in a 52-year cycle which we know as the "calendar round." This system was already widely distributed half a millennium before the Christian era, and estimates of its antiquity, or of its separate components, place its origins still earlier. It figures importantly in the earliest examples of writing in Middle America, as it does also in the more advanced varieties of the Classic and Postclassic Maya. Its essential components survive in some parts of the area, jointly or separately, even to the present day.

In addition to the calendars, a chronological system was also once widely shared, and dates given in this system formed an equally important component in the Mayan and in some pre-Mayan inscriptions. It consisted of a day count in which the days were numbered, one after another, starting from a far-distant epoch. In principle it was quite analogous to the so-called Julian day count, which is employed in the modern world for astronomical and other kinds of technical chronology and precise time reckoning. Both of these counts number the days in serial order. Both start from epochal dates that were projected far into prehistoric antiquity: the Middle American from a day that is equivalent to August 13 (retroactive Gregorian), or September 7 (Julian), of the year −3113 (3114 B.C.); the Julian from January 1 (Julian) of the year −4712 (4713 B.C.).[3] Both projections appear to represent reconciliations of concurrently running cycles of varying lengths and starting points: the Julian certainly so, the Middle American possibly and very probably so. But the Middle American invention antedates the European by more than sixteen centuries. Its earliest surviving examples (pre-Mayan, one from Chiapas and one from Vera Cruz) date from 36 and 32 B.C., and its invention must have preceded these by an appreciable length of time. The European on the other hand was a sixteenth-century invention, introduced by Joseph Justus Scaliger in 1583 as a framework for systematizing Old World historical chronology, and later adopted internationally by the astronomical profession.

The early Middle American inscriptions with chronological and calendrical data must be accounted as examples of true writing, for their numerals and the combinations of these with day signs are constructions in accord with the syntax of spoken languages, and they designate temporal phrases or clauses qualifying predications of events. The numeral system employed in these was vigesimal (base twenty, rather than ten), making use of "place notation" (successive places denoting successively higher powers of the base), and with "zero" symbols to occupy empty noninitial places. A modification of this numeral system, with 360 rather than 400 as the value of units in the third place, was employed in chrono-

logical recording, allowing the values of the higher-placed digits to be apprehended immediately—albeit only approximately—in terms of years.

The characteristics of Middle American writing can best be appreciated by examining a few specimens. For an introduction I have chosen one of the earliest Mayan examples; then, for brief comparison, a yet earlier, pre-Mayan, one; and finally, to illustrate more of the resources of the hieroglyphic system, a Classic Mayan inscription.

......

The Leiden Plaque

Figure 1 illustrates the Leiden plaque (named for the museum in which it is preserved), which is one of the two earliest specimens with identifiably Mayan hieroglyphic writing. It is a carved jade pendant, deriving from the region of Tikal in the northern Petén of Guatemala, commemorating the accession of an early ruler who stemmed from that site. The face of the plaque depicts the ruler, heavily attired in symbolic accoutrements, in a conventional stance before a bound captive who is destined to play a role on the occasion, while the inscription on the reverse describes the date and names the event and its protagonist in a properly constructed sentence of which the initial temporal clause, as was customary, is a predominating feature.

Standing at the head of the column of hieroglyphs is an early example of what is known as the "initial-series introducing glyph." It was a standard opening for

(a)

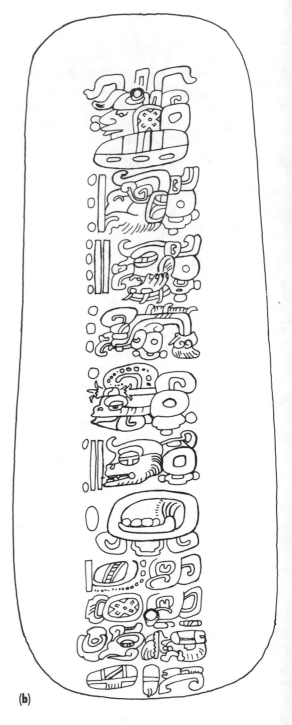

(b)

Figure 1 The Leiden plaque, from the northern Petén region of Guatemala. It bears the date 8.14.3.1.12, 1 Eb, G5, 0 Yaxkin, equal to A.D. 320 September 16 (Julian), and commemorates the accession of a ruler of the lineage of Tikal. Drawing by David Kiphuth, after M. D. Coe, *The Maya* (London: Thames and Hudson, 1966).

Mayan inscriptions of this type, and it has antecedents also in earlier, pre-Mayan, inscriptions. It is not known precisely what it meant or how it was read, though its lower component, a sign with a reading of *tun,* could imply reference either to the time periods or to their termination, and its central component, also as was customary, names the patron of the calendrical month in which the date occurs—in this case the patron of Yaxkin, which month is named further on in the inscription.

The next five hieroglyphs, with bar-and-dot numerical prefixes, name the units of time: eight periods of the fifth order of magnitude (144,000 days each), fourteen of the fourth order (7,200 days each), three of the third (360 each), one of the second (20 days), and twelve of the first order (single days). Their total is the number of days—1,253,912 in all—since day zero of the Middle American day count. This interval leads from the previously mentioned epoch to the day commemorated in the inscription, which is that of A.D. 320, September 16 in the Julian calendar, or September 17 in retroactive Gregorian for that year.

The next hieroglyph (the seventh from the top, and the last of the full, or double-width, glyphs) names the day "One Eb,"

placing the date now in the 260-day almanac. The almanac itself was the product of two lesser cycles running concurrently, a "trecena" of thirteen day numbers, and a "veintena" of twenty day names. The day recorded here belonged to the first of the thirteen and the twelfth of the twenty.

Following this, on the next line, in the first of the single-width glyphs, the "lord of the night" pertaining to this date is named, this one being the fifth in a cycle of nine. His glyph intervenes, as is most often though not always the case, between the name of the day in the almanac (1 Eb) and its name in the calendrical year (0 Yaxkin), which follows next.

The designation of the day in the year occupies two of the smaller glyph spaces here, the second space on the line with the lord of the night, and the first space on the next line below it. The former is a form of the "seating" glyph, made up of two constituents: (1) a much used conventional logogram for the root of that verb, whose inherent meaning is "to seat," "to set in place," or "to install," and (2), attached to it as a postfix, a phonetic sign of value *mu,* or more generally of the consonant *m* either before or after the vowel *u.* The latter functions here as a phonetic complement, confirming the final consonant of the root, and so permitting us to know that of two possible readings of the root sign—*cul* or *cum* if read in Yucatecan Maya, *chul* or *chum* if in Cholan—it is the second from one of these pairs that was intended, the one ending in *m* after *u.*

The second glyph in this year-day designation (on the next line) is the name glyph of the month Yaxkin, a compound consisting of the sign for *yax* and the sign for *kin,* the former treated graphically as a prefix to the latter. Yaxkin was the seventh of the so-called "months" of the calendar year. Of these there were eighteen, of twenty days each, with a residue period of five days at the end of the year.[4] The days of any such "month" were designated with the appropriate numerals, except that the last day— the twentieth of a full month or the fifth of the residue period—was usually described as the "seating" (i.e., "installation") of the next. The analogy is with the seating or installation in office of a ruler, and the seating of a new month regularly took place on the day of expiration of the preceding month. It is, so to speak, the zero day of the month, and so we customarily transcribe it. Thus the "Seating of Yaxkin" which is recorded here is in effect the last day of the preceding month, the sixth, which was Xul; and so it is the 120th day of the calendar year.

These calendrical specifications represent the coordinates of the date in four separate cyclical dimensions, resulting in a characterization which is unique within a period of nine calendar rounds, or 468 calendar years (lacking leap-year intercalations). Given the chronological day number which precedes them, and bearing in mind that the day zero of the era was a "4 Ahau 8 Cumku" (number 4 in the trecena, 20 or 0 in the veintena, and 348 or −17 in the calendar year) and that its lord of the night was "G9" (9 or 0 in that cycle), they are all predictable; a moment's calculation will show that they are

indeed what they should be. Lacking from this brief inscription, however, are the data pertinent to the lunar calendar. The earliest secure attestation of the recording of lunar data is from an inscription (Stela 18 of Uaxactun) dated thirty-seven years after this one, in A.D. 357.

Following after the glyph of the month Yaxkin, on the same line, another "seating" sign is readily recognized, but it has affixes different from the one that modified it in its previous occurrence. The larger postfix is identifiable as one that figures in one of the past-tense passive verbal inflections, allowing the sense of the glyph to be understood here as "was seated." The reference this time is to the seating of the ruler, that is, to the installation in office of the one who is depicted on the other side of the plaque, whose titles and name are represented in the glyphs of the remaining two lines of the inscription. These come at the end. They designate the subject of the sentence; and the subject in Mayan syntax is properly *after* the predicate, in final position.

The Leiden plaque was once the earliest-known dated artifact that was identifiably Mayan. But in 1959, during the excavations at Tikal, a monument with a yet earlier inscribed date came to light, which now holds that title. It is Stela 29 of Tikal, with the date 8.12.14.8.15, equal to A.D. 292, July 8 (both Julian and Gregorian, these being the same in the third century). Its lower portion is missing, however; so the Leiden plaque has served us better for illustration.[5]

Other monuments—one from Chiapas, two from Vera Cruz, and one from the southern highlands of Guatemala—bear inscribed dates yet earlier than either of these

from Tikal. The two earliest, 7.16.3.2.13 and
7.16.6.16.18, are from 32 B.C. and 36 B.C.
Though they exemplify the same day count
and calendrical system as the Mayan, and
with some of the same conventions (including two early specimens of the "initial-series
introducing glyph"), certain other features
of sign inventory and syntax imply a linguistic base different from the Mayan. We
speak of them as pre-Mayan. They attest to
the existence of the system for at least three
and a quarter centuries before the earliest
surviving Mayan examples. One point of interest in these is that none of them employ
period signs, such as accompanied each of
the separate digits of the day-count numeral
on the Leiden plaque. Rather, the numerical concept is given in these by means of
place notation alone. This more abstract
and elliptical representation is therefore at
least as old as the earliest surviving records.
An example of one of these, Stela C of Tres
Zapotes (Vera Cruz), with a now famous
history, is shown in figure 2.[6]

These examples of Middle American writing, one early Mayan and one yet earlier,

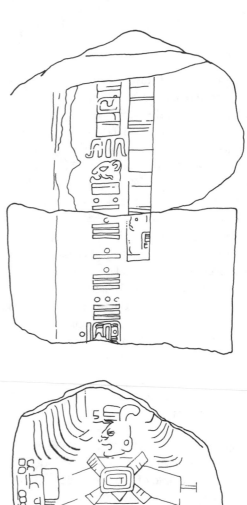

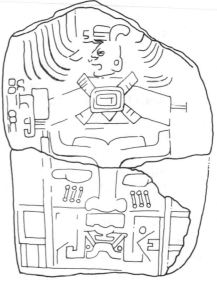

Figure 2   Stela C of Tres Zapotes, a pre-Mayan
monument from the state of Vera Cruz, Mexico.
The inscribed date, 7.16.6.16.18, 6 Etznab, is
equivalent to September 5 (Julian) of the year
32 B.C. Above the numeral series is an early example of the identifying "Introducing Glyph"
for such a series. Drawing by David Kiphuth,
after M. D. Coe, "Early Steps in the Evolution
of Maya Writing," in *Origins of Religious Art and
Iconography in Preclassic Mesoamerica*, ed. H. B.
Nicholson, UCLA Latin American Studies
Series 31 (Los Angeles: UCLA Latin American
Center Publications, 1976).

pre-Mayan, are illustrative of the special importance of calendar and chronology as a component of the subject matter of writing in this area. They also indicate something of its political content and the context of its use, as well as its antiquity. Yet earlier examples from the Zapotec region of the Valley of Oaxaca, in some respects similar in theme but different in character, exemplifying the almanac and another calendrical device but without the day count, and believed to go back as far as the fifth century B.C., might also be adduced.[7] But instead let us look ahead now to a later period for a sample of a longer hieroglyphic text from the Classic Maya florescence.

······

The Inscription of the Temple of the Cross at Palenque

Reproduced here, in figure 3, is a drawing of a portion of the main inscription from the Temple of the Cross at Palenque, Chiapas, Mexico. It is one of two panels of hieroglyphs, of six columns each, which flank a central panel filled with mythological and astrological iconography, two standing figures with ritual objects and symbols of political status, and some shorter hieroglyphic texts. The temple is one of a group of three—the others known as the Temple of the Foliated Cross and the Temple of the Sun—on three sides of a former plaza area, constructed in the late seventh cen-

Figure 3 The first panel of the inscription from the Temple of the Cross (late seventh century A.D.) at Palenque, Chiapas, Mexico. Drawing by Linda Schele.

tury (prior to 9.13.0.0.0, which was in A.D. 692). These also have similarly arranged inscriptions, each about two-thirds the length of the one of the Cross. A yet longer text (longer than all three of these together) is in a temple of earlier construction, known as the Temple of Inscriptions, facing another plaza. Yet other texts, of varying lengths, are found in constructions of later dates at this site.

The text of figure 3 is too long for a detailed analysis of its hieroglyphs. Much of it has been presented elsewhere.[8] Here it will suffice to summarize the structure and the content of the text and then to consider just a few of its glyphs in some detail in order to illustrate the nature of the writing system.

The writing of Mayan hieroglyphs was generally in paired columns, and from top down within the pair. To identify loci in an inscription it has become customary to label columns alphabetically and rows numerically; but the letters are to be taken in pairs: AB, CD, and so on. Thus, for example, the locus C1 is followed by D1, but D1 is followed by C2. That convention will be followed here, as it is necessary for the identification of hieroglyphs and for the demarcation of passages.

At the beginning of an inscription, the glyphs of an initial series are often of double width, with compound glyphs spanning two columns rather than one; and their "introducing glyph" is often of double height as well. In this manner it fills four glyph spaces, as it does here. In form this one from the Palenque Temple of the Cross is similar to the Leiden plaque and Stela C of Tres Zapotes; but this one has an "earth" sign, *cab* or "Caban," infixed into the central

position over the *tun* sign, in which position it symbolizes the patron of the month Tzec, the month whose own proper sign is thus to be found below.

Following this, occupying glyph spaces A3–B7, is the series of signs symbolizing the five digits and the periods of the chronological day number for the date that is highlighted in the inscription. In the examples seen previously (fig. 1 and 2) the digits were indicated by means of bar-and-dot numerals (bars for fives and dots for units); but here, in the four higher positions, they are faces. These are the faces of deities, the gods of the numbers twelve, nine, three, and four; but two of them, namely those of nine and three, are equipped with fleshless lower jaws, which adds ten to their respective values. Some of these are known in other contexts; for example, the god of the number four is the Mayan sun god. He is also the god of the day Ahau, and his hieroglyph has the capacity to symbolize either of these calendrical concepts, "four" and "Ahau," in addition to its primary function, which is to designate the deity himself. The sense intended is always clear from the context. The sign for the fifth digit, a shell sign held in a hand (in units position, at A7), is one of the signs for zero. The indicated day number is thus 12.19.13.4.0. The values of these signs have been known to Americanist antiquarians since the last decade of the nineteenth century, when they were determined by J. T. Goodman.[9] Their alternations with transparent bar-and-dot equivalents in identifiable contexts, and the internal redundancy of the combined calendrical and chronological system, made their decipherment possible and have proven its correctness many times over.

Comparing again with the earlier examples discussed above, it is apparent that the time periods are also indicated in a different manner in this inscription. As already noted, on Stela C of Tres Zapotes, and on some other pre-Mayan monuments, they are given by position alone, dispensing with explicit period signs, whereas on the Leiden plaque there are two bird heads with overlaid symbols, a fanciful reptilian head, a frog head with appurtenances, and a monkey head. But in the Temple of the Cross they are indicated by their primary signs. These are all standard and much-used alternatives for the representation of numerical and calendrical concepts in Mayan inscriptions, where primary signs and extravagant zoomorphic and anthropo-theomorphic variants freely alternate with one another, with the latter varieties presented either in facial or in full-figure portrait.

The long-count date 12.19.13.4.0, if it were intended to be in the current era, has not yet occurred. (It is due in another two decades, on April 19 of the year 2006.) But it is clear that it is not the current era that was intended here. If it were, the calendar-round day recorded at A8–B9 would have to be 8 Ahau 13 Pop; instead it is 8 Ahau 18 Tzec, which is the proper calendar-round position for this same day number in the "Old Era" that preceded the present one. That era, mythological, was conceived by the Maya as having had a duration of thirteen baktuns (5,200 "chronological years," or *tuns*), and its closing day—which is also the "zero" day of the current era—is

often so expressed in the inscriptions. For example, it is cited in this manner in the present inscription, at D3–C5, where it is referred to as "4 Ahau 8 Cumku, completion of 13 baktuns."

The event that is celebrated in the opening passage of the inscription is thus a mythological one, and it is said here to have taken place on a date that was some six years (6.14.0) before the epoch of the current era. This places it in the year 3120 B.C. It is recorded in three glyphs at A17–C1. But before these, there is more to the temporal clause which orients it in the cycles of time. After the calendar-round day of "8 Ahau 18 Tzec" (A8–B9) comes the placement of the date in the cycle of the nine lords of the night (at A10, this one being the eighth); then placement in the lunar calendar (B10–A13: moon age 5 days after first appearance of the crescent, after 2 prior months in the current lunar half-year, a 29-day month in the 29-day/30-day alternation); and then its placement in an 819-day cycle (B13–B16: 20 days after the last station of that cycle, which was of the south in a 4 × 819-day counterclockwise directional rotation, and which was on a calendar-round day 1 Ahau 18 Zotz).

With the day thus oriented in the coordinates of time, its event is announced. It was the "birth" of the ancient mother goddess. A17 is the birth glyph, B17 her title, and C1 her name glyph. One may wonder how they could be so specific about the time of an event in mythological antiquity. But there is more to the date than at first meets the eye. We return to it later.

This sets the theme. The next passage (D1–C13) records the birth of the ancient male progenitor deity on a date that was 8.5.0 before the epoch of the current era (i.e., before "4 Ahau 8 Cumhu, completion of 13 baktuns"), and then another event for which he was responsible and which had apparently some cosmological significance, on a day "13 Ik end-of-Mol," 1.9.2 after the epoch. The nature of that event is unclear; but the current hypothesis, shakily drawn from certain of the glyphs, is that it had something to do with the setting in order of the celestial universe, or its resetting for the current era in the order in which we now know it. Whatever the event, he, the ancient cause, was of age 9.14.2 when he accomplished it—not much more than nine and half years old!

The next passage (D13–F4) records the birth of the first of the offspring of this pair, the namesake of his sire, on a date that was some seven and a half centuries later. He was one of a set of triplets, the second of them coming four days later, and the third fourteen days after that one, these being celebrated, respectively, in the Temples of the Sun and the Foliated Cross.

The following passage (E5–F9) records the "accession to rulership" of the mother deity on a date that was some eight centuries after her birth. The hieroglyph employed for that legendary event is identical to those that designate accessions to rulership by historical kings in the second half of this inscription. What cosmic event this mythological "accession" was imagined to represent is unknown. As for its compatibility with the sex of the protagonist, it can be noted that the idea of a female acceding to rule would not have been strange to the Maya of Palenque. Their "king list" includes two female rulers who held the title and occupied that office, one for a reign of twenty-one years, until her death, and the other—a namesake of the ancient mother deity—for something less than three years, until her son had reached the age of 12.9.8 and was installed, still a boy, in that office.

Next is another mythological birth, followed by accession, some thirteen centuries later (E10 ff., continued on right-hand panel), and after that a somewhat similar sequence, not securely anchored in the chronology, which could be either mythological or historical.

After these begins the assuredly historical sequence, with a securely anchored date corresponding to August 9 of A.D. 422. The remainder of the text (on the panel of the right, not shown here) records the birth and accession dates, with ages at accession, for a series of six kings of Palenque. The series overlaps with another in the Temple of Inscriptions, which records in a different manner the accession dates of the last four of this sequence of rulers and of five others who followed them, together with the katun rites which they carried out, bringing the historical record up to a date in the year 684. Other inscriptions from the site carry it a century further.

This quick review of the content of the text has been included in order to permit an appreciation of the historical and cultural context in which the hieroglyphic writing flourished. Matters for whose recording it was employed included principally the important events in the lives of rulers: their births, rites of heir-designation, sometimes their marriages, their deaths, and apotheoses. Also recorded, and of particular importance, were the rites which they performed at the completions of katuns, half-katuns, and quarter-katuns (period of twenty chronological years and subdivisions thereof). Other important subjects were their military engagements with enemy kingdoms and the taking of high-ranking captives. Another serious matter at some sites was the ball game, staged on ceremonial occasions as a contest between warlords of rival principalities, and apparently often ending in sacrifice. There is less of explicitly astronomical matters (other than that entailed by the lunar calendar) than we might wish they had bequeathed to us, but if significant astronomical events happened to coincide with a katun-ending, these—at least at Palenque—were recorded. Thus we find references to the evening star Venus at its greatest elongation from the sun (the point at which it reverses its motion in the horizontal sphere, relative to the sun) in the katun-ending records of 9.9.0.0.0 and 9.12.0.0.0, and of the first appearance of the evening star Venus in the record of 9.10.0.0.0. This planetary deity appears to have been a war god. Important dynastic rituals and military undertakings, of sorts whose timings could be controlled, also coincided in a surprising number of instances with critical points in the synodic cycle either of Venus or of Jupiter.[10] One can only suspect that court astrologers must frequently have played a role in the setting of these dates.

If the astrologers had a part in determining dates, so also apparently did the numerologists; or perhaps they were the same personnel. The birth date of the ancient mother goddess, to which reference was made earlier, is a remarkable numerological contrivance, establishing a cosmic relationship between her birth date and the birth date of a great Palenque ruler. So also the dates of numerous other mythological events can be shown to have had numerological derivation.[11]

......

The Nature of Mayan Hieroglyphic Writing

The Mayan hieroglyphic writing system is still in the process of decipherment. Much has been accomplished; much remains to be done. The values of a majority of the numerical and calendrical signs, even in their multiplicity of substitutable forms, were determined in the latter part of the nineteenth century by J. T. Goodman, working with photographs and drawings of Mayan monuments made available by A. P. Maudslay, and also by Ernst Förstemann, working with a Mayan hieroglyphic codex which he had obtained in Italy for the Royal Public Library of Dresden. The semantic values of a few other signs, some with and some without iconic clues, were also determined at this time and in succeeding years as a consequence of their consistent associations with particular figures among those depicted in the surviving codices (the Dresden, another codex in Madrid, and one in Paris). These included the name-glyphs of many of the deities, the signs designating various birds and animals, and those relating to a few material objects, such as the house, the slit-log drum, and the hunting noose. The sign for the planet Venus was identifiable because of its repeated employment in the Venus tables of the Dresden Codex, where numerical relationships—subdivisions and multiples of the number 584 (the mean number of days in the synodic period of Venus)—give the clue. So also with the eclipse sign by virtue of its employment in the eclipse tables of the same codex, where again numerical relations reveal the subject matter. And the signs for the four directions and for the four colors associated with them were recognized from abundant circumstantial evidence, but especially from their appearance in the pages devoted to the Mayan New Year rites in the Dresden and Madrid Codices, together with information detailed by Diego de Landa in his *Relación de las Cosas de Yucatán* (ca. 1566).[12] But other hieroglyphs, the majority, with neither arithmetical nor pictorial associations to indicate their values, did not so easily give up their secrets.

Opinions have varied among scholars, and have shifted through time, as to the possible nature of this writing system and as to what might be the content of the texts inscribed on Mayan monuments. A few aspects of its character and subject matter have been indicated in the foregoing introduction to some illustrative specimens. These matters have not always been understood in that manner, however. In fact, they have been subjects of much dispute and controversy, almost to the present day. The earliest researchers did indeed expect that the writing system might be in substantial part phonetic, and some were optimistic that Bishop Landa's "abc"—a purported alphabet with a few additional signs given by example—might hold the key and lead to decipherments. But its failure led instead to abandonment of that hope, even by those who had once shared it and had invested effort in its pursuit. The conviction became general that the Mayan hieroglyphic signs were essentially nonphonetic in character and that they were exclusively ideograms. Occasional attempts to resurrect the phonetic hypothesis, such as those of the linguist Benjamin Lee Whorf, were brusquely and easily disposed of because of the many errors of identification that they contained—inevitable for an amateur venturing into this domain without having a long and thorough familiarity with the data. The net effect was to discredit linguistic approaches to decipherment. And it became a fixed dogma that there were no phonetic signs in Mayan hieroglyphic writing.

As for the content of the inscriptions, some early writers had expressed the expectation that they might contain historical accounts. Others expected astronomical information or religion. One thing, however, was certain: they contained an extraordinarily high proportion of hieroglyphs designating and enumerating periods of time and stations in the cycles of time. It was nearly always a series of these, at the beginning of an inscription, that received the most lavish embellishment. Often these commemorated the ending of a katun (20 × 360 days), or of a half- or a quarter-katun period. Gradually the view crystallized that the primary burden of the inscriptions was to do honor to the gods of time. The outlines of a hypothetically Mayan philosophy of time and number began to take shape. The gods were seen as ruling for foreordained durations in cyclic succession to one another, some periodically throughout eternity, others perhaps only in an era. Each exerted his unique influence, endowing his period with special benefits or hazards according to his nature. The katun rites were seen as "climaxes of the great mysteries, every whit as sacred as were those of Eleusis to the early Greeks."[13] Actually a fair amount of evidence supported such a view. There was a wealth of information in Landa's *Relación de las Cosas de Yucatán* and in the writings of other Spanish observers from the postconquest period; there was native testimony in the books of Chilam Balam—esoteric documents written by Mayans, in Mayan, in Roman letters; and there was the testimony of iconography on the stone monuments, especially in the full-figure portraiture of personified "Numbers" grappling with zoic or demonic "Periods." It was held by the leading Mayanist of the twentieth century and the one most influential and eloquent, Sir Eric Thompson, that events of human history were not recorded on Mayan monuments.[14] Apparent counterevidence—such as scenes of conquest, bound captives, depictions seeming to glorify individuals—were questioned as to their proper interpretation. Were these really captives and conquerors? Or were they actors in a ritual drama expressing astronomical or otherwise symbolic motifs? Mayan mythology is rich in just that kind of content. So also are the Mayan painted ceramics. And the figures depicted

on stelae, so heavily overlaid with symbols, could as well be deities as humans.

New evidence pertinent to the question of the content of the inscriptions appeared in 1958 and 1960 with the publication of two carefully reasoned studies, one by Heinrich Berlin, and one by Tatiana Proskouriakoff.[15] The evidence in each case came from their discovery of the significance of particular categories of hieroglyphs, defined in terms of composition and distribution in the first case, and in terms of a patterning of associated dates in the second case. These deserve special notice here because of their methodological interest and because they initiated one of the two main thrusts of the "recent" period in the history of Mayan decipherment.

Berlin isolated a category of hieroglyphs which, to be minimally committal at the outset, he labeled "emblem glyphs." They were defined as a category by virtue of their common possession of certain prefixed and superfixed elements (see fig. 4). They also shared a common distributional feature, namely, their occurrence in final position in an inscription, or in final position within an otherwise structurally defined segment of an inscription. But the "main signs" of these glyphs, that is, their principal components, which bear the diagnostic prefix and superfix, varied. Each of these principal components, he noted, was peculiar to a particular Mayan city, occurring frequently in its inscriptions but only rarely if ever in the inscriptions of other cities. From this it could be inferred that, whatever their general significance as a category, their particular significances were local. Possibilities might be place names, dynasty names, or

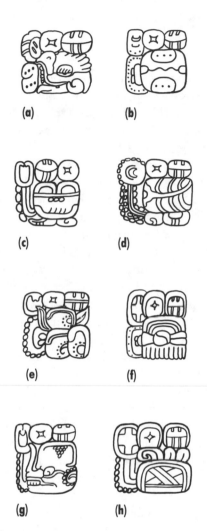

Figure 4 Emblem glyphs from several sites:
(a) Palenque, (b) a second variety from Palenque, (c) Yaxchilan, (d) Quirigua, (e) Seibal, (f) Tikal, (g) Copan, (h) Naranjo.

names of local tutelary divinities. This made it reasonable to consider now that matters of purely local concern might enter into the content of the inscriptions. Which suggests local history.

In the next development along this line, Proskouriakoff, working first with the inscriptions of a single site, focused attention on a few particular hieroglyphs which occurred repeatedly with dates (and therefore presumably designated events) but whose dated recurrences were at irregular intervals in time (rather than at regular intervals, as were those associated with period endings, or as would be expected if they designated recurrent astronomical phenomena). The dates associated with the hieroglyphs of this set, moreover, could be sorted into several separate series, based on the spatial distribution of the monuments on which they were inscribed at the site. (An alternative diagnostic for sorting, with the same result, would have been the hieroglyphs immediately following the ones in question.) With the dates thus sorted into several separate series, it could be observed that any particular hieroglyph from the set occurred but once in any given series (with a single explicable exception) and, further, that the hieroglyphs from the set, when occurring in different series, occurred in the same relative chronological order, though with different spacings in time. Next she was able to point out that the total time span of a series, from its earliest date to its latest, never exceeded a reasonable human lifetime. One of the glyphic phrases from the set had iconographic associations of a sort which suggested that, if it referred to an event in the life of a human being, the event would be the inauguration of that person into a high social or political status, such as one of rulership. Another glyph of the set, if it occurred in any given series, was always associated with the earliest date of the series. A reasonable supposition then would be that this designated the person's birth. Another, when occurring in a series, was always associated with the terminal date of the series. This, it could then be inferred, might refer to the individual's death, or to some event associated with his death. The exceptional one, which could occur more than once in a series, had iconographic associations which indubitably linked it to the taking of captives. Proskouriakoff showed also that there were similar series at a few other sites.

Eric Thompson, in writing a new preface for the second edition (1960) of his *Maya Hieroglyphic Writing*, took note of Berlin's study, which had just been published, and of Proskouriakoff's, which was still in manuscript as he wrote, and referred to them as a breakthrough of the greatest importance, remarking, "It may well be that they will lead me to revise my views on the impersonality of the texts on Maya monuments." And a little over a decade later, writing another preface for the third edition (1971), he acknowledged, "This work has shown that the generally held view, to which I subscribed, regarding the impersonality of the texts on Maya stelae, is completely mistaken." But he continued, "Possibly the personal and impersonal categories are not mutually exclusive; dates may have been chosen for civil events, such as

accessions of rulers, because of calendrical or astronomical associations. Such a practice was widespread in the Old World; there is some evidence of a similar interrelationship in the Maya area."

With these studies a new era in Mayan interpretive epigraphy was ushered in. Series of dates and associated hieroglyphs such as Proskouriakoff first brought to light have now been found throughout the entire Lowland Maya area. Hieroglyphs for other events, such as heir designation, marriage, and burial, have been added to the list, and many sets of substitutable synonymous glyphic forms and phrases have been verified. Hieroglyphs designating the relationships of child-to-father and child-to-mother (which many Mayan languages distinguish) have been determined, again including sets of synonyms. Dynastic sequences, with dates, and in some cases with partial genealogies, have been established for many of the major Mayan city-states. That the inscriptions refer to historical persons and to real human events can no longer be doubted.

But the last-cited remark of Thompson's was also prophetic; there is now a small but growing body of evidence for a role played by astronomical observations and predictions in the setting of dates for events whose timing was subject to human control. Dates of the first appearance of the evening-star Venus were choice occasions for initiating raids on enemies or for staging accessions to rulership. Other astronomical cues for important events included the inferior conjunction of Venus, the heliacal rising of the morning star Venus, the greatest eastern elongation of the evening star, the departure of the morning star from the second stationary point, and so on. The departure of Jupiter from its second stationary point was another such cue at some sites. But the degree to which such considerations entered into the planning of human undertakings seems to have varied with different sites, and within sites, with different rulers.

......

The Composition of the Hieroglyphs

As was noted earlier, it had become dogma among the specialists that the Mayan hieroglyphic writing system did not employ phonetic signs. That position requires clarification, however, for the notion of "phonetic sign" can easily be misunderstood. It did not mean that the phonetic features of Mayan words were thought never to have played a role in the formation of hieroglyphs used to represent them. For the so-called rebus principle, whereby a sign iconically suited to an object word is employed also for one more abstract that is phonetically similar, was recognized to have had a function in the system.

Such usage could be seen in the employment of the sign for "tree" or "wood," *te'*, not only for trees (of which there are numerous examples in the codices), or in compound glyphs for certain objects made of wood, but also as a prefix to the signs for certain other objects when these are enumerated, where a spoken Mayan language would require a numeral classifier of that same phonetic form. So also in the employment of the *tun* sign (which is considered to have been derived from a conventional-

ized representation of the slit-log drum) for the 360-day time period of that name, and occasionally also for the terminal day of a month, and yet further (with an iconically motivated superfix) for the month Pax; for that drum is *tun* in several of the Mayan languages, and *tunkul* or *pax* in Yucatec. Another example has been seen in the employment of the shark-head sign, apparently for "count," in a pair of signs for counting "days from" and "days to" particular dates. "Shark" and "count" are both *xoc*.[16] Yet another, known since the earliest work with the codices, is the employment of one and the same sign for "earth," "bee," "honey," and the day Caban ("Earth"). These are homonyms or near-homonyms in several of the Mayan languages (*cab* or *chab*, depending on the language).

The "no phonetic signs" hypothesis thus in no way applied to the employment of the rebus principle in extending the hieroglyphic inventory. Rather, it was concerned with the issue of whether any instance of the use of a hieroglyphic sign ever conveyed *phonetic value only*, without an inherently associated semantic or grammatical value; or more particularly, whether a sign could ever be employed for something *less than a morpheme*, that is, less than a linguistic unit which carried a meaning in its own right, whether as a full word, a word root, or a grammatically meaningful affix. In other words, the question reduces simply to that of whether the system had resources for what amounts to phonetic spelling (whether alphabetic or syllabic) as implied by Bishop Landa's "abc" and his examples.

The verdict was long an emphatic and often emotion-laden No!

The discoveries of Berlin and Proskouriakoff have been cited as a turning point in the interpretation of the content of the hieroglyphic inscriptions. A second new development, also amounting to a decisive turning point, has followed from the reopening of the long-tabooed question of "phoneticism." This was initiated in the early 1950s by Yurii V. Knorozov, who set out to demonstrate that Landa's data were valid, that several of the signs that he recorded could be confirmed in the values that he gave them, by reference to their occurrences in the illustrated Mayan codices and by comparison of these with lexicographic sources for Yucatec Maya, and that the different applications of these signs verified their role as phonetic in the strictest sense, that is, as frequently representing only portions of morphemes rather than complete ones, and as representing sounds independently of meaning.[17]

Except by a very few scholars, Knorozov's work was received with general hostility and with an equal amount of misunderstanding. His position, however, was not that the Mayan writing system was fundamentally phonetic but rather that it was in an authentic sense "hieroglyphic"; which is to say that it employed, of necessity, compositional devices analogous to those of the ancient Old World writing systems to which that characterization is commonly applied. According to this view it could be expected to exhibit the following features: (1) its sign inventory should be large, not the size of an alphabet or a syllabary, but of a magnitude such as to require the services of a specialized priestly-scholarly class; (2) the majority of its signs should be logograms, that is, word-signs, signifying unique associations of phonetic and semantic values, in which neither of these is free of the other; (3) some of its logograms, however, should inevitably be multivalued because of the necessary expedient of extending the application of a sign from one word value to another, exploiting either a phonetic similarity or a semantic connection as a basis for the extension; (4) some of its otherwise logographic signs might also, in appropriate contexts, be employed solely for their semantic values, not as logograms, but as keys to the interpretation of other signs with which they are compounded, or as category markers, to be left unpronounced (these are the "determinatives" of the Old World hieroglyphic systems); and (5) in addition to its logograms, the system should be expected to have also some signs that are employed primarily or exclusively as phonetic signs, mainly syllabic, without any necessarily implied semantic value, these having the three main functions of (*a*) serving as phonetic complements to logographic signs—especially when the latter are multivalued—offering additional cues for their recognition and for sign individuation, (*b*) representing the semantically less concrete elements of a sentence such as syntactic particles and the inflectional affixes of words, and (*c*) providing resources also for the construction of purely phonetically derived composite word-signs, which in effect amounts to phonetic spelling.

Knorozov attempted to show that the Mayan writing system conformed to this type, illustrating with examples these and certain other related compositional principles. Some of his proposed readings of hieroglyphs in the Mayan codices have proved viable; others have not. But the principles which he posited have proved to be correct; today they are accepted by most of the scholars who are actively engaged in this area of research. As guidelines for the formation and testing of hypotheses, they have been productive of many new discoveries of glyph values.

These compositional principles can best be appreciated if we see them in application to the system's graphic elements, which derive from the Mayan art tradition and its iconographic conventions. To this end, let us examine now a few hieroglyphs in some detail. The examination will also serve to convey an impression of where the process of decipherment stands at the present time, illustrating both something of what has been found out and something of what still remains obscure.

Mention has been made of Proskouriakoff's isolation of the glyph that accompanies the earliest date in each of the series that she identified, and of the inference that this glyph might signify "birth." There are seven of these birth glyphs in the left-hand panel of the inscription of the Temple of the Cross (fig. 3: A11, A17, C17, D2, E7, E13, E17) and twelve more in the right-hand panel (not shown here). Of these nineteen, nine are in reference to the births of gods in mythic time, nine to the births of historical rulers at Palenque, and one (at A11) to the "birth" of the current moon. This latter was a standard usage at Palenque and a number of other sites for placing a date in the lunar calendar (recall the content of the passage B10–A13 as given in the overview of this inscription in the previous section). Even to the present day in many Mayan communities the first visibility of a new crescent moon is referred to as the "birth of the moon," or the "birth of Our Grandmother," and the age of the moon on any given date is counted from her most recent rebirth.[18]

These "birth" glyphs have as their common central component an upturned head, which on the basis of certain of its diagnostics has been understood to derive from the representation of a frog of some variety. Examination of its occurrences (e.g., those in fig. 3 as listed in the preceding paragraph) shows that it occurs with several different combinations of affixes, as exemplified in figure 5. Closer study of their contexts, both here and elsewhere, shows further that the forms (d) and (e) of figure 5 are used in reference to a birth only when its date is related to the date of some other previous event, in a clause such as, "it was so-and-so many years, months, and days from such-and-such an event *to the birth* of so-and-so on such-and-such a date." Those of (a), (b), and (c), on the other hand, are found both in simple single-event statements ("on such-and-such a date *was the birth* of so-and-so") and in statements of the two-event variety where the birth in question is the *prior* of the two events ("it was so-and-so many years, months, and days *from the birth* of so-and-so to his accession on such-and-such a date"). This correlation allows the attribution of certain syntactic functions to the various combinations of affixes, some

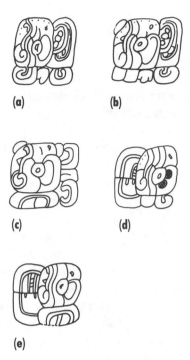

(a)　　　　**(b)**

(c)　　　　**(d)**

(e)

Figure 5　Hieroglyphs for "birth," with varying combinations of affixes. All are from the
first panel of the inscription of the Temple of
the Cross at Palenque (fig. 3), located (column
and row) as follows: (a) at E7, (b) at D2, (c) at
A11, (d) at E13, (e) at C17. Drawings by David
Kiphuth, after Linda Schele (Figure 3).

of them contrastive, others merely mutual
alternatives.

These examples illustrate the use of a
logogram with attached phonetic signs as
affixes. The characterization of the affixes
as phonetic rests on the grammatical nature
and the diversity of the functions associated
with their occurrences in different contexts, which exclude the possibility of any
common component of meaning. It in no
way excludes, however, the possibility of
their ultimate derivation from signs that
may once have served or may even continue

to serve also as logograms. For example,
the suffix to the right or upper right in (a)
and (b) of figure 5 is derived from a logographic "moon" sign; but the functions
associated with it as an affix are diverse,
lacking a common feature, and bearing no
relation to either of the two significations
of the logogram, which are "moon" and
"twenty." Even its apparent phonetic value,
ah (vowel with voiceless laryngeal spirant),
is of uncertain relation to its readings as a
logogram, which must have been *uh* and
k'al, and variants or alternates to these,
depending on the particular language.

As for the other affixes appearing on the
"birth" glyphs of figure 5, the following
can be noted. The prefix that is common
to forms (d) and (e) is the one that Landa
gave for the letter *i* in his purported alphabet. This phonetic value has been attested
in several other contexts, but as a "poste-
rior event" indicator, as exemplified here,
its identification with a linguistically documented or reconstructable grammatical
element is still a matter of question. For
the subfix that is common to (c) and (e),
two competing hypotheses—*ne* and *il*—
are still under consideration, neither having
been brought yet to definite proof or dis-
proof. For the affix that is found as a subfix
in (a) and as a postfix in (c), and in abbreviated form in (d) and (b), a value will be
illustrated later in the context of another
example.

The phonetic reading of the upturned-
frog-head logogram, which is central to
these "birth" glyphs, remains uncertain; it
might well have varied with the local language in which it was read, inasmuch as
words for birth are among the most vari-

able in the comparative Mayan lexicon. Neither is it known for sure whether there was any phonetic basis for the invention of a birth glyph with this frog-head form. Two rather tenuous rebus possibilities have been suggested by other writers. But a phonetic basis is hardly necessary; there are ample possibilities for a semantic motivation in the symbolism of frogs and in a related Mayan figure of speech. And the upturned orientation of the head has analogs in the iconography of birth in the surviving Mayan codices.[19]

Glyphs based on the upturned frog-head are not the only ones to signify birth. Some others are illustrated in figure 6. That those of (a) and (b) of figure 6 are synonymous with the upturned-frog-head variety is implied by their employment in certain texts at Palenque to designate events involving the same personages on exactly the same dates as are designated in other texts by upturned-frog-head glyphs. That there should be hieroglyphs of totally different appearance having the same meaning, or being at least coreferent, should not surprise us; for synonyms exist also in the spoken languages. There are "ordinary" words for birth, and there are other expressions of euphemistic or poetic derivation; for example, "come into existence," "sprout," "emerge," "become a person," "begin being," "appear on the earth," "arrive in the world," "see the light," "see the world," "touch the earth." In some of the languages, as spoken today, expressions of the latter sort have become the general terms employed for the births of humans, while the once basic words have come to be restricted to the births either of animals or of deities. In Chontal—one of the languages of the Cholan branch of Mayan (and the one most likely to have been the general language of hieroglyphic inscriptions outside of Yucatán)—the word used for the births of humans is a verb that is derived from the noun for "earth"; it can be glossed most literally as "to earth," in the sense of arriving or making one's appearance on the earth. But in this language, as also in Chol, the original simple word for "earth," *cab* (or *chab,* as would have been expected in Cholan) has been replaced by a compound expression meaning literally "the surface of

Figure 6 Additional varieties of "birth" hieroglyphs: (a) and (b) are from the alfardas of the Temples of the Sun and the Foliated Cross at Palenque; (c) is from the first panel of the Temple of the Cross (fig. 3: E2); (d) is from the hieroglyphic codices of Dresden and Madrid, generic form. Drawings by David Kiphuth.

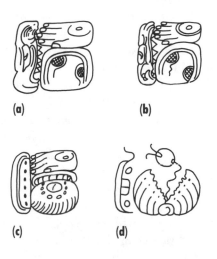

(a)   (b)

(c)   (d)

the earth." In Chontal this is *pancab* (*pani-mil* in Chol), where the first part of the compound, *pan,* is a noun that applies to any outer visible surface, flat exterior expanse, and so on. The Chontal expression for "birth" employs this same compound as a verb stem.

This is the verb that must have been the basis for the "birth" hieroglyphs of the form shown in figure 6 (a, b). The principal component (lower right) is the well-known Mayan logogram for "earth," as also for the day Caban (the day that is named for the earth). The sign placed over the earth sign is a straightforward depiction of the back of the right hand, with a conventional exaggeration of the wrist bone (a standard iconographic feature in Mayan glyphic forms based on the hand), and with the fingers extended in such a way as to present it as a flat surface. It is thus a suitable rebus for the noun *pan,* the primary sense of which includes both the notion of "outer surface" and that of "flat surface." The glyphic compound thus suggests a reading of *pancab,* either directly in the sense of "earth," or as a verb stem or deverbal noun in the sense of "birth." It should be noted, however, that the proof of the "*pan*" hypothesis for the back-of-the-hand sign is still incomplete; it can be considered secure only when all of the other occurrences of the sign, in contexts not yet fully understood, are shown also to require it—which may or may not turn out to be the case. The remaining element, the preposed sign to the left, is one of several different glyphic prefixes for a third-person pronoun. The several prefixes of this category, which alternate seemingly freely with one another, are well attested for their pronominal component; but whether they had homonymous readings or represented instead contractions of the pronoun with various preposed syntactic particles is still an unresolved question. The entire glyph must have been understood either nominally as "his birth" or verbally as "he was born"—two renderings whose difference is more one of English grammar than of Mayan.

Yet another hieroglyph for "birth" is that of figure 6 (c). (It can be seen also in the panel from the Temple of the Cross, fig. 3, at locus E2.) Its preposed element, at the left, is another of the pronominal category just mentioned. The upper element is again the back-of-the-hand sign. But below it are two different components. The one in the middle is one that Bishop Landa presented as having the value *ca.* In recent studies that phonetic value has been attested over and over again, in many different contexts; it is entirely secure. The one at the bottom is the logogram for the day Imix; but it is a glyphic form that has been shown to be multivalued. When employed as a phonetic sign its value is regularly *ba* if syllabic, or *b* after the vowel *a* if it is for a consonant in word-final position. These values too have been amply attested in diverse contexts and are known now to be secure. The two signs combined therefore yield *ca* plus either *ba* or *(a)b,* the latter giving a phonetic spelling of the syllable *cab.* Together they provide a phonetically derived alternative to the "earth" logogram, and they serve in the same function. The glyph of form (c) in figure 6 thus had the same reading and the same sense as that of (a) and (b); it exemplifies the phonetic derivation of an alternative logogram.

In the Mayan codices there is found yet another hieroglyph for birth, figure 6 (d), which portrays a seedling shooting forth from a split gourd. Though its form is based on the "sprout" metaphor, its reading was probably that of the ordinary verb for "birth" in Yucatec, the root of which was *sih*. A reason for this assumption, aside from the fact that Yucatec is the language of the surviving codices, is that another hieroglyphic sign, derived from this and consisting simply of one half of the split gourd, serves as a phonetic sign for the syllable *si* in other contexts in the codices (and only in the codices) in hieroglyphs for expressions such as "gift," "trap setting," and "rope pulling," which employ verb roots beginning with that consonant-vowel combination. The prefix at the left in figure 6(d) is the simplest and most frequent representation of the third-person possessive and ergative pronoun. Its phonetic value was given by Landa as *u,* and it has been amply attested in that value.

Of importance on a par with birth glyphs in Mayan dynastic inscriptions are those that denote accession to rulership. Of these also there are several varieties, some of which are totally different and others only partially different from one another in their makeup and appearance. They too carry suitably different inflectional or syntactic affixes according to their contexts. Synonymy can be identified among accession phrases in the same way as it can among birth hieroglyphs; for if a glyphic phrase in one passage ascribes such an event to a particular ruler on a particular date, and in another passage a different-appearing phrase ascribes an event to that same ruler on exactly the same date (and further, if alternations of this sort occur repeatedly), then the event named by the second glyphic phrase must be either the same as that named by the first, or else the two must be consistently associated—as part to whole, or as different aspects of the same totality.

For present purposes it will suffice to illustrate just two types of glyphic accession phrases, those of figure 7 and those of figure 8. An example of the first variety may be seen also in figure 3, at the loci F7–E8, where it records a mythological event in a "birth-to-accession" passage (E5–F9) that is typical—except for the magnitude of its interval(!)—of those recorded for several human rulers in the continuation of the inscription in the remaining panels from the temple. Accession phrases of this type, though well attested for their meaning, are still partially obscure in respect to their reading. Their analysis therefore will not be undertaken here, though some of their components will already be familiar. Their citation is only for the illustration of synonymy between two overtly unlike sets of forms (cf. figs. 7 and 8).

Accession phrases of the second variety (fig. 8) are of very frequent occurrence, at Palenque as well as elsewhere, with abundant confirmation of their functional equivalence to those of the first variety. The principal component of the first hieroglyph in each of these phrases of figure 8 will perhaps be recognized; it was encountered twice in the inscription of the Leiden

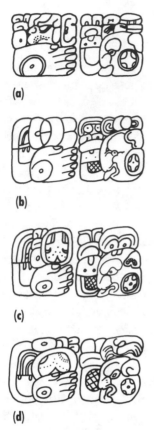

(a).

(b)

(c)

(d)

Figure 7 Some hieroglyphic "accession" phrases: (a) and (b) are from the third panel of the Palenque Temple of Inscriptions; (c) and (d) are from the third panel of the Temple of the Cross. Drawings by David Kiphuth.

plaque, which dates from about four centuries earlier. It is the logogram for the root of the "seating" verb, *cum* or *chum*, depending on the particular language. It is seen here in three different inflections, the first as indicated by the affixes of (a), the second by those of (b), and the third by those of the form (c–e).

The first of these examples is of especial interest because of the existence of historical evidence for its linguistic form and for the entire phrase in which it occurs. It mer-

its therefore a close examination. Affixed to the "seating" sign of the first glyph of the phrase (fig. 8,[a], first half) are three phonetic signs: *wa,* directly underneath (consisting of two conjoined parts); *ni,* the upper one of those to the right; and *hi,* in the lower right-hand corner of the composite glyph (with only two of its three parts showing, as if overlapped and partly hidden by *wa*). The values of all three of these affixes are well attested, so the reading of the first hieroglyph of the phrase is completely determined. It must have been *chumwanihi,* or *chumwanih* if the last sign was employed only for its consonantal value in word-final position. In most of the languages of the Cholan branch of Mayan, this is a third-person-singular perfective form, "(he/she/it) was seated," "was set in place," or "was installed." That the glyphic affixes are phonetic rather than logographic (morphemic) is proven by the fact that the graphic segmentation corresponds to the phonetic syllabification, *chum-wa-ni-hi,* and not to the morphemic segmentation of the form, which is *chum-wan-i-h(i)*.

The second glyph of the phrase (fig. 8[a], second half) is made up of three main constituents, of which the second and third are in turn each of two parts, making five in all. Of these, the tall prefix to the left is one of a set of several signs that alternate freely with one another in the value *ta,* or in final position simply *t* after a vowel *a.* (Some others can be seen either prefixed or superfixed in the examples of fig. 8[b–e].) The value of these is phonetic, often indicating only part of a morpheme; but at the beginning of a sign cluster they can also represent a locative preposition of that phonetic form. That

Figure 8 Hieroglyphic "accession" phrases based on the "seating" idiom. The last three examples (c–e) from the Tablet of the 96 Glyphs at Palenque, are from the drawing of that inscription by Linda Schele, conforming to a rubbing of the limestone tablet by Merle Greene Robertson. It reproduces accurately the calligraphy of the original.

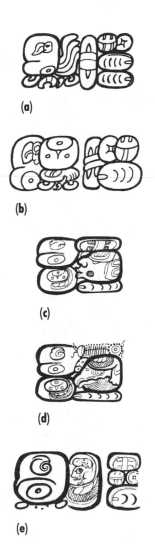

(a)

(b)

(c)

(d)

(e)

is their function here; in these examples each can be translated as "in" or "into."

To the right of the prefix, the pair of small signs on the top of the stack (▦⊠) is one of the ways of representing the word *ahaw,* which means "king," or "ruling lord." And the signs below it—two identical signs (⟨⟨⟨⟨⟨), one on top of the other—are identified as the inscribed equivalent of a sign given by Landa as a letter *l* in his Mayan "abc." But Landa's illustration of its use shows that its value was fundamentally syllabic, namely *le;* though like other such consonant-plus-vowel signs, it could be used just for its consonant when in word-final position after a vowel of quality similar to that of the one suppressed. Thus the reading of this second glyph of the phrase is also completely determined; it must have been *ta ahawlel.* The suffix *-lel* is derivational, forming an abstract noun. Taking the preposition and the derived noun together, the meaning is "into the kingship," or "into the office of ruling lord." With the preceding hieroglyph, the entire phrase must have been read *chumwanih ta ahawlel,* which can be understood as "he was seated in the royal office," or "he was installed as ruler."

These examples are from inscriptions of the late eighth century of our era. In a colonial manuscript of more than eight centuries later (1610–14), written in Chontal in a Latin script, we find almost the identical expressions. In the history recorded there we read statements such as *chumvanihix ta ahaulel Paxtun,* "Paxtun was installed as ruler"; and *chumvanix ta ahaulel Macvabin yidzin Pachimalhix,* "Macvabin, the younger brother of Pachimalhix, was installed as ruler." But for an additional enclitic on the verb, and the Spanish-based writing of *v* and *u* for the Mayan phoneme *w,* these are the same expressions as that of the hieroglyphic phrase just analyzed.[20]

It was noted that the pair of small signs on the top of the stack in the second glyph of figure 8(a) is "*one* of the ways" of representing the word *ahaw.* (It is also in the middle tier of the corresponding glyph in (e), and with reversal of the order of its components also in [b].) Two other *ahaw* logograms can be seen in corresponding positions in the remaining two examples, one of them a human head (c) and one a vulture head (d), each with diagnostic details. These all substitute freely for one another as designators of the "ahaw" status.

The glyphic suffix to *ahaw* appears doubled in (a) but single in (b–e). Whether an alternate linguistic form ending simply in -*le* or in -*el* existed in the language of the inscriptions or whether the single graphic element at that time could also represent the fuller ending -*lel* is uncertain. In either case, it is clear from the contexts and from the alternations of these phrases that the sense of the second glyph in each of the examples (b–e) was the same as it was in (a), and that their readings were closely similar if not identical. The graphic suffixes on the "seating" glyph in each of the phrases (b–e) correspond to yet other inflections of that verb but do not change its fundamental sense. Thus, all five of the glyphic phrases of figure 8 are essentially equivalent; all say "was seated in the status of *ahaw.*"

The "seating" idiom has had a long history. From its earliest surviving glyphic representations in the Leiden plaque to its last recorded uses in a political context in the seventeenth-century Chontal document is a span of thirteen centuries. The verb is still in use in the Cholan languages in other contexts; and in cognate forms with *cum* instead of *chum* it continues in use also in Yucatec.

The *ahaw* term and its graphic representations have an equally long history. In many of the Mayan languages to this day the word still means "king," though its hieroglyphs were forgotten three or four centuries ago. Only three of its glyphic forms have been illustrated in figure 8, the human-head *ahaw* of (c), the vulture-head *ahaw* of (d), and the two-part affix-like form of (a), (b), and (e). That the head forms of (c) and (d) were read as *ahaw* is assured by their frequent occurrence in calendrical contexts as alternative specifiers of the twentieth day of the veintena, which bore that name (conventionally transcribed as Ahau, in the Spanish manner). In this function they substituted for the basic calendrical Ahau sign (an example of which can be seen in the illustrated panel from the Palenque Temple of the Cross, fig. 3, at locus B8). And that the two-part form of (a), (b), and (e) was also read in this manner follows from several considerations: (1) from its alternation with the head forms (c) and (d) when functioning as a title; (2) from its frequent accompaniment by the affix *wa,* a phonetic complement, confirming its final consonant, *w,* after the vowel *a;* (3) from its occurrence in some other calendrical contexts and titles (not reviewed here) which require that reading; and (4) from the occasional replacement of one of its components by the calendrical "Ahau" sign. Its derivation and history offer a suitable subject with which to conclude this exemplification of the workings of the Mayan hieroglyphic writing system.

Of the two components in this form of the *ahaw* title, one of them (⊞), on the left in (a) and (e) but on the right in (b), is a logogram in its own right. It serves as the sign of the thirteenth day of the veintena, commonly known as Ben or Been (*be'n* or *be'en*) in Yucatec, Cholan, and a few other languages. But in most of the languages of the Highland Maya the name of this day is Ah, and its sign could convey that value also. The sense of the term *be'n,* which underlies the lowland name of the day, is akin to that of the term *ahaw,* designating an honored status of headman or ruler, or denoting a person of such status. That the sense underlying the highland name of the day, *ah,* may once have been similar is implied by the fact that in one of the recorded Quiché lists of day names the thirteenth day is given as Ahau rather than Ah (causing no confusion with the twentieth day, however, since in the languages of the eastern highlands the twentieth day is known as Ahpu or Hunahpu, rather than as Ahau as in the languages of the lowlands). The sign of the thirteenth day was thus multivalued, with readings *be'n, ah,* and *ahaw,* depending on the glyphic context. (An interesting instance supporting the last of these readings is found in the eclipse table of the Dresden Codex, where the Ben day sign occurs once in place of the proper Ahau. In this—apparently a slip of the pen betraying a common occasional reading and connotation—the sign of the thirteenth day of the veintena substituted for that of the twentieth.)

These are the potential values of one of the two components of this glyphic title. The other component (⊠), on the right in the examples of (a) and (e) but on the left in (b), is fundamentally a phonetic sign with the value *po.* It is employed in glyphic representations of words such as *pohp,* "mat"; *pom,* "copal incense"; and *pol,* "wood carver," either in outright phonetic spellings or as a phonetic complement to a phonetically generalized logogram. Its use in representations of the word for "mat" are pertinent here. The mat was the universal symbol of royal authority among the Maya. It was laid over the throne or dais upon which the ruler sat. In its original form it was a woven reed mat, but in Classic Maya times it was replaced or supplemented by a jaguar pelt; and in its more elaborate forms it had evolved into a cushion or hassock covered over with a jaguar skin. The ruler was known in many places as Ah Pohp, "He of the Mat." In numerous graphic representations of seated rulers, both on painted ceramics and in carved monuments, the throne or hassock itself is marked prominently with the phonetic *po* sign, or alternatively with an iconic "weave" or "plait" sign which could substitute for it. Sometimes the *po* sign is doubled, giving a fuller phonetic representation of the word *pohp,* with indication of both its initial and final consonants and of the vowel between them. When only the single sign was employed, it was an abbreviation, in the nature of a phonetic complement, marking the

(a)

(b)

Figure 9 Two examples of figures seated on phonetic "*po*" signs. The figure in (a), from a carved limestone panel apparently taken from Bonampak, Chiapas, Mexico, is an early historical ruler from that site. His name is in the first two hieroglyphs in front of his face; the third hieroglyph is the Bonampak emblem glyph. In the original panel he faces another named figure, also seated on a *po* sign, and between them is a four-column hieroglyphic inscription beginning with the date 9.4.6.14.9, 5 Muluc 12 Tzec, equivalent to A.D. 521, June 30 (Julian). The *po* sign substitutes for depiction of the throne. The figure in (b), from a painted ceramic plate of unknown provenience, probably of middle-Classic date, is mythological, the god of the number "Nine" and of the day "Chicchan," depicted as a ruler. He is seated on a double *po* hieroglyph, which spells the word for "mat" and substitutes for depiction of the mat-covered throne; at his back is the mat-weave or plaiting sign, substituting for depiction of the royal backrest. Drawing (b) from Nicholas Hellmuth, *Monster und Menschen in der Maya-Kunst* (Graz, Austria, 1987), 207. Courtesy of the Foundation for Latin American Archaeological Research and the Akademische Druck- u. Verlagsanstalt (ADEVA).

mat-covered seat of the ruler and making a point of its identification. In quite a number of examples, the *po* sign itself, either singly or doubled, completely substitutes for the throne; the ruler sits instead on the hieroglyph. The phonetic sign, single or doubled, becomes in effect a logogram; and the "word" then substitutes for the "thing" (fig. 9).

Given these usages, it is possible to consider that the two-part glyphic title of the form represented in (a) and (e) of figure 8 may have been read as Ah Pohp, or even simply as Ahpo (a cognate form in two

230

of the languages of the Highland Maya, historically well documented in the sense of "ruler" or "chieftain"). This is a late form of the hieroglyph, first appearing in the latter half of the eighth century. All earlier examples consisted of the same signs but arranged in the opposite order, as in (b) of figure 8, and as in most of the "emblem glyphs" of figure 4. This earlier order readily admits of being read as Pohp Ahaw, "Mat Lord," which also is a syntactically acceptable form in Mayan. It is an idiom apparently older than that of Ah Pohp or Ahpo. It is found iconically represented, in that order, in the symbolic costuming of lords on many Classic Mayan stelae. And the substitution of an iconic "jaguar-mat throne" sign for the *po* sign in a variant of this glyphic title supports further the possibility of a "Pohp Ahaw" reading. In speech, moreover, the idiom *pohp ahaw* still survives in the sense of "king" or "headman," having been documented in Chontal usage as recently as 1978.

This two-part sign is as old as Mayan hieroglyphic writing. (A minute and poorly etched early version of it appears as a superfix to the final glyph of the inscription of the Leiden plaque.) The original order of its components requires the reading of *pohp ahaw*, "mat lord." The reversed order, introduced in the late eighth century and continuing on through the usage of the codices of the thirteenth to fifteenth centuries, requires a reading as either *ah pohp* or *ahpo*, literally "he of the mat," if both signs are to be read. But in many instances, of both orders, there is clear evidence that the *po* or *pohp* sign was not intended to be read, that its function rather was that of a

determinative, as a key to the sense—and hence by implication also to the reading—of the *be'n/ah/ahaw* portion of the compound. Of the three potential values of that sign, it admits in these cases only the last, which is *ahaw*. This is often confirmed by means of the addition of a phonetic complement for its final *aw* (i.e., *w* after *a*). Its free alternation with other known *ahaw* signs, such as those of figure 8(c, d), offers further verification.[21]

These few examples, drawing upon some "birth" and "accession" phrases, may provide a glimpse into the character of the ancient Mayan writing. They show some of the resources of the hieroglyphic system, and they illustrate some of their modes of utilization. But they give no more than a hint of the wealth of alternatives that were available to the scribes and that on occasion were exploited by them to add variety and surprises to their inscriptions and to turn them into works of art. The language itself provided alternatives, and going beyond these, the graphic system offered opportunities for more. A ruler's name, for example, might appear sometimes as a logogram, or as a compound or conflation of logograms, sometimes as a form of partly logographic and partly phonetic composition, and at other times as one of totally phonetic derivation, these various forms bearing little or no overt resemblance to one another. And the graphic forms employed could range from the ordinary conventional symbols, to head-form equivalents of these, all the way to the most fanciful full-figure creations whose features required study and searching in order to

Figure 10 Full-figure personifications of the terms of a long-count date. They represent "9 baktuns, 16 katuns, 15 tuns, 0 uinals, 0 single days, and tzolkin day 7 Ahau," equivalent to A.D. 766, February 15 (Julian). They are from the east face of Stela D at Quirigua, Guatemala. Drawing by David Kiphuth, after A. P. Maudslay, *Archaeology* (1889–1902), vol. 2, pl. 25, with restoration of diagnostic details in the first two hieroglyphs.

find the diagnostics from which their intended values could be inferred (fig. 10 is an example). At some sites especially, scribal virtuosity seems to have been highly prized. One imagines that the unveiling of a new inscription must have been an exciting event.

This variability in modes of glyphic representation might make decipherment seem a next-to-impossible task; but in fact it works just the other way. The alternations between hieroglyphs different in form but equivalent in function provide the next best thing to a Rosetta stone. Fortunately, the Mayan penchant for exact dating of every event greatly facilitates the establishment of equivalences, both among event glyphs of unlike form and among alternative name glyphs. And a native literary convention, the "poetic couplet," grounded in an oral tradition that is still very much alive today and that in ancient times was carried over even into the unwieldy medium of hieroglyphic inscriptions, also serves to bring out equivalences. Passages which are in this form present parallel strophes, "rhyming" (so to speak) in meaning rather than in sound, and conveying their message twice but in different phrasings. It was

the recognition of this device that led to the discovery of the equivalence between some of the diverse forms of "birth" glyphs presented above. Other contextual clues have made it possible at times to distinguish between homonymy and synonymy of alternatives; and in cases of homonymy, phonetic alternatives reveal the readings of logograms.

In contrast to the flexibility of the system, and to the opportunities which it offered for innovation, there is a surprising uniformity in the inventory of primary signs throughout the entire Lowland Maya area. This is true not only of these, the ultimate building blocks (of which some 700 to 800 have been catalogued), but it is true also of a very large portion of the inventory of compound hieroglyphs constructed from them.[22] Such uniformity over so large an area would seem to indicate an intensity of communication quite beyond what might have been expected. And the preservation of these forms virtually intact over so many centuries reflects a remarkable continuity in Mayan culture.

......

Notes

1. See Michael D. Coe, "Early Steps in the Evolution of Maya Writing," in *Origins of Religious Art and Iconography in Preclassic Mesoamerica*, UCLA Latin American Studies Series, vol. 31, ed. H. B. Nicholson (Los Angeles: UCLA Latin American Center, 1976), 107–22.

2. For an introduction to some of these other Middle American systems of writing, see the articles by H. B. Nicholson and by Mary Elizabeth Smith in the collection *Mesoamerican Writing Systems*, ed. Elizabeth P.

Benson (Washington, D.C.: Dumbarton Oaks Research Library and Collections, 1973). For a readily available and inexpensive reproduction of a specimen, see *The Codex Nuttall: A Picture Manuscript from Ancient Mexico*, Peabody Museum Facsimile, ed. Zelia Nuttall, 1902, with a new introductory text by Arthur G. Miller (New York: Dover, 1975). For fuller studies see Jill Leslie Furst, *Codex Vindobonensis Mexicanus I: A Commentary*, Institute for Mesoamerican Studies, Publication 4 (Albany: State University of New York, 1978); and Mary Elizabeth Smith, *Picture Writing from Ancient Southern Mexico: Mixtec Place Signs and Maps* (Norman: University of Oklahoma Press, 1973).

3. The date of the Mayan epoch (as cited in the text) is equal to day number 584285 in the Julian day count. The addition of this constant to a Mayan day number yields the corresponding Julian day number, from which the equivalent Christian year and Julian or Gregorian calendar date can be derived.

The term "Julian" in calendrical and chronological terminology has two quite different senses. As a modifer of "calendar" it refers to the one that was instituted by Julius Caesar in the year 46 B.C. and that was employed until the institution of the Gregorian reformed calendar in Roman Catholic countries in 1582, in the British Isles and colonies (including American) in 1752, and in countries under the Orthodox church only in the twentieth century. As a modifier of "day count" the term "Julian" refers to the chronological system introduced by Joseph Justus Scaliger in 1583, in which context its rationale may have been either (or both) of two that have been alleged: the inventor named it in honor of his father, Julius Caesar Scaliger; or he intended it to be used in conjunction with the Julian calendar, being unsympathetic to the Gregorian reform.

4. The reasons for applying the term "month" to these periods are that (1) Bishop Landa, referring to their "two kinds of months" (lunar and vigesimal), used the corresponding Spanish word to translate both of the Yucatec Mayan words, *uh* and *winal;* and (2) at least some of the Mayans—the Jacaltec Maya of Guatemala—are known to have done the same, still into the twentieth century, applying to the twenty-day

"months" the same term in their language that they applied in other contexts to lunar months. The term is thus polysemous, the context of usage sufficing to identify the intended sense. The implied analogy is a native one. Pertinent to the point also is that the independent logogram for the numeral 20 is the moon sign. This suggests that the analogy is as old as the institution of the arithmetically subdivided year as an alternative to the incommensurable lunar subdivision.

5. An even earlier monument, known as the Hauberg stela, whose Mayan origin was previously in doubt but is now virtually certain, can perhaps now lay claim to the title of "earliest Mayan." Its date is A.D. 199.

6. When Stela C of Tres Zapotes was first discovered by Mathew Stirling in 1939 its top half (above the break shown in fig. 2) was missing, so that the uppermost digit of its day number was unattested. Assuming that the unfamiliar hieroglyph with a prefixed "6" (vertical bar and dot) at the bottom of the column was a day sign, and exploiting the redundancies in the calendrical-chronological system, Stirling reconstructed the missing fifth-order digit as a "7," which is the only possibility, given the four lower-order digits and a trecena value of six. This determines the date as 7.16.6.16.18, equivalent to September 5 (Julian) of the year -31 (32 B.C.). Disputed at the time, even ridiculed, this interpretation was later (prophetically) defended by M. D. Coe, and in 1971, when the top half of the monument was discovered, Stirling's original prediction was confirmed.

7. For accounts of the early pre-Mayan dated monuments, see the study by Michael D. Coe cited in n.1 above, and the review article by Joyce Marcus, "The Origins of Mesoamerican Writing," *Annual Review of Anthropology* 5 (1976): 35–67. A newly discovered pre-Mayan monument, Stela 1 of La Mojarra (Vera Cruz, Mexico), must be added now to those mentioned here and in the reviews by Coe and Marcus. It bears the dates 8.5.3.3.5 and 8.5.16.9.7 in the same chronological system as that employed in other pre-Mayan and Mayan inscriptions, corresponding thus to A.D. 143, May 22, and 156, July 14, resp. It has by far the longest pre-Mayan hieroglyphic text yet known, described as employing "some 140 different signs in a total of about 520 appearances combined graphically into 428 different hieroglyphs." See the recent publication by Fernando Winfield Capitaine, "La Estela 1 de La Mo-

jarra, Veracruz, México," in *Research Reports on Ancient Maya Writing* 16 (Washington, D.C.: Center for Maya Research, 1988).

8. The studies of the hieroglyphic text from the Temple of the Cross at Palenque include the *Notebook* by Linda Schele (listed in Further Readings) in its 1984 or 1987 editions, and the papers by the present author in the Palenque Round Table Series, namely, "A Rationale for the Initial Date of the Temple of the Cross at Palenque," vol. 3 (1976), pp. 211–24, "Some Problems in the Interpretation of the Mythological Portion of the Hieroglyphic Text of the Temple of the Cross at Palenque," vol. 5 (1980), pp. 99–115, and "The Identities of the Mythological Figures in the Cross Group Inscriptions of Palenque," vol. 6 (1985), pp. 45–58, Merle Green Robertson, gen. ed. (Austin: University of Texas Press; and San Francisco: Pre-Columbian Art Research Institute).

9. See the section entitled "The Face Numerals" in J. T. Goodman's *The Archaic Maya Inscriptions*, vol. 6 (appendix) of A. P. Maudslay's *Archaeology* (London, 1889–1902; repr., New York: Milpatron Publishing, and Arte Primitivo, 1974), 41–52.

10. See F. G. Lounsbury, "Astronomical Knowledge and Its Uses at Bonampak, Mexico," in *Archaeoastronomy in the New World*, ed. A. F. Aveni (Cambridge: Cambridge University Press, 1982), 143–68; and "A Palenque King and the Planet Jupiter," in *World Archaeoastronomy*, ed. A. F. Aveni (Cambridge: Cambridge University Press, in press).

11. See my 1976 article referenced in note 8; also the section "Numerology," in my article "Maya Numeration, Computation, and Calendrical Astronomy," in Charles Coulston Gillispie, ed., *Dictionary of Scientific Biography* (New York: Scribner's, 1973), 15:804–8.

12. The authoritative English translation of Landa, with exhaustive scholarly annotations and indexing, is Alfred M. Tozzer's *Landa's Relación de las Cosas de Yucatán*, Papers of the Peabody Museum of American Archaeology and Ethnology, Harvard University, vol. 18 (Cambridge, Mass.: Peabody Museum, Harvard University, 1941). Another English translation, well written, readily accessible, and inexpensive, is that of William Gates, *Yucatán before and after the Conquest* (1937; repr., New York: Dover, 1978).

13. Quotation from J. Eric S. Thompson, *Maya Hiero-*

glyphic Writing: An Introduction, p. 206 (see reference under "Further Readings," below).

14. Thompson, *Maya Hieroglyphic Writing*, 63–65. And in a similar vein, "It has been held by some that Maya dates recorded on stelae may refer to historical events or even recount the deeds of individuals; to me such a possibility is well-nigh inconceivable. The dates on stelae surely narrate the stages of the journey of time with a reverence befitting such a solemn theme. I conceive the endless progress of time as the supreme mystery of Maya religion, a subject which pervaded Maya thought to an extent without parallel in the history of mankind. In such a setting there was no place for personal records, for, in relation to the vastness of time, man and his doings shrink to insignificance. To add details of war or peace, of marriage or giving in marriage, to the solemn roll call of the periods of time is as though a tourist were to carve his initials on Donatello's David" (ibid., 155). As noted later, Thompson eventually had to retract that view.

15. Heinrich Berlin, "El glifo 'emblema' en las inscripciones mayas," *Journal de la Société des Americanistes*, n.s. 47 (1958): 111–19; Tatiana Proskouriakoff, "Historical Implications of a Pattern of Dates at Piedras Negras," *American Antiquity* 25 (1960): 454–75.

16. The letter x in transcriptions of Mayan words is for phonetic $\check{s}$ (English *sh*), as in the early sixteenth-century pronunciation of Spanish, and as also in Portuguese, Galician, Catalan, and Ladino. For a delightful account of the circumstances under which the Mayan word *xoc* entered the English language (becoming *shark*), see the study by Tom Jones, "The Xoc, the Sharke, and the Sea Dogs: An Historical Encounter," in *Fifth Palenque Round Table, 1983*, Palenque Round Table Series, vol. 7, ed. Merle Greene Robertson and Virginia M. Fields (San Francisco: Pre-Columbian Art Research Institute, 1985), 211–22.

17. Yurii V. Knorozov, "Drevniaia Pis'mennost' Tsentral'noĭ Ameriki," in *Sovetskaia Etnografiia*, 1952, no. 3 (Moscow: Academy of Sciences, 1952), 100–18. An English translation of this article, by Sophie Coe, "The Ancient Writing of Central America," circulated in manuscript carbon and mimeographed copies, and a Spanish translation, "La antigua escritura de America Central," was published in Mexico. Other articles by

Knorozov appeared in 1954, 1955, and 1957; and in 1963 his monograph *Pis'mennost' Indeitsev Maiia* (Moscow: Academy of Sciences) was published, portions of which were translated by Sophie Coe under the title *Selected Chapters from "The Writing of the Maya Indians,"* Russian Translation Series of the Peabody Museum of Archaeology and Ethnology, Harvard University, vol. 4 (Cambridge, Mass.: Peabody Museum, Harvard University 1967).

18. See Helen Neuenswander, "Vestiges of Early Maya Time Concepts in a Contemporary Maya (Cubulco Achi) Community: Implications for Epigraphy," *Estudios de Cultura Maya* 13 (1981): 125–63.

19. Upturned god-C and reptilian heads with deity emergence and associated "birth" hieroglyphs of the type of fig. 6 are on pp. 18–20a of the Madrid Codex. Other examples are with the serpent numbers of the Dresden Codex, pp. 61–62 and 69–70.

20. For the text of this document and an analysis of the text, see Ortwin Smailus, *El Maya-Chontal de Acalan*, Centro de Estudios Mayas, Cuaderno 9 (Mexico City: Universidad Nacional Autonomo de Mexico, 1975). The correspondence of the hieroglyph to the textually documented Chontal form was first pointed out to me by Peter Mathews in 1977. He presented it publicly in April 1979 at the Conference on Phoneticism in Mayan Hieroglyphic Writing held at the State University of New York in Albany. A definitive study of status hieroglyphs in Mayan accession phrases is contained in an expansion of that paper, "Patterns of Sign Substitution in Mayan Hieroglyphic Writing: The Affix Cluster," jointly authored by Peter Mathews and John Justeson and published in the proceedings of the conference (John S. Justeson and Lyle Campbell, eds., *Phoneticism in Mayan Hieroglyphic Writing*, Publication 9, Institute for Mesoamerican Studies [Albany: State University of New York, 1984], 185–231).

21. This two-part sign was first known in Mayanist literature as "Ben Ik," on the basis of a misidentification of its second component (*ik,* "wind," day name "Ik"); then, following Thompson (*Maya Hieroglyphic Writing*, 1950 ed.) as "Ben Ich" on the basis of another misidentification (Yucatec *ich,* "eye"). By 1971 Thompson had changed his mind about this, and proposed

reading the entire compound as the title "Ah," as a rebus extension from the highland Mayan day name of that form, supposedly meaning "reed," and corresponding to Yucatec "Ben" and to Aztec "Acatl," the latter also meaning "reed," and ignoring altogether the other component of the compound. The proper sense that must be attributed to the "Ben" sign in this context was first pointed out by Thomas S. Barthel, still retaining, however, Thompson's earlier reading; see his "El complejo 'emblema,'" *Estudios de Cultura Maya* 7 (1968): 159–93. The phonetic value of the questionable component was demonstrated and the "Ah Pohp," "Ahpo," and "Ahaw" readings of the compound were suggested in my paper "On the Derivation and Reading of the 'Ben-Ich' Prefix," in *Mesoamerican Writing Systems,* ed. Elizabeth P. Benson (Washington, D.C.: Dumbarton Oaks Research Library and Collections, 1973), 99–143. The "Pohp Ahaw" reading for the reverse order of the components was proposed immediately thereafter and has had word-of-mouth currency since then, but as far as I am aware it appears in print for the first time in the present book. The critical substitution of the "jaguar-mat-throne" sign for the phonetic *po* sign in the glyphic compound is on the Naranjo hieroglyphic stairway, step 9, at T1. The documentation of the still-current speech idiom was by John Justeson, in fieldwork carried out in December 1978, when he was given the mixed Spanish-Maya expression *gran pohp ahaw* as meaning "king" or "important personage" by a native speaker of Chontal from San Carlos (Benito Juarez), Tabasco, Mexico.

22. J. Eric S. Thompson, *A Catalog of Maya Hieroglyphs* (Norman: University of Oklahoma Press, 1962).

• • • • • •

Further Readings

Kelley, David H. *Deciphering the Maya Script.* Austin: University of Texas Press, 1976. An introduction to the study of Maya writing, taking into account the reorientation that began with the discoveries of Berlin and Proskouriakoff regarding the content of Mayan inscriptions, and those of Knorozov regarding the nature of the hieroglyphic writing system. The most comprehensive recent treatment, though already dated in some points of detail.

Lounsbury, Floyd G. "Some Problems in the Interpretation of the Mythological Portion of the Hieroglyphic Text of the Temple of the Cross at Palenque." In *Third Palenque Round Table, 1978*. Part 2. Palenque Round Table Series, vol. 5, ed. Merle Greene Robertson, pp. 99–115. Austin: University of Texas Press, 1980). Analysis of the structure and content of the hieroglyphic text that is illustrated here in fig. 3.

Schele, Linda. *Notebook for the Maya Hieroglyphic Writing Workshop at Texas*. Annual. Austin: Institute of Latin American Studies, University of Texas, 1977–. Introductory material, with illustrations and analyses, intended to accompany a series of lectures and workshop sessions, but useful in its own right as an introduction. The 1980, 1983, and 1986 editions focus on the texts of Temple of the Inscriptions at Palenque (Chiapas, Mexico); those of 1981, 1984, and 1987 on the inscriptions of the three temples of the Cross group at Palenque; and those of 1982, 1985, and 1988 on inscriptions of the several remaining tablets at that site. The 1989 edition will concern mainly the inscriptions of Copan (Honduras).

Schele, Linda, and Mary Ellen Miller. *The Blood of Kings: Dynasty and Ritual in Maya Art*, with photographs by Justin Kerr. Fort Worth: Kimbell Art Museum, 1986. A special exhibition catalog, superbly illustrated and analyzed, which serves also as a general introduction to the culture, art, and hieroglyphic writing of the ancient Maya, taking into account the recent discoveries relating to these topics.

J. Eric S. Thompson. *Maya Hieroglyphic Writing: An Introduction*. Washington, D.C.: Carnegie Institution of Washington, 1950; 2d and 3d eds., Norman: University of Oklahoma Press, 1960, 1971). The most comprehensive study of Maya writing ever undertaken, representing what was known or believed about this subject *before* the discoveries of the past three decades; invaluable nonetheless, in spite of the recent drastic reversals in interpretation of the writing system.

The Contributors

......

Elmer H. Antonsen is a professor of Germanic languages and of linguistics at the University of Illinois at Urbana-Champaign. He is the author of *A Concise Grammar of the Older Runic Inscriptions* (1975) and of numerous articles dealing with runes, the history of the Germanic languages, and the structure of modern German.

James A. Bellamy is a professor of Arabic literature at the University of Michigan. He is the editor of *The Noble Qualities of Character* by Ibn Abī d-Dunyā (1973). His major research interests are in medieval Arabic literature, Arabic papyrology, and textual criticism.

Frank Moore Cross is Hancock Professor of Hebrew and other Oriental Languages at Harvard University and sometime Director of the Harvard Semitic Museum. His publications include *The Ancient Library of Qumran* (1957), *The Development of the Jewish Scripts* (1961), and *Canaanite Myth and Hebrew Epic* (1973). He is an editor of the so-called Dead Sea Scrolls of Qumran, Cave IV, of the Samaria Papyri, and has written extensively in the fields of Northwest Semitic epigraphy and paleography, and in the history of Canaanite, Phoenician, and Israelite religions.

Henry George Fischer is Lila Acheson Wallace Research Curator in Egyptology at the Metropolitan Museum of Art, New York. His publications include *Dendera in the Third Millennium B.C.* (1968), *The Orientation of Hieroglyphs*, Part I: *Reversals* (1977), *L'écriture et l'art de l'Egypte ancienne* (1986), and *Ancient Egyptian Calligraphy* (1979; rev. 1983, 1988).

M. W. Green received her Ph.D. in cuneiform studies from the University of Chicago in 1975. She has worked on the decipherment of Archaic cuneiform at the Free University of Berlin and in Philadelphia as one of the collaborating editors of the *Pennsylvania Sumerian Dictionary*. She has published text editions of Sumerian literary works and articles on Archaic cuneiform.

David N. Keightley is a professor of history at the University of California at Berkeley, where he has taught since 1969. He is the author of *Sources of Shang History: The Oracle-Bone Inscriptions of Bronze Age China* (1978) and editor of *The Origins of Chinese Civilization* (1983). One of the editors and founders of the journal *Early China*, he has published articles on the religion and history of the Chinese Neolithic and Bronze ages.

Ruth P. M. Lehmann is a professor emeritus of English at the University of Texas at Austin. She is the author of *Fled Duin na nGed* (1964), *Introduction to Old Irish* (with W. P. Lehmann, 1975), *Early Irish Verse* (1982), and *Beowulf: An Imitative Translation* (1988).

Floyd G. Lounsbury is Sterling Professor Emeritus of Anthropology at Yale University. He is the author of *Oneida Verb Morphology* (1953), *A Formal Account of the Crow- and Omaha-Type Kinship Terminologies* (1964), *Maya Numeration, Computation, and Calendrical Astronomy* (1973), and a series of papers on the decipherment of hieroglyphic inscriptions at Palenque and Copan (1973–88).

Denise Schmandt-Besserat is a professor of art and Middle Eastern studies at the University of Texas at Austin. Her articles have appeared in *Scientific American*, *Science*, the *American Anthropologist*, *Archaeology*, and other journals. She is an advisory editor for *Technology and Culture* and is on the advisory board of *Visible Language*.

Wayne M. Senner is a professor of German and Scandinavian studies at Arizona State University. He is the author of *Reception of German Literature in Iceland* (1985) and is writing a book on the history of Icelandic literary criticism.

Ronald S. Stroud is a professor of classics at the University of California at Berkeley, where he has taught since 1965. He has published articles on Greek archaeology, epigraphy, and topography in addition to *Drakon's Law on Homicide* (1968) and *The Axones and Kyrbeis of Drakon and Solon* (1979). He is coeditor, with H. W. Pleket of Leiden, of *Supplementum Epigraphicum Graecum*.

Rex Wallace is an assistant professor of classics at the University of Massachusetts, Amherst. His research interests include historical and comparative linguistics and Indo-European linguistics, focusing primarily on the languages of the Italic branch. He is preparing a work on Etruscan, the Etruscan alphabet, and the spread of this alphabet to the various Indo-European–speaking tribes in ancient Italy.

Index